ADVANCE PRAISES

"Hopefully this book can inspire the younger generation to be more courageous, not to be complacent, but to compete, struggle and fight for their beliefs. Don't let there be a spoon-fed generation. Pak Mochtar is a great inspiration for our generation."

Joko Widodo
President, Republic of Indonesia

"I would like to express my gratitude and appreciation to Pak Mochtar, for the many things that he has done for this country, especially during the 10 years I was president. I am confident that Bung Karno (Sukarno), Pak Harto (Suharto), Pak (B.J.) Habibie, Gus Dur (Abdurrahman Wahid) and Ibu Megawati (Soekarnoputri) would say the same thing: thank him for his work.

I've read about his life, from the time he moved to Jakarta from Malang, and even until now and hopefully I will continue to read about his works in the future. After reading his book, having joined him on the journey of his life, it is clear that Pak Mochtar is not just a Man of Ideas, but also certainly a Man of Action. Normally success starts with ideas but then those ideas need to be fought and worked hard for, until the goal is finally achieved.

He is certainly a man of ideas, a hardworking man, a persistent man, and an accomplished man. Thomas Alva Edison has said that genius is just 1 percent inspiration, and 99 percent perspiration, hard work. I am sure that the road he travelled has been like that—and this book is a witness to that journey."

Dr. Susilo Bambang Yudhoyono
Former President, Republic of Indonesia

i

"Many people have aspirations, but Pak Mochtar understands the art of implementation and management, and that takes special skills and expertise which is detailed in the book."

Jusuf Kalla
Vice-President, Republic of Indonesia

"Pak Mochtar and the Lippo Group have made a huge contribution to the development of Indonesia, especially in the field of health and education. When I travel to the remote areas of eastern Indonesia, they are dotted with many of Lippo's affordable hospitals and schools. This book is instrumental in understanding the person behind this great vision."

Gen. Luhut Binsar Pandjaitan
Coordinating Minister for Political, Legal and Security Affairs
Republic of Indonesia

"I was surprised to find myself resonating so strongly to Mochtar Riady's life story. Throughout his autobiography, he keeps going back to what animates him deep inside—his Chinese-ness, his love of Indonesia, his Christian values and his Taoist philosophy. Around this core, he responds flexibly and creatively to an incredible range of life experiences. He talks about his personal disappointments, the pursuit of his wife, his devotion to family, the cry of revolution, his mastery of finance, the challenge of new technologies and, always, his passion for education and social justice. He shows neither rancour when bad things happen nor overweening pride with success. There is in him a profound humility despite huge achievement. Mochtar Riady's book is both inspiring and edifying."

George Yeo
Chairman, Kerry Logistics
Former Singapore Foreign Minister

"Pak Mochtar Riady's autobiography makes a fascinating read. The account of his formative years and his values and business principles helps one realise the basis of his business acumen and success. His many philanthropic endeavours, some of which are recounted in the book, bear testimony to the impact Pak Mochtar has had on many. The Lippo group has thrived not just in Indonesia and China, but also across much of South-East Asia and beyond. His story explains so much, stands witness to many interesting events, and teaches and guides."

Lee Hsien Yang

Special Advisor, General Atlantic

"The autobiography of Mochtar Riady can be read either as an adventure story or a story about succeeding in life. As an adventure, the book flows with energy, each page bringing about a new twist and yet another turn. But we can benefit most by absorbing Riady's lessons on what brings success: imagination, hard work, willingness to roll up the sleeves and get the hands dirty, persistence, honour, responsibility, patience, seizing opportunities, making opportunities, admitting failure, and appreciating the good fortune of having a wonderful wife and mother who emphasises values, morality, clean hands and clear minds. Riady brings to life the principle of making good things happen: OTTLLSS—Observe carefully, Think deliberately, Try out ideas, Learn from mistakes, Lead your people, Stand for truth and right, and Serve country and society. Don't miss these great lessons of life and leadership."

Lim Siong Guan

Co-author of *The Leader, The Teacher & You and Winning With Honour*

"Mochtar Riady is synonymous with the Indonesian banking industry. A pioneer who built up the country's largest private sector bank, Bank Central Asia, he went on to establish his own Lippo Group. He continues to be a giant in the banking circles, widely known and regarded in the region. His life story would encapsulate an important part of Indonesian history and give a glimpse of how members of the pioneer generation helped built up the economy of their country through passion, commitment and hard work."

Peter Seah

Chairman, DBS Group Holdings

"Brimming with personal insights, Dr. Riady's book chronicles how his tumultuous childhood, career choices and the various cultures he lived through laid the foundation for his love for life, devotion to education and development of a profound sense of social responsibility. This is a journey of humble beginnings and the teachings of his grandmother and father have resonated across generations. Dr. Riady ultimately forges his own path, overcoming dire circumstances through will and determination. I found the book an honest and engaging read."

Samuel Tsien

Group Chief Executive Officer
Overseas-Chinese Banking Corporation Limited

"Mochtar Riady is one of Asia's business legends, and his autobiography details the hard work, perseverance and ingenuity that has helped him build Lippo Group into a global conglomerate of diversified businesses including real estate, hospitality and F&B, some of which are listed on the Singapore Exchange. I enjoyed the wide-ranging wisdom and insights from workflow processes to management philosophy from the patriarch of a family that has left a significant imprint on both Singapore's business and CSR landscapes, including through the Stephen Riady Group of Foundations."

Loh Boon Chye
Chief Executive Officer
Singapore Exchange

"Dr. Mochtar Riady is one of Asia's foremost entrepreneurs and philanthropists. He is a generous benefactor who has made impactful and far-sighted contributions, particularly in educational philanthropy. In his biography, he shares the rich insights and lessons gleaned from a remarkable life and career. Dr. Riady lived through tumultuous times, and faced many trials and circumstances that tested his character and abilities. Undaunted, he took on each challenge and opportunity with passion, fierce integrity, and an entrepreneur's flair and daring. Dr. Riady's biography offers many inspiring life lessons we can all draw upon on our own journeys."

Professor Tan Chorh Chuan
President, National University of Singapore
Deputy Chairman, Agency for Science, Technology & Research, Singapore

"Dr. Riady has dedicated himself to making a positive contribution to humanity and society. His autobiography is a wonderful read in understanding the events and experiences that helped shape Dr. Riady's illustrious life."

Ms. Yenny Wahid
Director, The Wahid Institute

"Dr. Mochtar Riady's memoirs is a highly educational and inspiring book in which a leader shares his passion and insights based on decades of experience in entrepreneurship, banking, health care and education as well as building a prosperous family business in the midst of globalisation and uncertain economic development. The book illustrates the power of perseverance, an inquisitive mind, empirically-based causal thinking, win-win compromises in conflicts and seeking opportunities out of adversity. More importantly, it demonstrates the virtues of dedicated parenting, family values, and serving people. Pak Mochtar epitomises the Chinese wisdom that societal peace and prosperity arises from the righteous cultivation of oneself and a harmonious household."

Professor Bernard Yeung
Dean and Stephen Riady Distinguished Professor
NUS Business School, National University of Singapore

"This book succinctly captures the essence of a man who has not forgotten his roots, and who leaves an indelible legacy for the future. The account of his arduous journey from humble beginnings to his current business empire spanning the globe, his unwavering reliance on his faith, is undoubtedly an inspiration to readers of all ages and all walks of life."

Kwa Kim Li
Managing Partner
Lee and Lee

MOCHTAR RIADY
MY LIFE STORY

MOCHTAR RIADY
MY LIFE STORY

Mochtar Riady

WILEY

Copyright © 2017 by Mochtar Riady
Cover Design: Cynlinder
Cover Image: Margio Juwono

Published by John Wiley & Sons Singapore Pte. Ltd.
1 Fusionopolis Walk, #07-01, Solaris South Tower, Singapore 138628

Other Wiley Editorial Offices

John Wiley & Sons, 111 River Street, Hoboken, NJ 07030, USA
John Wiley & Sons, The Atrium, Southern Gate, Chichester, West Sussex, P019 8SQ, United Kingdom
John Wiley& Sons (Canada) Ltd., 5353 Dundas Street West, Suite 400, Toronto, Ontario, M9B 6HB, Canada
John Wiley& Sons Australia Ltd., 42 McDougall Street, Milton, Queensland 4064, Australia
Wiley-VCH, Boschstrasse 12, D-69469 Weinheim, Germany

Library of Congress Cataloging-in-Publication Data

ISBN 9781119256366 (Paperback)
ISBN 9781119256380 (ePDF)
ISBN 9781119256373 (ePub)

Typeset in 11.5/17 pt, Arno Pro Regular by SPi Global

Printed in Singapore by Markono Print Media Pte Ltd

10   9   8   7   6   5   4   3   2   1

"To my father, my teacher Luo Yitian, and my wife."

HARMONY

Harmony is reflected in the reality of disharmony

All things exist relative to each other, and they develop in relation
to each other

Yin and yang are formed in relation to each other

Being and non-being are born from each other and are the
opposite of each other

In this works the Way

From amidst this are derived all things

This is the philosophy of the origin of all things in the universe

Knead all that is inharmonious into harmony

Combine the disparate into the unified

Make the other your own

Interacting with each other in the same space, enriching each
other at the same time

Collaborating over the same goal

This is the true meaning of harmonious management

—Dr. Mochtar Riady

CONTENTS

INTRODUCTION

M any businessmen, the world over, have written books about building empires, despite being born into poverty. This book traces a similar arc of stunning success from humble origins, yet it is a truly unique account of an exceptional life. It is the autobiography of an Indonesian Chinese businessman who has an indomitable spirit and a great capacity for overcoming adversity. This book describes his occasional missteps as well as a lifetime of achievements spanning Southeast Asia, China, Korea and the West. At the same time it provides a lively and first-hand account of Indonesia's economic development after years of stagnation and decline. It is also a well-organised guide for aspiring businessmen that also grips the reader with its entertaining anecdotes. In 1935, his grandmother tells him that he must leave the family village: "You must leave to come back—study and equip yourself with skills before coming back," she says. Thus begins this fascinating tale of the man behind the Lippo empire.

In these memoirs, we are given an insight into his analytical mind as we follow his personal story as well as the developments of one of Indonesia's most globalised conglomerates. Dr. Riady describes how he came to learn about banking, trade and numerous other economic ventures. He shares his views on the five imbalances of China, his passion for education and his philanthropic work in Indonesia, Singapore, Hong Kong, China and the West. He is a passionate advocate for understanding the unpredictable nature of the economy and preparing for disruptive global changes, particularly the digital technological revolution which has already transformed the way we live and work.

On the more personal side, he shares details of the hardships he faced and overcame, offering his experience of four wars and five "dynasties" and the pain endured under Japan's World War II occupation of what is now Indonesia.

His first step was the hardest. Along the way, he embraced the business and work practices of the West, Indonesia and China, and this helped lay the groundwork for the growth of his numerous banks and ultimately, the building of the Lippo Group. He also muses on the friendships that helped him succeed, including his ties with business titans such as Li Ka-shing of Hong Kong and Jack Stephens of the US. From them, he learnt to play his role in international banking and commerce. It is these experiences that helped him set the course for his Group and adapt to the often bewildering global changes over the years.

Growing up in Indonesia and developing his business, even in hard times, he appreciated the vastness of his country—which stretches from Sumatra in the west to Papua in the east. He learnt how it was a cauldron of conflict between various religious groups even before the arrival of Dutch colonialists and their oppressive rule over Java. He learnt and understood real revolution and war, playing his own modest part in the nation's drive for independence from the Dutch. He did all this out of a profound love for Indonesia—his home.

He concludes that the future is in one's family. He ends by saying "All I have is hope", a short phrase that is reflective of his optimism and general enthusiasm for life and his work.

Today, the Lippo Group is one of Asia's largest business groups, with its main businesses in Indonesia. It is the biggest consumer services group in Indonesia and manages the country's largest portfolio of retail malls. It is also the leader in department stores, hypermarkets, broadband internet service, and hospitals. Beyond its market leadership and scale, it is also establishing itself as the partner of choice for many blue chip foreign investors looking to participate in the growth of Indonesia's vibrant economy.

Dr. Riady has many stories and life lessons to reflect on, but at 87 years old, he is still a man excited about what is to come and always looking into the future.

S. R. Nathan
Former President of Singapore

REFLECTIONS

In my years of public service, I was fortunate enough to bear witness to Pak Mochtar's lifetime of contributions to our country. Few people can say that they have endured the chaos of civil war, the feuds of rival warlords, a harsh military occupation and a revolutionary struggle for independence. Fewer still can say that in addition to witnessing these earth-shaking events, they also managed to overcome personal grief and hardship in their childhood before finding the inner strength to build a conglomerate that compete on the international stage and directly employs over 115,000 people across Asia. Pak Mochtar is a rare breed of man that exemplifies true grit. He is someone who can legitimately make all of these claims—but the Pak Mochtar I know would be too modest.

Pak Mochtar could be credited as being one of the most influential figures in the modernisation of the nation's banking sector. He firmly believed that the business of banking is about trust. Like myself, he also believed in the power of technology, and introduced the first ATM machines. Pak Mochtar made banking into a science, but equally understood the art of banking, and in doing so, the banks Pak Mochtar built grew to become amongst the country's largest, even to this day. Beyond banking, he has also unofficially negotiated on the government's behalf on issues of trade and capital flows. Pak Mochtar's Lippo is largely seen as an Indonesian blue chip company and is a trusted household name. Millions of people enjoy daily the quality services Lippo provides across sectors from telecommunication to retail to healthcare and education. Lippo strives to meet needs that the government has not yet been able to address, working closely with the government in both conceptualisation and implementation.

More important than the hardships he has weathered and the successes he has achieved, is the fact that he has always had his sights fixed on more than his own welfare and empire. Even as he strived to build his businesses from nothing, he never forgot the importance of being "good" and not merely "successful". He has demonstrated what it means to act in the larger interests of community and country. As a banker, he had the utmost integrity in his dealings despite the many temptations and moral hazards. In his book, he talks about the differences between being a "good" and "successful" banker—I can testify to this unshaking veracity to serve meaningfully. Even the township in Indonesia that was built by Pak Mochtar—Lippo Karawaci—stands as a unique example of a responsibly built township. Lippo Karawaci is actually built at a lower elevation than the surrounding villages so as to serve as a water catchment for the area, diverting flooding in the flood-prone neighbouring villages. It is also the greenest township. Pak Mochtar has also made it his mission to bring quality healthcare and education to Indonesians everywhere—establishing hospitals and schools in places where few other companies have wanted to venture—such as Papua and NTT. Furthermore, in everything that he does, he has emphasised the need to invest in human capital and employ modern technology— two key pillars for any country's development, a conviction which I deeply share.

I am reminded of the past, when I was asked by President Suharto to return to Indonesia in 1974. At that time, Indonesia was about to embark on an industrialisation drive. It was a tall order and achieving this vision would require massive amount of capital investment, but more importantly an investment in human capital and technology. In 1976, I was appointed Chief Executive of the new state-owned enterprise Industri Pesawat Terbang Nusantara (IPTN), later on named Indonesian Aerospace (Dirgantara). Two years later, President Suharto appointed me as Minister of Research and Technology. By this time, IPTN had grown considerably, specialising in the manufacture of helicopters and small passenger planes. And by the early 90s, Indonesia began to see the fruits of our labour, and I oversaw 10 state-owned industries including ship- and train-building, steel, arms, communications, and energy. Over the years, I have seen the importance of human capital and technology in enabling any country to achieve their full potential. As President of Indonesia, it is this transformation in human capital and technology—and the impact they have on people's lives—that is amongst my proudest achievements. Pak Mochtar has been an excellent entrepreneur in his endeavour to build up our country in these two areas and I am grateful that our country has such enlightened community leaders.

Indonesia has come a long way, but the journey never ends. As I reflect on the journey of our great nation and the challenges that lie ahead, Indonesia is grateful for the service and dedication of individuals such as Pak Mochtar. If future generations of Indonesians will read this book and find an example to emulate, I am as hopeful as Pak Mochtar that Indonesia has a bright future ahead.

B. J. Habibie
Former President of Indonesia

FOREWORD

The biggest story unfolding in our world today is the return of Asia. As Larry Summers, the former President of Harvard University, has said, "The rise of Asia and all that follows it will be the dominant story in history books written 300 years from now, with the Cold War and rise of Islam as secondary stories." After having lain dormant for almost two centuries, many Asian societies are waking up and resuming their natural roles in the world order. This massive Asian resurgence is truly a remarkable story.

No-one would have predicted this massive Asian resurgence in the year 1929, when Dr. Riady was born. Asia lay totally prostrate then. The two great Asian nations, China and India, had fallen. India had been completely colonised. China was completely defenceless as the Western colonial powers seized territories. It lay like a fallen animal being torn apart by wolves. China's travails were to become worse in the 1930s, as the Japanese began an occupation of much of the country—an occupation that would endure until the end of World War II.

Southeast Asia, with the exception of Thailand, had also been fully colonised. As Dr. Riady moved between Indonesia and China in his childhood, he seemed to move between two universes which were devoid of hope. All over Asia, people were suffering from foreign colonial occupation, conflict and poverty. As Dr. Riady says, "During my first 20 years, I had experienced four wars. At the age of eight I lost my mother."

This is what makes the Mochtar Riady story so fascinating. He was not born with a silver spoon in his mouth. Nor was he born in promising times or in a hospitable place. During his first 20 years, as both China and

Indonesia experienced tragedy after tragedy, he should have felt discouraged and despondent. In his early adulthood, he also lived in tumultuous times. From 1949 to 1965, under Sukarno's rule, Indonesia seemed to go from crisis to crisis.

Yet, even if Indonesia had been stable then, Dr. Riady would still have suffered a major disadvantage in Indonesia. The Indonesian Chinese population was viewed with suspicion as economic exploiters. From time to time, massive anti-Chinese riots would break out. Dr. Riady has experienced many in his life, including one as recently as 1998. In almost every dimension of his life, Dr. Riady had to struggle against the odds. The result of these massive struggles was magnificent success. The success of Asian businessmen like Li Ka-shing and Dr. Riady, both of whom are good friends, is one key reason why Asia is experiencing a great resurgence. This volume therefore should not be read as the story of one man. It provides a window into the extraordinary story of the return of Asia.

Memoirs can be boring. This one isn't. It combines remarkable personal anecdotes with many wise insights into the nature of life. Dr. Riady could have died in 1949, at the age of 20. Just before he was about to board a boat to the northern Chinese city of Tianjin to join China's communist forces, a letter appeared from his girlfriend in Indonesia, Li Limei. This led him to decide to return to Indonesia instead. Fortunately, he didn't board the boat. It sank and all the passengers died.

He also explains how he persuaded his reluctant father and future mother-in-law to allow him to marry Limei. Shrewd as ever, he offered his future mother-in-law business advice. It worked. She consented to the marriage. The business anecdotes are equally revealing. Dr. Riady has tried all kinds of businesses, from shipping to banking, from real estate to the new digital world. Along the way, he faced many near-death experiences. However, as he wisely observes in the beginning, "Experiencing failure gave me stamina, and my ideals gave me the courage to face hardship.

It later became clear to me that within crisis there is opportunity, and from suffering springs limitless vitality." Having experienced a difficult childhood myself, I agree completely with his observations. Equally importantly, the success of entrepreneurs like Dr. Riady explains why Indonesia has made continuous economic progress over several decades. These entrepreneurs were instrumental as partners of the government in bringing industrialisation and modernisation to Indonesia. It was their ingenuity, financial prowess and guts that contributed to Indonesia's transformation. So, as much as it has been an Asian resurgence, it has also been a remarkable Indonesian story.

This memoir also contains valuable political insights. Dr. Riady describes his meetings with two key Asian political leaders, Xi Jinping and Joko Widodo. Dr. Riady describes Xi Jinping's eagerness to learn about economic development when he was a young official in Fujian province. Similarly, President Joko Widodo told him that in terms of development, Indonesia needed to look to China. These two remarkable leaders, Xi and Widodo, also explain why the great Asian resurgence is moving ahead steadily.

Successful fathers can sometimes stifle the growth of their sons. Dr. Riady explains how he allowed his children to fly on their own wings. He watched on television how eagles teach their young to fly. They pick them up, hoist them in the air, and then let go. As Dr. Riady says, "In teaching your children to make their own way in business, you have to be brave enough to let them learn from their failures. . . Failure is indeed the mother of success." This is wise advice that all parents should heed.

From the deeply personal to the larger economic and political stories, this book is full of valuable insights into how Asia has undergone such a remarkable transformation in the past few decades. A lot of this was the result of brave men like Dr. Riady taking brave decisions when others ran away. In 1984, many panicked and left Hong Kong when the British announced their impending withdrawal. Dr. Riady's sixth sense told him instead that there was great opportunity in Hong Kong. The rest, as they say, is history.

Dr. Riady has done Asia, and the world, a big favour by writing this candid memoir. Future historians will learn a lot from his insights. Future generations will also benefit from his wise observations on how to succeed in life and how to deal with failure. Dr. Riady and his family have also supported many worthy philanthropic causes. Clearly, his life story will inspire many generations to come.

Kishore Mahbubani
Dean of the LKY School of Public Policy
National University of Singapore
Author of *The Great Convergence: Asia, the West and the Logic of One World*

ABOUT THE AUTHOR

Dr. Mochtar Riady, founder and Chairman of the Lippo Group, is one of Southeast Asia's best known and most respected business titans.

Born in Indonesia in 1929, Dr. Riady graduated from Southeast University in Nanjing, China. Despite his humble beginnings, Dr. Riady built one of Indonesia's biggest and most international conglomerates. He has been a key figure in the development of many of Indonesia's most important banks, gaining a reputation as a "bank doctor " who was able to bring ailing institutions back to financial health. Today, the Lippo Group is a pan-Asian investment holding company with interests across a vast array of industries including real estate, telecommunications, retail, healthcare, banking and e-commerce.

An avid philanthropist, Dr. Riady has taken a keen interest in promoting education and public health. His foundation manages 52 schools and three universities, as well as a nanotechnology research centre, which bears his name. He has served as chairman of the board of trustees of Universitas Indonesia, and held positions on the boards of Xiamen University, the Fulbright College of Arts & Sciences of the University of Arkansas and the University of Southern California, where Dr. Riady became the first foreigner to serve as a trustee. The National University of Singapore's business school building is named after Dr. Riady as a tribute to his exemplary life.

The Lippo Group has played a critical role in providing affordable medical care in Indonesia, working closely with the government health programme. The group has built state-of-the-art hospitals, including one of the nation's top cancer treatment centres, while its medical school helps train future doctors and nurses needed to staff the nation's hospital system.

Dr. Riady was the recipient of an honorary Doctor of Laws from Golden Gate University of San Francisco and an honorary professorship from his alma mater, Southeast University.

Dr. Riady resides in Jakarta with his wife, Limei, and enjoys the company of his 6 children, 20 grandchildren, 46 great grandchildren, and their spouses.

FAMILY TREE

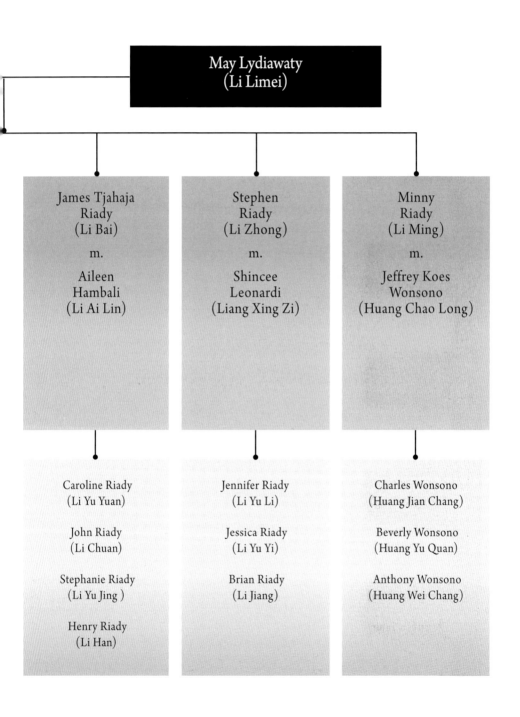

May Lydiawaty
(Li Limei)

James Tjahaja
Riady
(Li Bai)

m.

Aileen
Hambali
(Li Ai Lin)

Stephen
Riady
(Li Zhong)

m.

Shincee
Leonardi
(Liang Xing Zi)

Minny
Riady
(Li Ming)

m.

Jeffrey Koes
Wonsono
(Huang Chao Long)

Caroline Riady
(Li Yu Yuan)

John Riady
(Li Chuan)

Stephanie Riady
(Li Yu Jing)

Henry Riady
(Li Han)

Jennifer Riady
(Li Yu Li)

Jessica Riady
(Li Yu Yi)

Brian Riady
(Li Jiang)

Charles Wonsono
(Huang Jian Chang)

Beverly Wonsono
(Huang Yu Quan)

Anthony Wonsono
(Huang Wei Chang)

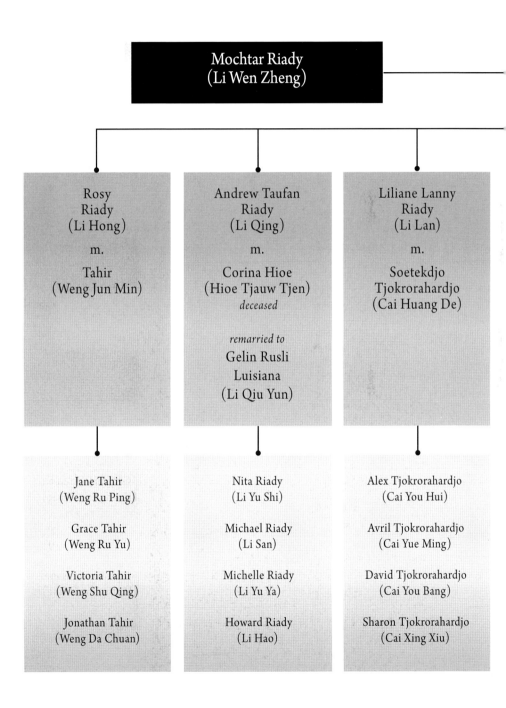

Mochtar Riady
(Li Wen Zheng)

Rosy
Riady
(Li Hong)

m.

Tahir
(Weng Jun Min)

Andrew Taufan
Riady
(Li Qing)

m.

Corina Hioe
(Hioe Tjauw Tjen)
deceased

remarried to
Gelin Rusli
Luisiana
(Li Qiu Yun)

Liliane Lanny
Riady
(Li Lan)

m.

Soetekdjo
Tjokrorahardjo
(Cai Huang De)

Jane Tahir
(Weng Ru Ping)

Grace Tahir
(Weng Ru Yu)

Victoria Tahir
(Weng Shu Qing)

Jonathan Tahir
(Weng Da Chuan)

Nita Riady
(Li Yu Shi)

Michael Riady
(Li San)

Michelle Riady
(Li Yu Ya)

Howard Riady
(Li Hao)

Alex Tjokrorahardjo
(Cai You Hui)

Avril Tjokrorahardjo
(Cai Yue Ming)

David Tjokrorahardjo
(Cai You Bang)

Sharon Tjokrorahardjo
(Cai Xing Xiu)

PREFACE

My story is a tale of two countries. First and foremost it is about Indonesia, the land of my birth and the country that has given me so many opportunities over the years. But I must also acknowledge the birthplace of my father, who left his homeland, China, in search of a better life elsewhere. These two countries—and their distinct cultures—have been a constant source of strength for me over the more than eight decades of my life.

Even my name reflects this debt to two cultures. To many people, I am Mochtar Riady while to others I am Li Wenzheng. In fact, I am both of them. (I will explain how this came about in the first chapter of this book).

The early years of this story were marked by poverty, warfare, political upheaval and economic chaos. At times, death was not far away. Tragedy came early as my mother died when I was only eight years old, tearing a huge hole in the fabric of our family. But my father's wisdom and guidance helped me endure this profound sorrow, and enabled me to make my way in the world. Later on, my Christian faith became my guiding light. It taught me that as I built an increasingly global corporation known as the Lippo Group, there was more than one way to judge success. We are merely temporal stewards of the blessings that we have been graciously given and we must use these blessings to bless others for the eternal glory of God.

My early life of suffering and hardship could not be farther from my comfortable circumstances of today. Even in the wildest dreams of my youth, I could never have imagined the path that I would take or the years of health and happiness that I would be able to enjoy. I now find my greatest pleasure in my expanding family. Counting my wife and myself—and three more generations of direct descendents—there are 97 of us as I write this account. And later this year we may be blessed with one more great-grandchildren.

I also find great pleasure in the numerous schools and hospitals that have been built by the Lippo Group and the Riady family foundation. These continue to serve their communities across Indonesia, giving youngsters the educational tools they will rely on in the future and providing medical care to those in need. I am filled with joy when I gaze upon the letters of thanks and the photos of healthy former patients that now adorn the walls at the Mochtar Riady Comprehensive Cancer Center in Jakarta. These are vivid testament to the inspiring service of the doctors, nurses and other dedicated employees at that leading provider of medical care. And I find similar satisfaction in the fact that the Lippo Group continues to provide a livelihood for more than 110,000 employees and contributes to the economic development of Indonesia as well as China and places beyond.

Over the last 20 years, many friends—both old and new—have suggested that I write an autobiography. One of the most persistent was the late Gu Guanqun, the dean of my alma mater Southeast University (formerly Chung Yang or National Central University) in the Chinese city of Nanjing. In the past, I have resisted such suggestions in the belief that fortune is fickle, and a final assessment would be best left to someone else after I am gone.

But in the spring of 2014 I accepted an invitation from a friend and fellow Christian, Brother Yu Jieling, to go on a trip to the Middle East in search of the origins of the Bible. During that trip I found my friend and travelling companion frequently directing the conversation to my past experiences. I began speaking freely about events of long ago and giving a candid account of my life. Soon after our stimulating journey came to an end, I received a 106-page transcript of our conversations entitled *Brother Riady's Oral Account of His Life*. Reading it left me both delighted and moved by my friend's effort. The transcript inspired me to seriously consider compiling an account of my own. Looking back at the past would at the very least let the younger members of my family learn more about my tumultuous life. And perhaps the stories of how I was guided by my father's dedicated hand would one day aid them in their own role as parents.

The eight decades of my life can roughly be divided into four distinct 20-year periods.

- The first period (1929–1950) covers the hardship and suffering of my early years.
- The second (1951–1970) saw the creation of a business that grew in step with the young Republic of Indonesia.
- The third (1971–1990) witnessed the progress of an outward-looking business amid the great tide of globalisation.
- The fourth (1991–2010) saw a global adjustment to the rise of China.

In my book, I also describe the most recent years of my life where I have focused on trying to be a role model for my children, grandchildren and great-grandchildren.

These years have passed in what seems like the blink of an eye. My memories of the past are like unfiled records in an archive, chaotic and disordered. For someone who never even kept a diary, compiling this history is a humbling task. I ask my readers to forgive my oversights and any inaccuracies. And I sincerely hope this tale will be of interest and of use to a broader audience.

HISTORICAL BACKGROUND: INDONESIA GAINS INDEPENDENCE

B efore I begin my personal story, I would like to offer a brief account of some of the events that helped shape the modern state of Indonesia. In sharing my perspective of the economic and political developments of these early years, I hope to provide a sense of the difficulties that had to be overcome as I tried to start a trading business, break into the world of banking and finally build a company that became the Lippo Group of today.

The first chapter of this book explores my years as a young boy in China, yet most of the events I describe actually took place in Indonesia, the country of my birth and my home for more than eight decades. The world has certainly become familiar with China's dramatic emergence as a global power, but not many people know of Indonesia's story. For example, how many know that the country, the world's fourth most populous, played a pivotal role between the great powers in the Cold War era, or that Indonesia's role in the Asian financial crisis of 1997–1998 was critical?

Certainly, Indonesia, even prior to the early years of the Republic, was not isolated from world politics or events. The country's struggle for independence was fuelled by a history of occupation and colonial rule—first by the Dutch and then the Japanese. However, it was Japan's occupation of Indonesia during World War II that helped set the stage for the end of colonial rule in what was then known as the Dutch East Indies. The Japanese encouraged nationalist sentiment to counter Dutch influence while the nationalist movement saw Japan as a useful tool in the drive to throw off Dutch colonial rule. Just two days after the announcement of Japan's surrender in August 1945, the Indonesian revolutionary leaders Sukarno and Mohammad Hatta declared independence. But it took more than four years of bloody struggle before a peace treaty formally ended colonial rule in what is now Indonesia.

It is hard to overstate the importance of the anti-colonial movement. This was seen as a just cause and part of an international drive to break the grip of Western colonial powers over much of what became known as the Third World. A new group of political leaders emerged to unite disparate peoples and forge new national identities in many parts of the world, including Indonesia. Even from my vantage point as a young student on the periphery of Indonesia's struggle, the importance of this movement was clear. My classmates and I were swept up in the political tide of the times, joining in public protests and adding our voices to the chorus of opposition to Dutch colonial rule.

The man who embodied this new political consciousness in Indonesia was Sukarno, a leader who had fought against colonialism his entire life and became the nation's first president. He championed Pancasila, the five major principles of the foundation of the Indonesian state. These principles, which fused socialism, nationalism and social justice among other ideas, became the nation's official ideology.

Nations born from armed struggle are fundamentally different from those created through peaceful means. Divisions are often deeper, particularly when the struggle is a prolonged one. In Indonesia, the struggle did not end at independence. The new nation continued to contest Dutch rule over Western New Guinea, and it was not until 1963 that the territory was incorporated into Indonesia.

President Sukarno achieved significant victories on the political front, establishing an international standing for the Indonesian people and strengthening their national pride. I believe we should recognise him as a hero who is worthy of our esteem and deserving of our respect and admiration. However, his political victories came at a price. The new nation's hostility to colonialism, combined with Indonesia's increasingly warm ties to the former Soviet Union and the People's Republic of China, eventually led to antagonism with the West. And that spilled over into relations with Indonesia's neighbours: confrontations with the newly independent state of Malaysia, and later Singapore, which were viewed in Jakarta as mere puppets of British imperialism, were protracted.

ECONOMIC PROBLEMS IN A YOUNG NATION

Economic problems plagued the young nation from its earliest days. The announcement of Indonesian independence was closely followed by the introduction of a new currency known as the Oeang Republik Indonesia (ORI). This gradually replaced the banknotes issued by the Japanese Government during the war. The Dutch-occupied area had also issued its own Netherlands Indies Civil Administration (NICA) banknotes. So, from 1949 to 1951, there were three different currencies circulating in the Indonesian market. The poor printing quality of the ORI made for easy counterfeiting, and as a result fake notes in circulation were plentiful.

In March 1950, the Indonesian Government adopted "currency reforms" in which all NICA notes with a face value above 2.50 rupiah were cut in half—literally. The left half of the note remained in circulation at 50 per cent of its original value, and the right half was exchanged at the central bank for a 40-year government bond. The measure was aimed at withdrawing the NICA notes from circulation to unify the nation's currencies. It was also supposed to keep inflation in check, but the benefits were limited and short-lived.

Another "reform" followed in 1959 when banknotes were reduced to 10 per cent of their original value. In 1965, the value of banknotes was again reduced—this time to a mere one-thousandth of what they had been. This too was supposed to deal with mounting inflation. Instead, it made inflation worse and led to capital flight. It wasn't much help in encouraging savings either, and this was particularly important to me as I was trying to build a banking business. That same year, inflation reached around 600 per cent and monthly interest on bank savings was as high as a staggering 20 per cent. Indonesia's economy was nearly bankrupt, and bank runs and bank failures were all too common.

During these protracted periods of high inflation, the salaried class, particularly civil servants, struggled to make ends meet as salaries failed to cover expenses. However, when civil servants finally discovered that there was a market for the power they held, even for the simplest government approvals, they began to live more comfortably. The selling of authority spread through the ranks of the bureaucracy and Indonesia was ensnared in widespread official corruption. The Indonesian people are still grappling with the effects of this history of corrupt behaviour.

Economic problems, the growing influence of the country's communist party, Partai Komunis Indonesia (PKI), and hostility from the West, brought an end to the Sukarno era. The transitional period near the end of Sukarno's rule was one of great instability, with deadly attacks on communists—suspected and real. Many of those in Indonesia's Chinese community were targeted as well.

By 1967, one of the nation's military leaders, General Suharto, had consolidated power, becoming Indonesia's second president. Suharto introduced more market-oriented policies and encouraged foreign investment. During his more than three-decade rule he also adopted a more pro-Western foreign policy and ended the confrontation with Malaysia and Singapore.

While the Suharto era had a far better economic track record, it too experienced deep problems. In 1997–1998, the Asian financial crisis hit Indonesia, and the banking system was one of its major casualties. Companies faltered, banks failed and the nation's currency collapsed. The country was forced to turn to the International Monetary Fund and World Bank for aid, ultimately leading to the fall of Suharto.

The political and economic storms of the last 65 years have been a harsh test for Indonesia. But we the Indonesian people can say that we have weathered this storm, emerging stronger from this protracted struggle. In the account of my life story on the pages that follow, I hope to show what that struggle was like on a personal level. I also hope it makes clear why I feel so optimistic about the future of my family, my company and my country.

THE FIRST PERIOD
1929–1950

CHAPTER ONE

HARDSHIP
AND SUFFERING

"You must go away in order to come back."

In 1928 my father, Li Yamei, made the bold decision to pack his bags and leave his ancestral village, Xindian, in China's Putian County. Putian, in the southern province of Fujian, lies along the west coast of the Taiwan Strait and is known to Chinese around the world for its role in mythology as the birthplace of the goddess Mazu, the protector of seafarers. When my father made his decision to leave, Putian was mostly a farm county with little industry and few homegrown opportunities. But there was a good port not too far away at Xiamen and that had enabled the region to become a source of outward migration. Many of those who decided to leave headed for Southeast Asia, particularly the island of Java in what was then a Dutch colony and is now Indonesia. My father had heard stories of others who went before him, and there was a network of people from this region who spoke the same distinct dialect of Chinese known as Xinghuanese (this dialect is also known as Henghua in Southeast Asia). Xinghua was actually the main town in the prefecture that included Putian at that time. My father, along with my mother, boarded a ship at Xiamen, and when the two-week journey ended they were in Surabaya, the main port and commercial centre in East Java. Eventually, my parents settled in Malang, to the south, where my father ran a small shop selling batik fabric and clothing.

In 1929, the year after my parents reached Indonesia, I was born in a hill town near Malang. I was the only son in a family that eventually had a total of eight children, seven of them girls. In a Chinese family, even one in another country, it meant everything to have a male heir who could continue the family line. In those days, girls were effectively second-class citizens. They were considered less important because it was expected that they would marry and begin a new life with their husband and his family. Of my four elder sisters, none of them made the trip to Indonesia; in fact three of them had been placed with other Chinese families at a very early age. This was painful for all concerned, but not uncommon at the time, as attention and resources were concentrated on the male offspring. After I was born, there was yet more family building to be done—my mother gave birth to three more daughters.

At the time of my birth, I was given the name 李文正, which these days would be romanised as Li Wenzheng. Li was our family name and Wenzheng combined the Chinese characters for "knowledge" and "integrity". Moreover, these same characters may also have been an allusion to an honorific bestowed on eminent Chinese officials of the past.

I should also point out that Li Wenzheng is a romanisation of these same Chinese characters based on their pronunciation in Mandarin—or what is now called "Putonghua" in mainland China. But in the Xinghua dialect, which we spoke at home, the pronunciation was closer to "Li Mong Ding". My birth registration reflected this pronunciation and was recorded as "Li Mo Di", which eventually became Riady on all official documents issued under the Dutch colonial government. It was all quite confusing, particularly for a young child. Occasionally, though, it had its benefits. As a teenager I was active in a student movement that opposed Dutch rule in Indonesia. I was picked up by police who were looking for an ethnic Chinese whose name was Li Wenzheng. They mistakenly thought I was someone else and let me go when they saw my identification card, which gave my name simply as Riady.

Some two decades later, matters became even more complicated. At that point, ethnic Chinese were strongly encouraged to take an Indonesian name if they wanted to enjoy the rights of an Indonesian citizen. This was a time of great hostility between China and Indonesia which was a factor in social unrest and ethnic tensions. These were the early years of President Suharto's rule and I will talk about the political and economic disruptions at the time he took power in a later chapter. But I will just say here that I added "Mochtar" to my name to become Mochtar Riady. And that name stuck.

But let me return to the very early part of my life. When I was five months old, my grandfather fell seriously ill. He still lived in our family's village of Xindian, so my father took my mother and I from Malang to visit him. Not long after our arrival, my grandfather succumbed to his illness, and my father returned to Malang, while my mother and I remained in the village with my grandmother.

We stayed in Xindian for six years. During that period, there was constant fighting among the local warlords, which left the countryside in turmoil. Xindian was located close to the Fuzhou-Xiamen Highway, which was the main road used by an assortment of armed groups whenever they were on the move. This meant that in the daytime we feared soldiers and the police, and at night we feared bandits.

The village consisted of a long street with a fortified building at either end. At night, the villagers took turns standing guard, on the lookout for bandits. It seemed like everyone carried firearms for protection. At times the fighting between warlords was so intense we were forced to flee to the shelter of a cemetery in the mountains. With war raging all around us, my loving grandmother urged my father to take us back to Indonesia as soon as possible.

There were around 200 families living in the village, and with the exception of one household with the surname Chen, all others were named Li. All of the Lis had moved there from surrounding villages, and my father belonged to the sixth generation to make its home in Xindian.

There was little to distinguish Xindian from other villages across China's rural heartland. These were poor farming areas with few resources and fewer opportunities. The only villagers to get a university education were two younger cousins on my father's side. They both went to Shanghai. Another villager distinguished himself by graduating from a military academy. He later became a battalion commander in the army of the Nationalist— or Kuomintang government.

My grandfather was the second wealthiest farmer in the village, and it was said that he owned 30 mu (two hectares) of farmland. My family had traditionally been carpenters by trade and had acquired enough wealth to become landowners, as well as the village moneylenders. I remember my grandmother as a wise and capable woman, who was greatly respected in the village.

Being the only grandson in the family, I was my grandmother's favourite. She showered me with affection, always watching over me and making sure that no harm came to the family's precious young boy. She always saved the best food for me, and with grandma around, no one dared scold me—even when I clearly deserved it. During those six years in the village, I almost always slept in her room.

One day my grandmother took me to a temple, a serene place set amidst beautiful scenery. I clearly remember her saying: "Child, our home is very beautiful, but look how poor everyone is here. It's because they have no skills. You must go abroad to study. You can come back once you are done and do things for the village. You must go away in order to come back, my child."

I never forgot my grandmother's words. However, it would not be until I returned to Putian in 1990 that I finally understood the true meaning behind them. As I set foot on the warm soil of my hometown, I realised what my grandmother had wanted to convey to me: the village was poor because there was no industry. And I could see then that there was no industry because there was no running water or electricity. It was after that trip that I decided to approach the Asian Development Bank and the International Finance Corporation—an arm of the World Bank—to raise funds to build a power plant in Putian, at nearby Meizhou Bay. I thought that Meizhou could one day become a centre of industry. I also helped the local residents build a water supply plant so they would have reliable drinking water. In gratitude, residents placed a large commemorative stone outside the front entrance of the water plant, inscribed with the words: "When drinking water, think of the source." While the words were a flattering reference to me, they also reminded me of my family's humble origins in this part of China. I recalled what my grandmother had told me: "You must go away in order to come back."

In 1935, my father wanted us to return to Indonesia. I cried for days and wouldn't let go of my grandmother—I couldn't bear to leave her. However, it had been decided that we would return and that decision was final. At the port of Xiamen, we boarded a boat laden with cargo and jammed with passengers, and two weeks later disembarked at Surabaya. At our destination and drenched in sweat, we patiently waited in line for inspection by the Dutch colonial immigration officials.

This was the first time I had seen white Europeans, and they made an especially deep impression on me with their red hair, blue eyes and tall, bulky frames. The Dutch officials had an arrogant and intimidating way about them, and treated Chinese with obvious disdain. I was hot and frightened and started to cry. As I thought of my grandmother and our familiar home town, my mother held me close and told me not to be afraid.

In Malang, I went to the Nan Qiang primary school, where I made many friends. One schoolmate's family ran a restaurant in their home. One day, when we were playing there, we heard the sound of a Dutch customer cursing and screaming. It turned out that the Dutchman was unhappy with a waiter who had dipped his thumb into the dish while carrying it to the table. He was right to be upset over this disregard for basic hygiene but there was no need to make such a fuss. Some Dutch colonialists saw themselves as members of a superior race. I would see more of this kind of behaviour in the years to come. It would contribute to the anti-Dutch sentiment that would eventually boil over into armed resistance.

THE PAIN OF LOSING MY MOTHER AT AN EARLY AGE

" [My father] adopted the roles of both a stern father and a caring mother. "

When I was eight years old, my mother became pregnant with my sister. In those days there were no hospitals in the countryside, and women would give birth at home with the help of a midwife. When my mother went into labour, the whole family waited outside the house, listening to her screams of pain from within. My father could not bear the tension, but there was nothing we could do to help. Finally, my sister was born—but my mother was lost to us forever. I became a child without a mother.

My father hung a picture of her in the centre of the living room. In keeping with Chinese custom, for 49 days he rose before 5.00 A.M. to prepare food as an offering to her spirit. He would burn incense, light candles, and recite prayers. For a long time after the period of mourning, he would often gaze at his wife's picture, and tears would roll down his cheeks. After my mother's death, my father adopted the roles of both a stern father and a caring mother. He would often mend my clothes and bathe me. In the evening, he would urge me to use the bathroom before bed, and in the morning, he would send me off to school. In the afternoon, allowing me a brief rest after class, he would make me write one page of small *xiaokai* (小楷) Chinese script, and two pages of the large *dakai* (大楷) script, instructing me to copy the works of Liu Gongquan, one of the great masters of late Tang dynasty (618–907 AD) calligraphy. My father tutored me in the proper brush strokes of Chinese characters. He said that each character was a painting, and that one could only learn to write Chinese characters by understanding a character's composition and structure.

Among the Putian natives in Malang, my father was the only one who knew how to read and write in Chinese. Every day, villagers would bring letters from their families back in China, asking my father to explain the contents and help write a reply.

In this way, and as time went on, I too became familiar with the villagers' correspondence, gaining an understanding of their social status and relationships with other family members, and learning the proper form of address for the sender and the recipient. Though I was still a young boy, my father would ask me to write on behalf of the villagers. I was delighted to help. At the same time this allowed me to better understand the issues that affected my neighbours and see how family problems could be resolved. It also helped me organise my thoughts and put them on paper. At school, I was appointed the class monitor and served as the editor for the monthly magazine.

THE STORY OF THE LOTTERY TICKET

" Wealth comes from sweat and toil, not from gambling. "

I heard that you could get rich by playing the lottery, and I figured I would try my luck. I had saved up a tiny bit of money and used it to buy a lottery ticket. As I was carefully checking to see if I had won, my father spotted me and angrily snatched the ticket from me. He tore it up and gave me a good scolding. "Wealth comes from sweat and toil, not from gambling," he said. "Gambling is the road to ruin."

Gambling wasn't the only lecture I got. My father also warned me not to accept gifts from others because that would become a debt that would have to be repaid. He insisted that this was also a crucial part of maintaining one's self-respect.

On one occasion, my third uncle gave me a packet of sweets, but when I showed them to my father, he insisted I return them. Even a small debt to someone should be avoided.

Although my father was stern at times, he was also caring. Whenever my clothes were torn or a button was lost, it was my father who would stay up at night, patching or sewing. If my shoes needed mending, he would make the repairs himself. In his spare time, he would often read me *The Twenty-Four Stories of Filial Piety*, a classic of Confucian precepts written in the 13th century. Another favourite was *The Twenty-Four Business Principles* of Tao Zhugong, an adviser to the ancient state of Yue whose skills as a businessman were legendary. And he bought me a children's picture edition of *The Romance of the Three Kingdoms*, a tale of battles and intrigues that is considered one of the great novels of Chinese literature. When I had finished the picture version, he started me on the original.

Step by step, my father guided me in my study of the Chinese classics and the assimilation of Chinese culture. Whenever I reflect on the richness of China's past, I always think of him.

THE CRUELTY OF THE JAPANESE ARMY

" My father was arrested and thrown into prison. "

After occupying much of northern and eastern China in the 1930s, the Japanese military turned its sights elsewhere. Soon after Japan's attack on Pearl Harbor in December 1941, the Japanese attacked the Dutch East Indies and by early 1942 they had occupied Java. The first time I saw Japanese soldiers, they were putting up checkpoints at key crossroads in our town. The locals had to bow deeply as they passed, and anyone who angered a soldier risked a slap in the face or being forced to stand in the blazing sun. The Japanese invaders, it seemed, were even more brutal and unreasonable than the Dutch colonialists.

In the Malang district at that time, 62 natives of Xinghua had organised the Fujian Xinghua Association, a social and business group commonly known as the Fuxing Association. This group continued to meet during the occupation, but the Japanese mistakenly concluded it was a front for anti-Japanese activity. One morning at 5.00 A.M., all members, including my father and third uncle, were rounded up and thrown into prison. They were held for over three years, until Japan's surrender at the end of the war. All these men were tortured; they were hung upside down, forced to walk on glass, and had water poured down their throat. Beatings, burnings, starvation, and being forced to stand in the hot sun all day were some of the techniques the Japanese liked to use. The chairman of the Xinghua Association died in prison, and it took over a year for many of the others to recover from their injuries after their release.

WAR-TIME SCHOOLING

"Social unrest. . .an inevitable consequence of the antagonism between rich and poor."

During the Japanese occupation of Malang, only primary schools were allowed to stay open and Japanese language classes were added to the curriculum. Every morning in the playground we had to raise the Japanese flag and sing the Japanese national anthem. Without any secondary school to go to, I remained in primary school, where I eventually "graduated" three times. Nan Qiang primary school's principal, Luo Yitian, helped me continue my education despite these difficult circumstances. He was a veteran teacher who was highly accomplished in classical Chinese literature. He had a knack for explaining the profound in simple terms. I remember how I had difficulty with the use of the character 而 (pronounced "er", and meaning, among other things, "yet" and "whereas"). Principal Luo wrote out a long sentence that included several examples of 而 in my homework book. After reading it, I immediately understood its uses and grasped its nuances. Luo Yitian also taught me the true meaning of the "Three Principles of the People"—the political philosophy developed by Chinese revolutionary leader Sun Yat-sen. On one occasion, I asked my teacher why some people were poor, while others were rich. He made me read *Messages of the Wanderer* by Zou Taofen, a Chinese journalist who was critical of wartime leader Chiang Kai-shek as well as the Japanese. In his book, Zou described the tyranny of imperialism, the inequalities of the American capitalist system, the enslavement of African-Americans and discrimination against Asians. The book left me with the profound sense that a nation needed to be self-reliant before it could free itself from imperialist oppression.

During the early stages of the Japanese assault on East Java, there was widespread looting and social unrest. At the time, this was widely blamed on anti-Chinese sentiment on the part of indigenous Indonesians. Principal Luo, however, taught me that this was not racial discrimination, but the result of a social and political vacuum, and an inevitable consequence of the antagonism between rich and poor. It was a lesson I would remember.

ATTENDING NATIONAL CENTRAL UNIVERSITY IN NANJING

"War is savage and brutal."

I n September 1945, Japan formally surrendered, bringing an end to World War Two. But as that great struggle drew to its dramatic conclusion, another was already intensifying as Indonesia sought to gain independence from its colonial masters. In Surabaya, there was fighting in the streets between Indonesian revolutionary forces and the British army, which had arrived to repatriate the defeated Japanese troops. The British soon transferred Surabaya back to Dutch rule. Dutch armed forces later attacked and occupied Malang, forcing the Indonesian revolutionaries to retreat into the surrounding villages, where they continued to fight. At the time, Commander Imam Soekarto led a division of the army near Malang. I met him by chance and we became good friends, despite the fact that I was only 15 or 16 and he was probably in his forties. Sometimes I was sent to reconnoitre the Dutch barracks and report back to the revolutionary army; at other times I would buy medical supplies for them in Surabaya. I felt I was part of an important cause.

The Dutch colonial government planned to continue its rule by partitioning the country and creating a Republic of East Indonesia. I heard that an organisation led by activist Siauw Giok Tjhan was trying to block this plan. Siauw mobilised East Java's Chinese students, urging them to take to the streets and demonstrate. I immediately responded to the call.

The Dutch colonial government arrested members of the organisation, and around 100 of them were imprisoned in Malang's Lowokwaru Prison. I managed to escape, after which I left Indonesia and travelled to Nanjing (known as Nanking at the time) in eastern China.

In Surabaya, my great uncle, Li Yajin, had a wide circle of acquaintances and he gave me an introduction to a fellow Xinghuanese who lived in Shanghai. This man appeared to be a businessman of considerable influence. Three days after I met him, he sent me to Nanjing to meet Commander Wu Heyun, a ranking officer in the Nationalist government's Ministry of Defence. At the time, I was hoping to secure a place at Nanjing's National Central University, but because I had left Indonesia in such a hurry, I hadn't brought any documents with me. Luckily, with Commander Wu's help, the university's rules were relaxed and I was permitted to sit the entrance examination. After an interview, I was ultimately accepted. For this, I am grateful to my father and Principal Luo, for without their invaluable help and guidance I would never have been able to get into university.

The National Central University had only recently moved back to Nanjing from Chongqing—the wartime capital—and things had yet to return to normal. In 1946, reports that an American soldier had raped a university student in Beijing (at that time known as Peiping) sparked nationwide protests. Students from all over Nanjing went out onto the streets to take part in anti-American demonstrations and I joined in. While questions later surfaced about the incident, my participation in the protests confirmed my left-leaning sentiments.

During the Japanese occupation, China was subjected to brutality and destruction at the hands of the Imperial Army. But in 1945, after eight years of nationwide resistance and the overwhelming power of the Allied forces, the Japanese were finally defeated. Life briefly returned to normal, lost territory was reclaimed, and the nation rejoiced.

During and after the war, the Americans directed generous amounts of aid to the Nationalist government of Chiang Kai-shek, supplying it with money, weapons and equipment. But Chiang's government was despised for its corruption and economic mismanagement. The Nationalists gradually lost public support as they became locked in a struggle with communist forces for control of the country. Hyperinflation took hold and it seemed that the price of goods rose by several hundred per cent each day. Legal tender depreciated so much that it was no longer circulating, and the government was compelled to issue gold-backed coupons. However, these gold coupons soon had no value either. The government tried to replace the gold coupons with new silver coupons, but their lifespan was even shorter. People had no choice but to try to get by using barter trade. There were food shortages and the public was desperate. Morale had nearly collapsed.

The Nationalist army, at least on paper, consisted of more than three million men at the time, but in less than two years the weaker Communist army had brought it to its knees. In 1948 and 1949, the communists' decisive Huaihai Campaign finally sealed the Nationalist government's fate. As the conflict approached Nanjing, the city teemed with refugees; public order disappeared and looting was widespread. Combined with the devalued currency and shortages of supplies, this meant that Nanjing was very soon out of food. As the weather turned cold, refugees in the city's Xinjiekou district froze to death by the roadside.

With most of the teachers and students gone, classes at the university were suspended and only a handful of us remained in the dormitories. At one point we had nothing to eat for three days. I found myself with no one to turn to and nowhere to go. Eventually, I decided to approach the Dutch embassy in Nanjing for help. It would be a bitter pill to swallow, but at least asking the embassy for assistance offered a glimmer of hope. To my surprise, after some intense questioning, the embassy arranged for me to go to

Hong Kong. War is savage and brutal, and it leads to starvation, poverty and death. Only after arriving in Hong Kong from that cruel and bloody battle-field was I able to appreciate just how precious peace is.

At the Indonesian consulate, I applied to return to Indonesia, but was unable to obtain approval because I had left all my newly acquired papers behind while fleeing Nanjing. I heard news that an old comrade-in-arms of mine, Imam Soekarto, was now a young general and the Republic of Indonesia's ambassador to Burma. I wrote a letter asking for his help, and he confirmed my identity. Finally, I was nearing my objective of returning to the place of my birth, my beloved homeland—Indonesia. While waiting in Hong Kong for permission to return, I came across another native of Xinghua who offered a helping hand. At the time he was working in a rela-tive's store in Hong Kong, and he let me sleep on one of the counters at night. Each day at dawn I would have to run to Sai Wan market to use the bathroom and have a wash, but at least I had a place to stay.

LIMEI'S LETTER SAVES MY LIFE

*"*Within crisis there is opportunity.*"*

B efore I returned to Indonesia I had one more brush with danger. It was an incident that to this day reminds me of how different things might have been. While waiting in Hong Kong for word on my return to Indonesia, I would go to a bookshop or library, deliberately picking out anti-Marxist books and magazines to aid my study of *Das Kapital*, the foundational text in communist philosophy by Karl Marx. Because most of the authors of these publications were likely to be well-versed in the subject, I could use their anti-Marxist essays to verify the truth of Marx's theories. I also had vigorous discussions with friends about social-ist ideas. This all contributed to my belief that the great problems of the world all stemmed from imperialism and that only the Communist Party could save mankind. I was very young, my emotions easily stirred. Encouraged by my friends and bolstered by a naive impulsiveness, I decided to go with them to Yan'an—the remote headquarters of the Chinese com-munist forces. I planned to take a boat to Tianjin in north China and travel overland from there. In hindsight, the decision to leave was probably more immaturity than a real understanding of communist ideology.

Before departing, I wrote a letter to my girlfriend, Li Limei, who had been in China but had returned to Indonesia ahead of me. Every night she was in my dreams. I hated being apart from her, yet for the sake of my ideals I felt I had no choice. My heart was full of conflict and pain, and everyone remarked on how thin I had grown. I waited anxiously for her reply. Every day I would check the mailbox, and every day there would be no letter. I was anxious and unsure of what to do. But then a miracle happened. The day before I was about to leave for Tianjin, Limei's letter finally arrived. She wrote that she, too, had waited every day for my letter, and for my return to Indonesia. She was worried that she would never see me again once I got to Yan'an. Of course, she could not predict the future, but she felt helpless. Her words left me heartbroken, and I spent the whole night in tears.

The next day, my friends told me to hurry and board the boat to Tianjin. A storm warning had been posted, and I told my friends to go ahead without me as I thought about Limei. The storm worsened and boarding the ship was by then out of the question. As the already fierce storm became truly terrifying, a loud boom came from the dock. There had been an onboard explosion before the ship had even set sail. It was a whole day before the typhoon passed, and the next day's paper broke the news: the Tianjin-bound ship had been carrying drums filled with chemicals, which had slammed against each other in the crashing of the rough waves. In the resulting blast, every one of the passengers on board was lost. After reading the news, my entire body went cold.

"Dear Limei," I thought at the time, "Thank you—your letter saved my life."

"Dear God," I thought, "Thank You for Your grace."

In the first 20 years of my life, I had encountered numerous difficulties. I experienced four wars and at the age of eight I lost my mother. During the Japanese occupation, my father was arrested, and I was suddenly alone and forced to stand on my own two feet. These years had been difficult and painful but they toughened me. Experiencing failure gave me stamina, and my ideals gave me the courage to face hardship. I later understood that within crisis there is opportunity, and from suffering springs limitless vitality.

THE SECOND PERIOD
1951–1970

CHAPTER TWO

TOURING JAVA AND ESTABLISHING A BUSINESS IN A DEVELOPING INDONESIA

"All rivers run to the sea."

I n 1950, I returned to Indonesia. The country had defeated the Dutch colonialists and officially become independent. It had experienced three-and-a-half years of Japanese occupation, followed by more than four years of struggle known as the Indonesian National Revolution. So the new republic, which finally won Dutch recognition in December 1949, had been through nearly eight years of conflict. The economy was in ruins, and both the government and people were destitute. It was against this backdrop that I set out to build my own business—one that, as it turned out, would be a first of its kind for Indonesia and which would grow in tandem with the republic's own development.

But that was in the future. The first issue I had to settle on my return was where I should base my business operations. I decided to travel around Java to see how people lived and how they made ends meet. Full of confidence, I set off on my expedition with only a small suitcase and some pocket money to cover travel costs.

I took the train from Banyuwangi in East Java and visited township after township (called *kecamatan* in Indonesian) along the route. In those days, very few towns and villages had hotels, and I would often head to the local bicycle shop to ask for directions or to enquire whether there was a hotel. Knowing that it was people from Xinghua who ran more than 90 per cent of Java's bicycle businesses, I would talk to them in the Xinghua dialect and immediately feel a bond between us. Instead of having to go to a hotel, I was always welcome to stay in their shop. This saved me a lot of trouble and expense, allowing me to spend six months travelling around Java and to accomplish my plan.

At the end of the six months, I came to the conclusion that "all rivers run to the sea": the nation's trade and business activity all ended up in the capital. Jakarta would be my business base.

MY MARRIAGE

"Adopting a 'retreat in order to advance' strategy."

I had always envisaged Li Limei as my future wife, but my father had other ideas. He was against a match with Limei because we shared the same surname. Instead, he wanted me to marry a local girl whose family name was Chen. Worried that provoking him might damage his health, I had no choice but to wait patiently and make no further mention of marriage.

Limei's family was also opposed to the marriage—firstly, because we shared the same surname, and secondly, because I had taken part in the revolution and had been the leader of student protests in Malang. I was seen as an extremist, a dangerous person and a loafer.

The heads of both families may have been against our marriage but I didn't give up. I decided I would go to Jember, also on Java, to see Limei's mother (her father had already passed away). I had heard that my prospective mother-in-law was sharp, capable and held in high regard by the community. Her 15 m × 50 m shop was located right in the middle of the town's busiest street. A Japanese-owned department store before the war, it was Jember's largest shop. For a widow to occupy such a commanding space was testament to her business acumen.

I went to see her as soon as I arrived in Jember, but when I introduced myself to her, I didn't come straight out and say I wanted to marry her daughter. That's because when I arrived at the store I was amazed that only a small part of its huge area was being used, and that most of the store was completely empty.

An idea sprang to mind. Rather than mentioning marriage, I decided to ask her about her business. In reply, she haughtily asked what it had to do with me. I replied that it was a great pity, such a waste, a great loss, and muttered to myself as I looked around and sighed, completely ignoring her. This piqued her interest and she asked me how I thought it should be run.

I calmly explained my opinion. I believed a shop should function as the intermediary between the supplier and consumer. In times when goods are plentiful, supply exceeds demand; it's an intermediary's market, and suppliers need shops to sell their goods for them. Provided that the shop is in a good location and has the right layout, there should be no problem finding suppliers. In addition, the goods could be sold on a consignment basis.

I suggested that the entire length of the shop be fully utilised. One side should sell fabrics and merchandise related to textiles and clothing. On the other side there could be male and female salons and men's tailoring, and at the front and right in the middle, women's cosmetics and shoes. The rear-middle section, meanwhile, could be made over to sporting goods. I explained that products should be arranged by colour to create an eye-catching effect.

After listening to my ideas, the expression on her face softened and a hint of a smile appeared. She went on to ask several questions, and mentioned the problem of capital. I replied that suppliers needed display areas for their goods. That meant she could fill her shop using very little of her own capital.

She seemed delighted with my suggestions, and invited me to stay at her home, where I had dinner with the family. We continued our talk well into the night. I rose early the next day, and it wasn't until I was about to leave that I asked for her consent to the marriage. I expressed my deep love for her daughter, and told her that I was confident I could run a large business—that I had the means for Limei to live a happy life.

After listening to my proposal she agreed, but on the condition that I help her with the store for three years. I thought for a moment before consenting to her request. I was both excited and happy—I had achieved my goal.

I knew my father dearly wanted a grandson, and hoped that I would marry soon, but I adopted a "retreat in order to advance" strategy, never mentioning marriage and making sure I stayed on his good side. After I had kept this up for several months, my father finally agreed to let me choose my own wife.

I then had to proceed with the arrangements for the wedding. I rented a room in a nearby street, which I fixed up and cleaned myself, and bought some basic furnishings. I borrowed a gold ring, a pair of earrings and a bracelet from my aunt and sister-in-law. I booked a hotel and decorated the wedding venue. I made a guest list, printed the invitations and sent them out. I did all this on my own with great fervour. I was finally going to get married, and I was overjoyed!

However, throughout all this I kept my three-year deal with Limei's mother a secret from my father, not wanting to upset him. I persuaded my uncle to come to Jember and open a lollipop store with me, which gave me an excuse to settle in the town and fulfil my commitment to my mother-in-law. After helping her for three years, my plan of extending the store was realised. It became Jember's largest department store and business boomed. Limei and her family were delighted, and she was very proud of me.

A POTTED TREE
WON'T GROW

"For the first time I had grown a successful business from nothing."

D uring these three years, I began planning how to set up a business in Jakarta. My father was very anxious about this, and urged me not to be rash. He feared that I would be going into a complex and unfamiliar environment, and that without sufficient capital, establishing a new venture would be risky.

One day, one of my great uncles from Surabaya, Li Yajin, arrived in Malang. We became good friends even though I was still in my early twenties and he was in his fifties. He agreed with my idea of starting a business in Jakarta, saying that if a tree is planted in a pot, it won't grow very big—but if it is planted in the earth, it can reach a great size.

In the beginning, I was quite conservative: I only wanted to start a bicycle parts business, like most Xinghuanese in Indonesia. My first thought was to research the bicycle business network. I wanted to know which of Jakarta's importers obtained their supplies from wholesalers in Surabaya, and how much the wholesale price was. I then discovered that the goods in Jakarta actually came from Medan on the island of Sumatra, and after going to Medan I found out the original source was Langsa in Aceh Province, at the northwest tip of the same island.

I pressed on to Langsa, thinking it must be a large city, only to discover that it was a small, isolated port. The road was nothing more than an uneven mud track. The tyres of the car I was travelling in had to be fitted with iron chains to keep the wheels from spinning uselessly. The car swayed and bounced along at barely more than 20 kilometres per hour; on three occasions it got stuck in mud and the driver had to push it out. The journey was only around 200 kilometres, but it took eight whole hours to get to our destination.

Despite having only two roads, Langsa boasted many guest houses and hotels, all of them full every day. The water in the guest houses was a turbid yellow colour and tasted of salt. The beds were infested with bedbugs and mosquitoes buzzed around everywhere. Nonetheless, this was a thriving market town, with vehicles busily coming and going and apparently more visitors than locals.

The wharf was small but the warehouses were overflowing. Any space was stacked sky-high with wooden crates piled one on top of the other. I was astonished that so many people flocked to a town where the living conditions were so poor. Even more incomprehensible was why this remote little port, rather than Jakarta or Surabaya, had become such a successful import-export hub. I was intrigued by it all.

It was only after a few days of asking around that I learned that customs duties were based solely on the volume of the crate they were packed in. Duties did not take into account the weight, value or type of goods each crate contained. This made importing and exporting extremely easy. In effect, it was an unofficial free port. Little wonder, then, that so many merchants had no qualms about doing business in such an inconvenient location. I quickly worked out that by operating here it would be possible to earn a 50 per cent profit—a very attractive margin.

I realised that if I could find some small but high-value items to sell, then the profits would be even higher. High-grade textiles or electrical goods, for example, would make more money than bicycle parts.

Back in Jakarta, I immediately fixed my eye on several high-value products that were in demand. Then I went to Singapore to check market prices before deciding what business to do.

Jakarta and Surabaya had many large import agents for several major bicycle importers, and they reportedly went to Singapore every month to buy their stock. Singaporean merchants would then load the purchased stock onto a lorry bound for the harbour. Then the goods would be transferred to a small freighter and shipped to Langsa. For this service, they would charge a fixed commission. Whenever these buyers arrived at Singapore airport, a crowd of merchants would meet them, waiting to take them to a hotel.

I'd heard that these merchants' usual method of doing business was to let the Indonesian buyers rest for a few hours before taking them to dinner, followed by a visit to a local nightclub and a night with a hostess. The next day, the Singapore merchants would invite the buyers to lunch, and then, after an afternoon nap, they would again have dinner, before going to another nightclub.

This routine would be repeated daily for six days, when, in a dazed stupor, the buyers would purchase their stock. There would be no negotiation on price and the next day they would depart for Surabaya. In those days the Singapore immigration department only allowed Indonesian nationals to stay for six days; they had to leave on the seventh, otherwise they might not have gone home, because they were enjoying themselves too much.

My great aunt's son (my father's cousin), Huang Yaxin, was Singapore's second largest bicycle wholesaler and also vice chairman of Far East Bank. He was a prudent and extremely conservative man who did not trust people easily. As he was my only relative in Singapore, I would always stay in his shop when I visited, and in the evenings he would often ask me about Indonesia's economy and politics. He also took a keen interest in my business.

I went to see him in Singapore to ask him about Langsa's import trade. He was very knowledgeable on the subject, and provided me with some invaluable tips. I told him about my plan to import small, high-value goods such as high-quality textiles or electrical goods. He endorsed the idea, introduced me to some wholesalers and agreed to act as a guarantor.

I imported two shipments and made a profit of around S$200,000—a significant sum at the time. Of that amount, I spent S$60,000 to buy a shop in Krekot Bunder in Jakarta. Limei and I officially moved to the capital as man and wife. I had laid the foundations of my business career.

This had been my first large acquisition, but I felt I was pushing my luck and decided to wash my hands of this business. Later, my great uncle said that I was destined for great things. Later still, I also learned that this had been the first time he had agreed to be a guarantor. It was a welcome show of confidence in me.

Moving goods to Jakarta proved no easy task and involved high transport costs. This got me interested in inter-island shipping. After doing some research, I decided to buy a 90-tonne wooden boat and have it sailed to Palembang, also on the island of Sumatra, since that was one stop on a very popular shipping route. However, things did not go according to plan. I was too new to the business and no one would take a chance on chartering my boat. It remained idle in Jakarta's Sunda Kelapa port. It seemed that despite a lot of hard work, all my efforts were coming to nothing. Desperate for contacts, I asked the husband of my former primary school teacher if he had any friends who ran businesses in Sumatra and Jakarta, and he promptly introduced me to Xu Naichang. Xu operated rubber and coconut ventures in Tembilahan on Sumatra, and his business was booming. Everyone said there were three kingpins in the business world in Jakarta and they were known as the three "Changs": Xu Naichang, Lin Dechang and Huang

Yuanchang. A common saying among the locals was, "Nothing gets done without the Changs."

I had found the right person, as Xu Naichang was an exceptionally honest, prudent and obliging businessman. He immediately made arrangements for me to go to Tembilahan and stay in his shop. His local manager accompanied me on a visit to firms that supplied a large amount of cargo, both in Tembilahan and Rengat, and I was able to introduce my freight company and my regular shipping policy to the local merchants.

At the wharf, I personally supervised the loading and unloading of goods, and took great pains to ensure that nothing was damaged. I also accompanied my boat to Rengat in order to learn as much as I could about the business. I personally directed unloading to ensure there was no theft on board and I introduced incentives for the crew to make sure all of the cargo got to its proper destination.

After accompanying my boat on three voyages, I knew everything I needed to know about the route. We became the most trusted shipping company in Tembilahan and Rengat. Before long we were shipping more and more freight—more than we could handle, and I eventually began chartering vessels from all over Palembang.

Within the space of six months, I had gone from one vessel to a total of 17. My company was the busiest shipping company in the Jakarta port of Pasar Ikan, and it wasn't long before I bought another boat. The business kept getting better and better. This was the first time I had grown a successful venture from nothing, and I was extremely proud.

MY FATHER'S
INSTRUCTIONS

" Do not mistreat or take advantage
of others. *"*

In the autumn of 1958, my father began to look very thin. Eating made him nauseous and he gradually lost interest in food. He was initially diagnosed as having a stomach disorder, but none of the treatments he tried had any effect. After consulting three different doctors, his condition was getting steadily worse.

Finally, he saw a renowned doctor in Surabaya, and after an X-ray, my father was diagnosed with stage-three oesophageal cancer. He was burning up and needed ice cubes to cool him down, as well as morphine shots for the pain. In the beginning, he would have one shot a day, but he soon needed one every few hours.

The Western-trained doctor had already informed us there was nothing that could be done for him. We decided to turn to traditional Chinese medicine, and tried doctors from China to Singapore. Later on, we heard that a village in Malang had an Indonesian shaman who could cure cancer, and I made a special trip to see him and invite him to Jakarta to treat my father. However, no treatment seemed to work and my father's condition continued to deteriorate. He would cry out in agony, his whole body wracked with pain.

Seeing my father like this was heartbreaking, but I didn't dare tell him outright that he had terminal cancer for fear of the distress it would cause.

He misunderstood, thinking that I didn't care, and would get very angry that he wasn't being treated using Western medicine. I couldn't bear to see my father sick and in pain, and in the end, I summoned the courage to tell him that his illness was terminal and nothing more could be done. He rebuked me for not telling him earlier, but soon an unusual calm came over him. He had accepted his fate.

The next morning he refused to eat or take medicine. Two days later my father left us forever.

My father was a widower at 41 years old, yet he never remarried because he worried that I wouldn't get on with a stepmother. He had educated me and looked after me for all those years but near the end of his life when he was sick and in need of help there was nothing I could do. I felt ashamed.

My father's name was Li Yamei, but he was known as "Chengfu", meaning "bearer of fortune".

He was born 28 September 1898 in China's Xindian village and died on 22 August 1959 in his adopted country. In keeping with Chinese tradition, his body was placed in a coffin and kept in our home for seven days. Then he was buried in Malang alongside my mother.

At that time I was still in the trading business. During the final two months of my father's illness, I suspended almost all my business activities to look after him.

But I soon had to fix my attention on business once again. As the saying goes: "Luck comes but once, but trouble comes in droves." Almost immediately after my father's death, the government announced one of its currency "reform" measures. The rupiah's exchange rate was drastically devalued, the nation's 500 and 100 rupiah bank notes were reduced to one-tenth of their original value and large bank deposits were frozen. Moreover, debts still had to be repaid at their original value. At this point of my life I found myself facing bankruptcy.

I responded by quickly clearing some small debts, which left three larger sums owed to key creditors. I explained my predicament to my creditors and told them I was willing to give up my house and inventory as payment in kind. My sincerity earned me their sympathy. They declined the offer of my house and stock, and suspended interest on the money I owed them. They gave me two years to repay the money I owed them, and I was extremely grateful for their kindness.

At that time, the market was in chaos and import costs were higher than the price of goods. After a lot of research, I concluded that commodity prices and import costs would tally after a year or so of adjustments, and the market would return to normal. Therefore, I insisted on not selling goods that did not cover import costs, and within six months my judgement was proved correct as prices began to recover to above import cost levels. I then began to sell and settled my debts early.

After two years, my business was revitalised and I had the funds to pay the interest I owed to my creditors. Although the lenders had waived the interest, I insisted on paying them. I recalled my father's instructions: "Do not take advantage of others."

LIMEI:
WIFE AND MOTHER

"It was Limei who supported me through the difficult times. "

I n times of adversity it is necessary to be patient and analyse the situation carefully. It is also important that you not take what you have for granted. I told Limei about my business problems and asked her to cut down on her household expenditures. She was very understanding. She not only comforted and encouraged me, she also secretly put aside fabric to make children's clothes, which she sold to a department store in Jakarta.

Limei had never learned to sew, but in our time of need she had developed the sewing skills needed to launch her own business. Baby clothes were very popular and sold well. Initially, Limei would sew day and night, but as the business grew she hired a seamstress, and then another, until after six months there were more than 100 people working in the house. Later on, she also contracted out the work to local women. Business was booming. My wife's hard work and willingness to share my burden gave me the chance to get my business back on its feet.

MY DREAM OF
BECOMING A BANKER

" I would often linger outside the bank when I passed it, dreaming of the future. "

When I was at primary school, I would pass a European-style building on my way to class. It had a grand façade, and the people inside were all dressed very formally and had an air of self-importance about them. They all looked extremely busy, yet the place didn't seem to sell goods of any kind—all of which I found very intriguing.

One day I asked Principal Luo what kind of business it was, and after finding the address, he told me that it was a Dutch bank. He explained that banks accepted deposits from the public, paid interest on the money and then lent out the funds at a higher rate to businesses that were in need of capital. Banks distributed society's funds and were intermediaries in commercial operations. They enjoyed a special status because many businesses relied on them for financial support.

I half understood what he said: banks, it seemed, took money from some people and lent it to others, and a profit could be made simply by this exchange of money. It seemed like such a good business that I asked Principal Luo why he had chosen to be a school principal instead of opening a bank.

At that time we lived in poverty, and I thought to myself that when I grew up I would be a banker as I found the idea very exciting. From then on, I would often linger outside the bank when I passed it, dreaming of my future as a successful banker.

As I got older, I learned more of the banking business from books and magazines. I would engross myself in anything to do with banking. I discovered that even one of the treasured books from my school days, *The Messages of the Wanderer* by Zou Taofen, touched on banking themes. Banking became my dream.

A BANK'S COMMODITY
IS CREDIT

"To do business, one must thoroughly research the nature of the product of that business."

W ang Yalu was a fellow Xinghuanese, the wealthiest in Indonesia. After running an agricultural produce business, he opened Dadong Bank together with several other business people from the same part of China. Within just a few years, Dadong had become Indonesia's largest private commercial bank, and boasted almost all of Jakarta's Chinese businessmen as its clients.

Wang did not have much formal education but he was good at getting things done and was upright in his business dealings. He served as the bank's chairman and his success strengthened my conviction to go into the banking industry.

My neighbour and fellow Xinghuanese, Chen Defa, had been in the bicycle business. Later, Chen opened the Bank of Benteng on the site of his former bicycle shop—right next to my house. He was also very capable, and after just three years the bank was already doing well. Like Wang Yalu, he had little formal education, yet he had turned his small bicycle shop into a bank and achieved success.

I was more determined than ever to go into banking. Wang Yalu and Chen Defa's successes had spurred my ambitions. I started discussing the theories and concept behind opening a bank with a few friends whom I felt had the potential to be business partners.

My father was worried when he heard of my plans. He thought I was overextending myself—that the scheme was not feasible—and warned me not to jump into it blindly. He said that in life, you have to be pragmatic. Opening a bank required large amounts of capital. Where would this capital come from?

I did not want him to worry, so I gently explained my ideas about banking to try to change his mind. I told my father that banks are merely intermediaries. Banks take in people's superfluous capital and every month pay them a fixed "capital-leasing commission"—called interest, in everyday terms. They then provide loans to businesses in need of capital, and charge them a higher rate of interest, making a profit from the difference. In effect, they were taking an intermediary's commission. Banking does not involve the buying and selling of capital. If it did, then that would involve handing ownership rights to another party.

So, the core function of a bank is to act as an intermediary, and an intermediary's capital is principally reliant on credit. Therefore, the business of banks is buying and selling "credit", and not "money". Provided I had credit, I could become a banker. The basic principles of banking are how to package and maintain credit.

From this, it is easy to see that the key principle of banking is creditworthiness. If you can limit risk and stay clear of speculation, you can become a banker.

If we look at the hotel business, we can see similar logic. The essence of the business is not the letting of rooms, it is the travel industry. If we position a hotel as a business that simply "leases rooms to visitors", then the location you choose for the hotel would have to be in a city centre. However, if you view a hotel's commodity as catering to the travel industry, then not only can you do business in bustling urban centres, you can also open hotels in scenic spots or near a port or even a factory. You can provide a service that caters to both business meetings and tourists. In this way, the scope of your business is much broader, costs are lower, profits are higher, and there are no limits to your potential for expansion.

As such, defining a bank's commodity as credit means that it is not subject to any limitations; its operations can be expanded and repeated over and over. That was the conviction I would hold on to when I later started expanding my bank. I stuck closely to the principle that creditworthiness would provide the foundation for successful growth.

In the course of my deliberations and analysis of the nature of banking, I ended up with my own philosophy: to do business, one must thoroughly research the nature of the product of that business. If you understand the nature of a product, you know how to make the most of it.

RIDE A HORSE
TO CATCH A HORSE

"If I wished to pursue credit, I needed to approach businessmen in society who had credit."

I have mentioned that a bank's commodity is credit. I was young, with no connections, and without any experience in banking, so how could I get anyone to trust me and give me credit?

I thought of Batu, a tourist town in the mountains of Malang that offers horse treks to visitors, which also happened to be the place where I was born. The owner of the horses was forever tiring himself out chasing after the horses, and sometimes he did not even manage to catch them. It would have been far easier if he had been riding a horse himself. I drew some inspiration from this: if I wished to pursue credit, I needed to approach businessmen who had credit (and thus status) and, through them, I could gain creditworthiness. If I could ride a horse to catch a horse, I could accomplish the task with half the effort.

In 1959, I saw the first glimmer of hope. Wu Wenrong, a fellow Xinghuanese, had heard that I wanted to start a bank. One day he came to see me to introduce Andi Gappa, the proprietor of Bank Kemakmuran, a small bank that was struggling and in need of fresh capital.

Gappa was from a prominent family in the Makassar region on the island of Sulawesi. The family was very honest, but lacked a thorough understanding of the business, and this kept their bank from growing faster. They were willing to let an outsider buy shares in the bank and help it grow.

At that time, the bank's total assets were worth approximately US$3 million and it had around US$100,000 in capital. The deal called for a new shareholder to inject US$200,000 in return for a 66 per cent stake. I agreed to these conditions, but waited for a financial due diligence investigation before investing any funds.

After discussing the terms, I went to see Wu Wenrong's father and his uncle who were successful businessmen. I lobbied them to join me and asked them also to invite three more influential merchants—all of them from Fujian. They proposed that I hold the position of chairman of the board and general manager. My dream had come true: I had become a banker.

On my first day as the bank's general manager, my colleagues presented me with the bank's financial report. After fumbling through the report for the whole day, I still could not understand it. I had no choice but to feign comprehension and sign my name.

I knew that I did not understand finance, so I had to find someone who did. I finally managed to persuade Yang Dingliu, the director of the foreign exchange department of Dadong Bank, to be my assistant and take charge of finance and the bank's administration. This breathed new life into Bank Kemakmuran, and in just 16 months, the bank was back from the brink of failure and business was booming.

I did not understand accounting, but it is something that every banker needs to know, so I invited a head accountant from Charter Bank, the forerunner of today's Standard Chartered Bank, to teach me. After six months, I was still struggling. What I found hardest was how the debit had to be entered into accounts at the same time as the credit. "Debit" and "credit" made my head spin—I had no idea. I was so slow to learn!

But I persevered: if I wanted to be a banker, I had to learn to read financial reports and be able to understand accounting. I had decided that there was no shame in starting from the bottom, so I watched and learned, and eventually I grasped the concept of "credit" and "debit".

After learning accounting theory, I once more threw myself into studying the banking business. I discovered that many of the bank's operating procedures were inefficient. So I asked Yang Dingliu and other professional bankers to help make improvements. It took me over a year to gain a true understanding of banking and acquire experience in running a bank.

Emboldened, I then focused my attention on growing the business. Above all, I worked according to the logic of tackling the easy things first, starting small, and prioritising the tasks that were near completion before the tasks that were far from completion. I asked every shareholder and manager to list all of their friends and relatives, and endeavoured to make each one of them a bank customer. The second step was to ask these new customers to introduce their friends and clients to the bank. From there we looked into what services customers needed most from a bank.

One by one, we studied and analysed the work procedures for each of the bank's services, then proposed the most rational methods and fees. After less than two years of this tireless work, Bank Kemakmuran had become one of Jakarta's most prestigious banks.

The bank was beginning to grow, but I noticed that some of the shareholders were acting unwisely. Some of the younger ones had started partying all night in nightclubs with clients. Having built up a close relationship, the shareholders would raise no objections when these clients requested overdrafts, which inevitably resulted in bad debt.

Older shareholders also started running their own banks within the bank, using its infrastructure to accept personal deposits and make their own loans. If this resulted in bad debt, it was passed on to the bank. After my repeated warnings went unheeded, I decided to leave Bank Kemakmuran.

From my time there I had gained a specialist knowledge of banking, as well as an understanding of the nature of greed. My powerlessness in the face of the bank's problems left me no choice but to move on.

Now I needed to find new banking partners and business people with influence. After doing some research, I turned once more to my old primary school teacher. Yang Xiulian was her name and she was the chairperson of the Jakarta Overseas Chinese Women's Association. Her husband, Wang Dayue, was secretary of the Indonesian Overseas Chinese General Association. Wang was very well connected and had a large circle of friends and acquaintances. I went to see him and shared what I had in mind, then asked if he would introduce some of Indonesia's honest business owners to help build a bank.

Most people would never imagine they could get involved in banking because they think it involves a large amount of capital, but I patiently explained to Wang Dayue the theory behind opening a bank. He agreed with my ideas, strongly recommending I meet Huang Yuanchang, one of the three influential Changs.

At the time, Huang Yuanchang was the chairman of the Indonesia Cloth Merchants Guild (the cloth business was Indonesia's biggest industry). He loved to play tennis and had a court at his home. After I was introduced, we played tennis early every morning.

During this time, I did all I could to explain how important and necessary banking was for the growth of Chinese businesses. I made a point of explaining that a bank's commodity was credit and not money, and that all that was needed to start a bank was credit.

After several months of patient explanation, one of Indonesia's more influential merchants, Lin Dechang, also one of the three Changs, became the first to get involved in this project. He then worked hard to bring on board Huang Yuanchang, who in turn convinced two of the biggest Chinese suppliers of local produce to join us.

In the end, I managed to form a shadow "banking corporation" with some of the country's key business people as its shareholders. These men were Indonesia's coffee, pepper, rubber, cloth and glass moguls. As the prospective company founder and general manager, I then went out to purchase a bank.

When I left Bank Kemakmuran, I had already found a bank that might be suitable for my next venture. It was Bank Buana. An old school friend from Malang had started it, but it had not been run well and was losing money fast. I quickly reached a purchase agreement and it was soon signed over to me.

THE STORY OF BANK BUANA

"I was hailed as the saviour of the banks."

In 1962, a newly reorganised Bank Buana officially opened for business. I had learned from my experiences at Bank Kemakmuran, so I started small and dealt with the easier and more immediate issues first. I asked the shareholders to draw up a list of all their customers, family and friends, then gradually began to canvas for business, advertising the opening of the bank in the newspapers.

The bank's deposit interest rate was half a point higher than that of other banks and the lending interest rate half a point lower. The bank also offered a greater variety of services while trained staff boosted the quality of these services. All of the bank's cheque and single bill formats were updated, and taken together this introduced a sense of freshness at the bank and boosted staff morale.

After more than a year of hard work, Bank Buana became Indonesia's largest Chinese bank, with branches in Bandung, Semarang, Surabaya, Malang, Makassar, Solo, Yogyakarta, Palembang, Telok Betong, Pekanbaru, Jambi, Medan and Manado. It also established a foreign exchange business in partnership with another small bank, Bank Dagang Negara. Business was thriving, and I had won the trust of all the shareholders. At this point, I must thank Wang Dayue for having faith in me and becoming one of the bank shareholders. He frequently settled misunderstandings among the members of the group, helping us achieve the harmony and unity needed to record solid growth.

Indonesia had just been through an unrelenting and violent struggle for independence. From 1950, the fledgling republic had begun to try to construct a national economy from scratch, but constant political infighting among its numerous political parties was a serious hurdle.

By 1965, Sukarno's economic and political problems were mounting. At this point inflation had reached around 600 per cent, and people were desperate for change. It was then that Suharto rose to power. Several University of Indonesia professors who had recently returned from their training overseas shared with us in class that the government wanted to reform the economic system and open it up, and that the plan had won the approval of the World Bank. I was very confident that the reform would be a success.

Knowing that we would be faced with the pressures of liberalising the economy, after much thought I decided to adopt a plan of strategic reform for the bank.

The main idea was that "in times of inflation, it is a seller's market; in stable times, it is a buyer's market". Because there had been crippling inflation in Indonesia prior to 1965, businesses could easily sell goods in order to pay back loans. Prices could be counted on to rise quickly. As a consequence, most loans were unsecured. Rising commodity prices offset the high interest, meaning that there were few bad debts at the time.

However, in a free and open economy—with its institutional improvements, surplus goods and materials, and inflation under control— commodity prices were likely to fall. Businesses would no doubt hold back goods to prop up prices, leading to losses all round.

I made a proposal to the board of directors to stay one step ahead by adopting a new low-interest, secured-loan policy. The board did not agree. It had grave concerns that in an environment of increasingly tighter credit at that time, lower interest rates on loans could result in losses and a shortage of funds for the bank.

In reality, my low-interest strategy would not encourage customers to take out cheap loans that would lead to a liquidity shortage at the bank. In fact, the lower interest rates would be offered in exchange for collateral to secure the loans. I explained to the board that if I were taking out an advertisement for my strategy in the newspapers, it would read as follows:

"In order to improve service to customers, Bank Buana will be lowering its monthly lending interest rate to 12 per cent, starting from the first day of next month. To enjoy the new interest rate, all bank customers must settle their existing loans and sign a new loan agreement. New customers are also requested to provide sufficient collateral on their borrowings."

I was confident the new lending policy would attract a lot of attention, and that businesses would be scrambling to open accounts in the hope of securing a loan at 12 per cent interest—half the market interest rate of 24 per cent at that time.

In the end, the board acquiesced. I drafted an advertisement for the newspapers, and as soon as the word got out, new customers were queuing outside every day to open accounts. The number of loans doubled within three months. Existing customers settled their old loans and provided collateral in exchange for the new 12 per cent interest loans. In a short space of time, Bank Buana became a very healthy bank with abundant capital. In the three short years between 1962 and 1965, it had become the largest non-state owned bank in Indonesia and the country's sixth largest.

By 1967, the Suharto government effectively controlled Indonesia. It soon adopted the ideas of the Western-trained academics who had returned from overseas. The government had implemented reforms aimed at creating a free and open economy. Commodity prices tumbled and the rupiah gained in value. This new trend led to a sharp rise in bad loans in the banking sector, and resulted in runs on banks throughout the country. Every day, one or two private banks went into liquidation. The market was in turmoil, and eventually the central bank had no alternative but to bail out more banks. Only Bank Buana, Bank Kemakmuran and Bank Industri Dagang Indonesia managed to escape the crisis.

During the period 1962–1966, bad loans led to three successive crises at Bank Kemakmuran. On each occasion, I helped resolve the situation, often providing financing. In 1966, a major banking crisis occurred in Indonesia that once more put Bank Kemakmuran in danger of bankruptcy. I had no choice but to take over the business. Wu Wenrong continued to run the bank while I supervised lending.

Around the same time, Bank Industri Dagang Indonesia—which was run by another fellow Xinghuanese—was also plunged into crisis. The owners approached me for assistance and I ended up taking control of the bank. On hearing the news, my mother-in-law travelled to Jakarta immediately to push for the inclusion of my brothers-in-law, Li Wenguang and Li Wenming in my business. Out of respect for her, I agreed to the request and granted them a 25 per cent shareholding. I found them to be capable young men and appointed them as chairman and manager.

Before long, the Indonesian government adopted a more open policy towards banks that allowed eligible businesses to apply for a new banking licence. My mother-in-law also requested that I set up a bank in Surabaya (which became Bank Industri Dagang Indonesia Surabaya) and give Limei's nephew Li Zhenliang the opportunity to go into banking.

These developments meant that when the Indonesian financial crisis hit in 1966, I was presiding over four banks, which put me under a tremendous amount of pressure. For almost a month, I managed to get only two or three hours' sleep a night as I worked constantly in an effort to get customers to repay a portion of their loans and take some of the financial pressure off us. Eventually, I was able to stabilise the banks, and all four were regarded as healthy.

THE STORY OF
PANIN BANK

" I asked myself whether I wanted to be a successful banker, or a good banker. "

The 1966 Indonesian banking crisis was primarily due to an excessive number of banks, not enough capital, and regulatory safeguards that were too weak. There was also a lack of management talent, meaning banks were poorly run. In addition to this, supervision by Bank Indonesia (Indonesia's central bank) was weak, inflation was high, and there had been a sudden rise in commodity prices. Convinced that prices were headed even higher, businessmen were borrowing whatever they could in a speculative binge and buying up anything they could get their hands on. This led to a shortage of funds at the banks and lending interest rates as high as 2 per cent a day.

It put a huge strain on the banks and day after day banks were closing down. The market was in turmoil and there was widespread panic. Within 17 days, nearly 20 banks had shut their doors, and it was only after Bank Indonesia stepped in to provide relief that order was restored.

In order to prevent another financial crisis, I represented the Indonesian Association of Banks in joint talks with the central bank and the Ministry of Finance. The result of the discussions was to encourage the consolidation of banks; if three or more merged and were able to increase their capital to US$20 million, they would be granted a foreign exchange licence. Aware that I controlled four banks (Bank Buana, Bank Kemakmuran, Bank Industri Dagang Indonesia and Bank Industri Dagang Indonesia Surabaya) the governor of Bank Indonesia, Radius Prawiro, proposed that I carry out the first merger.

I wasted no time in discussing the merger with the shareholders of the four banks. The shareholders of Bank Kemakmuran, Bank Industri Dagang Indonesia, and Bank Industri Dagang Indonesia Surabaya all agreed, but Bank Buana's shareholders did not. I did everything I could to persuade them—but to no avail, and in the end I was only able to consolidate three banks under the name of Pan Indonesia Bank, also known as Panin Bank. It was the first bank in the country's history born of a merger, and the first privately run foreign exchange bank since the founding of the Republic of Indonesia.

At that time, Indonesia had no regulations regarding business mergers, and the bank merger involved the state tax bureau, the Ministry of Finance's banking division, Bank Indonesia and parliament. The hardest part of all this was the fact that, in order for the merger to go ahead, the value of the assets of all three first had to be estimated using equivalent standards. However, the income tax payable on the profit from assets, re-evaluated to reflect market prices, would mean losses for the bank.

Consequently, the tax bureau needed to adapt and modify the relevant laws. However, it was reluctant to do so, necessitating patient explanation and persuasion. In addition, all three banks needed to hold a joint shareholders' meeting, agree to the merger, and establish a new corporate body. At the same time, the Ministry of Finance and Bank Indonesia needed to cancel the banks' old licences and issue a new one for Panin Bank. Each stage of the process presented its own difficulties. It took me a whole year before I was able to complete the merger and my hopes finally became a reality.

While preparing to consolidate the three banks into one foreign exchange bank, I asked Bank Indonesia if they would approach several global banks (among them, Bank of America, Citibank, Chemical Bank and Irving Trust Bank) for talks about establishing correspondent banking agreements. I also fought to obtain a small amount of financing to support letters of credit and currency exchanges.

Meanwhile, I was busy looking for locations to open new branches in various cities around Indonesia, as well as training staff, learning about new financial services, designing new cheque and bill formats and refurbishing the old site of the Bank Kemakmuran to become our new head office. The internal layout and fixtures were all inspired by the style of Citibank.

The result of these efforts was the transformation of Panin Bank into Indonesia's most modern bank. The new approach appealed to the entire staff, instilling them with new drive and spirit. With so many commendations and good wishes, the business made rapid progress. Within a year, it had superseded Bank Buana as Indonesia's largest and most profitable private bank. It brought me new hope and made me extremely proud.

Yet not long after, there occurred a string of unfortunate events.

The following account of Panin Bank covers the period 1971–1975. In theory, it should appear in the third period of my life; however, for the sake of coherence, I will recount it here.

Two of the Pan Indonesia shareholders started an illegal banking operation, using the address and name of the bank to secretly take customer deposits and lend this money to other customers in need of short-term loans. The customers had signed collateral loan agreements with Panin Bank. These customers had given the unscrupulous shareholders their Panin Bank account cheques as loan collateral; if a lender failed to repay the loan on time, then these shareholders had the power to cash the cheques with the bank. They would then shift the bad debt to the bank, which would bear the loss.

On one occasion, these two individuals secretly issued a high-interest loan to a Jakarta steel merchant who later fell into financial difficulty, leaving him unable to repay. The two shareholders posted the collateral cheques and the bad debt was transferred to the bank. The two of them earned high interest from the loan, while the bank bore the loss.

When the steel merchant was ultimately unable to overcome his financial difficulties, the two shareholders secretly colluded with prosecutors, asking them to demand payment from the man and send officials to investigate his premises. After the confiscation of several years of his documents, he was eventually accused of tax evasion and fraud. The documents also led authorities to uncover large-scale tax evasion by many of the steel merchants and businesses that he had dealings with. This led to many of them being implicated.

The affair caused quite a stir in the market, and there were rumours that Panin Bank was secretly working with the tax bureau against its own clients. Fears about the confidentiality of bank customers' business secrets caused widespread panic and a succession of customers closed their accounts, leading to a life-threatening run on the bank.

Disaster loomed. This was the third time I had experienced a bank run, and it was only after I asked Bank Indonesia to step in that the crisis was averted.

In addition to violating regulations and harming the bank, these two individuals had also been smuggling goods to Singapore. At Jakarta's Pasar Ikan wharf, they would declare they were transporting textiles to Bagan, on Sumatra, when in reality the shipment would contain tin ingots and rubber. Halfway into the voyage out of Jakarta, the ship would turn and head for Singapore, unload the ingots and rubber in exchange for textiles, and then continue on to Bagan. They really were an incurably foolhardy pair.

Not only did the two of them fail to mend their ways, they became even more brazen in their illegal behaviour. They convinced a female director in the foreign exchange department to make unauthorised transfers of deposits from one of our accounts at the United Overseas Bank in Singapore into their private accounts, which almost led to our cheques bouncing due to a lack of funds. Their contempt for the law knew no bounds. The simplest solution would have been to inform the authorities—but after thinking it over, I concluded this would be tantamount to announcing Panin Bank's internal failings to the world. Misunderstandings could easily arise and blow the affair out of all proportion, leading to a crisis for the bank and the possibility of another bank run. This would not only harm Panin Bank, but could also endanger all of Indonesia's banks. For a nation at a critical time in its economic reconstruction, this could be a fatal blow. Moreover, one of the two was in fact an in-law. My love and respect for my family was too important to me to risk making this public.

While this was a painful episode, it made me wary of the dangers of hiring family members. This was a warning that I kept in mind in the future.

After giving this immediate issue a great deal of thought, I eventually decided that I had no choice but to leave the bank. I had enough faith to believe that I could start another, even bigger one. I could only pray to the Lord to protect and be merciful towards Panin Bank, and hoped that my departure would cause those two individuals who were so cavalier with the law to come to their senses.

When I decided to leave the bank, I asked myself whether I wanted to be a successful banker, or a good banker. A successful banker would lend to any customer who could provide sufficient collateral and pay higher interest rates on borrowings. This kind of banker does not care what a loan is used for.

A bank grows when it makes money, regardless of whether its customers use loans for smuggling or opening gambling dens or starting businesses that are detrimental to society or harmful to the environment. Successful bankers don't care as long as they receive higher interest income.

A good banker, however, must at all times consider how to ease the financial burden of the customer and how to create more jobs by effectively utilising the savings of the public. A good banker should also help customers make it through difficult times, and assist them in growing their business and increasing their income.

Higher incomes, in turn, mean that the government can collect more tax. Collecting more tax means a full treasury, which in turn allows the country to build needed infrastructure and provide more healthcare services and educational facilities. This results in peace and prosperity for society as a whole. The answer to my question was that I wanted to be a good banker. That was my ambition.

THE THIRD PERIOD
1971–1990

CHAPTER THREE

DEVELOPING A BUSINESS AMID THE GREAT TIDE OF GLOBALISATION

"In the third 20-year period of my life, I had to learn how to adapt to economic globalisation."

The shareholders of Panin Bank were young and short-sighted. They were not the partners I needed for the long-term growth of a bank. I spent several months in introspection, discussion and deliberation. What had I learned from my 15 years in the banking profession? What kind of bank did I want to create in the future?

In the formation, history and course of economic globalisation, we see the following: in the late 18th century, the Industrial Revolution began in Great Britain. It was a time of great technological innovation—a time that witnessed the invention of the steam engine and the rise of the factory system. The British became the world's foremost traders and the British pound became the pricing mechanism for global commodities. The pound was also the world's reserve currency and the Bank of England naturally became the clearing house for world trade. Britain enjoyed interest-free international capital and this economic dominance lasted until World War II.

The war left Britain financially exhausted while much of Europe was in ruins. The US, however, saw relatively little conflict on its own soil due to its distance from the main theatres of war. Its economy emerged from the war stronger than ever, and this allowed the US to assume Britain's leading role in global affairs. The Bretton Woods Agreement after the war put the dollar at the centre of the global financial system, replacing the pound. Ultimately, the Federal Reserve Bank supplanted the Bank of England as the clearing institution for world trade. From this we can see the immense power held by national clearing banks.

While Indonesia was in no position to dominate world trade, the importance of a clearing bank was obvious. I was determined to create Indonesia's second clearing bank after the central bank. Panin Bank's share-holding structure prevented the bank from taking on this important role, so I decided to look elsewhere to achieve my goals in the local financial sector.

At the time in Indonesia, the tobacco industry enjoyed far-reaching economic clout. It involved a large number of people, a broad market and a long production chain. I concluded that whoever controlled this industry would have the best prospect of establishing a clearing bank. This became my objective, and I decided that my future partners should be business owners with links to this industry.

On 1 May 1975, I was finally able to make my departure from Panin Bank. Soon after, I was on a flight to Hong Kong and I found myself sitting next to one of Indonesia's most successful businessmen, Sudono Salim (who was widely known by his Chinese name, Liem Sioe Liong). We later became close friends and formed a business partnership that lasted some

16 years. Sudono Salim was the dominant figure in Indonesia's tobacco industry, as one of two merchants authorised by the Indonesian government to import cloves, which were widely used in locally made cigarettes. He dominated distribution of cloves to cigarette manufacturers, effectively holding the lifeline of what was known as the *kretek* industry in his hands. He would make the perfect partner to help establish Indonesia's second clearing bank. Through him, I would be able to concentrate the tobacco industry's payments and currency exchanges in one bank.

We started discussing Indonesia's economic prospects and the latest political developments. He also asked me about Panin Bank and my plans for creating a new bank.

I told him about my idea for a clearing bank, and gave him a rundown of my competencies. I explained that in my 15-year career in banking, I had accumulated around 500 loyal customers and tens of thousands of customer accounts, and gained genuine insight into the running of a bank. I had also trained nearly 100 teams of management executives, and had established connections with five foreign banks that would support our foreign currency operations. Moreover, I had already contacted five small banks that wished to merge with us—meeting a key requirement for conducting foreign currency operations. Salim asked me to join one of his banks. At the time, he had three of them: Bank Windu Kencana, the Salim family flagship bank, overseen by his younger brother, Liem Sioe Kong; Bank Dewa Ruci, run by his cousin, Lin Wanzong; and Bank Central Asia, a bank that was going through some difficulties.

President Suharto's son and daughter each had a 15 per cent shareholding in Bank Central Asia, with another 10 per cent owned by a retired general. Salim and three of his relatives held the remaining 60 per cent. He told me that I could choose any of the three banks and have a shareholding of 17.5 per cent. I chose to become a partner in Bank Central Asia.

THE SECRET OF BANK CENTRAL ASIA'S GROWTH

"The master anticipates things that are difficult while they are easy, and does things that would become great while they are small."

In June of 1975, I walked into the Bank Central Asia building and held my first business meeting there. The focus of the meeting was on reformulating the bank's organisational structure and allocating staff to management departments. In this, Salim showed the utmost confidence in me, and I was touched by his generosity and sincerity.

During the meeting, I organised a 10-person administrative work-flow compilation committee—with myself as its head—to undertake the task of compiling an outline of the bank's business and administrative work procedures. We used system operating procedures that involved a narrative format. First they described the work tasks for each unit, and then detailed the tasks and operating method for each staff member.

I discovered that within the same work processes there would sometimes be several identical work practices. These had to be patiently explained over and over again, on top of which the format was inconsistent with no real standardisation. As a result, a simple workflow took 10 or more pages to describe. This narrative style made the work of compilation extremely onerous. One error anywhere in the document would require a complete rewriting.

Furthermore, each staff member would need to read the procedures from start to finish; they would be unable to focus all of their energies on their own tasks and work procedures, and would be unsure about their own responsibilities. I felt that there was ample room for improvement.

After much research and deliberation, I proposed a new way of compiling working procedures.

First, we would use diagrams to depict workflows. I said these should use a rectangular box format to be laid out according to workflow sequences. Each box should provide a simple and concise description of the tasks related to each staff member's position. In this way, the division of labour within the entire workflow could easily be understood at a glance.

Second, we would collate the operating procedures of all workflows, record any discrepancies item by item, and combine entries for procedures that were the same. Workflow descriptions could then be amended based on this screening procedure, and could serve as an outline for workflow operating procedures, each of which would receive an identifying number.

Finally, at the bottom of each of the boxes mentioned above there should be a circle with a number identifying the work procedure for each staff member. Individuals could then access their own work procedure based on its allotted number.

There were several advantages in using this method.

A diagram could be understood at a glance and every new staff member could easily understand his or her own tasks and how to perform them, meaning a new bank employee could gain a basic understanding of the job in just 20 minutes.

The work of compiling workflows was also simplified. If a task or work procedure for a particular position needed to be deleted, then revisions could be made to the relevant explanation without affecting the whole outline.

There is a secret to compiling workflows. What it comes down to is this: it is very easy to erroneously assume that certain work posts involve only a single task or procedure when in fact they are far more complex.

To give a simple example: on the face of it, the task of a bank teller is to handle deposits and withdrawals from customers. For deposits it looks like there is only one workflow involved. However, on closer inspection, we see that customer deposits use six different financial instruments (also referred to as payment bills), including cash, foreign currency, cheques from one's own bank, other bank cheques, national money orders and foreign money orders.

Each financial instrument has its own handling procedures. Therefore, there are six different workflows. It is very easy to teach a cashier six different workflows, but what is even more important is simplifying the work of compiling those workflows. This is the secret.

Within 12 months, the task of compiling workflows at Bank Central Asia was complete. These had the following 10 functions:

- Reviewing of existing workflows to remedy problems with outmoded practices
- Ascertaining the number of staff in each work unit
- Ascertaining the number of working hours needed for each unit
- Ascertaining the resources needed for each unit
- Calculating the costs of products and services based on staffing, working hours needed and the resources needed
- Drawing up a budget based on the calculation
- Forming the basis for the digitisation of workflows
- Forming the basis for management of each work unit
- Forming the basis for the standardisation of flow operations
- Forming the basis for each work unit's daily financial report.

This fundamental procedure dramatically improves work efficiency, saves on operational time and costs, and prepares the bank for large-scale expansion in the future. Rapid expansion, however, required another basic process: file management.

On my second day at the bank, I inspected the archives office, which looked like it hadn't been swept and cleaned for years. Files were all over the place: in boxes, on the floor and in filing cabinets. Different types of files and files from different time periods were mixed together, covered by a thin layer of dust. Cobwebs dangled from the ceiling. I was astonished—why had the management department been so neglectful of company property?

In fact, archives are the foundation of a bank, and sound file management can improve bank efficiency and increase profits. Complete and orderly files provide a record of the bank's operations, which is vital to business expansion. The lack of attention to organising the filing system was affecting Bank Central Asia's ability to grow. I immediately organised a team of six to put the files in order, giving them a deadline of three months to complete the task.

Three months later I went to the archive office to check on their progress, and found that little had been accomplished. I had no choice but to look into it myself and come up with a solution. I discovered that the reason for the lack of progress was that there was no logic to the ordering of the files. After giving it a day's thought, I asked for 15 empty boxes. On each box a year was written (from 1960 to 1974). Each file was then placed in the box corresponding to its year.

Within 20 days, all of the files in the archive office had been packed into 15 boxes. I then requested 180 medium-sized boxes. On each of these boxes a year and month was written (from January 1960 to December 1974). I arranged the files based on their year and month. The process took 70 days to complete. Fifteen years of files were bound into 180 file books, which were then packed into 15 large boxes according to year. In this way, the archives room went from being dirty and chaotic to clean and orderly.

THE ROLE
OF ACCOUNTING

"
A 'big-picture' view of an organisation's operation "

A ccounting plays a crucial role in banking. As a discipline, it has a history stretching back several thousand years; it can provide a wealth of information for business owners and serve as a guide for business strategy.

A financial statement can give a "big picture" view of an organisation's operations or it can be used to drill down into the details of individual components. To give an example: a bank's profit and loss statement can simply record profits, but at a deeper level it can show whether these profits come from interest, commissions, foreign currency exchange or elsewhere. It can give a detailed breakdown of income from interest: mortgage loan interest, car loan interest, long-term loan interest and inter-bank loan interest, among other sources. If required, it can paint an even more detailed picture, breaking down mortgage interest into commercial and residential mortgage loan interest, for example. And if that's still not enough, it can even identify income from different bank branches.

With so much information, an operational-level understanding can be gained about the business and profit of different branches. Decisions can then be made about how to best encourage and reward branch management, or to warn management that problems need to be addressed.

Executive and management staff can use the information from their accounting reports to analyse past business, determine business policies for the future, and draft annual budgets. For head offices, budgets allow them to stay on top of their overall operations, and evaluate whether managers have met their targets or are underperforming. This plays a vital role in determining staff bonuses.

The function of accounts, budgets and workflows is to tell the general manager about the overall operating circumstances and financial situation of the bank, allowing him or her to immediately issue a warning or suggest a solution to underperforming staff and branch managers. They allow general managers to be everywhere all at once.

Executives possess an intangible power that can motivate staff; even when they are not physically present, employees can always feel their presence. In this way, a leader's power and charisma can intangibly spur subordinates to perform their duties more effectively. This is the highest realm of management philosophy.

As the technological revolution led the world into the era of the information society, the digitisation of administrative and accounting operations became inevitable. At the core of this process were workflows and modularisation.

From 1976, Bank Central Asia began the process of compiling workflows and developing accounting functions, a project that took around 20 months to complete. Starting from 1978, I made workflows the blueprint for the digitisation of our operations. This would form the foundation of the rapid opening of new branches and the establishment of a nationwide network of banks. In addition, it would also serve as the foundation of Bank Central Asia's transformation into Indonesia's second clearing bank.

Pushing forward this fundamental task of compiling workflows, formulating accounting systems and establishing an archive management system meant that we had to overcome numerous difficulties, which required a vast amount of work. However, it was my profound belief that the firmer these foundations, the more Bank Central Asia would be able to grow.

As the ancient Chinese philosopher Lao Tzu said, "The master anticipates things that are difficult while they are easy, and does things that would become great while they are small. All difficult things in the world are sure to arise from a previous state in which they were easy, and all great things from one in which they were small. Therefore, the sage, while he never does what is great, is able on that account to accomplish the greatest things."

As I pushed ahead with these time-consuming efforts, I drew inspiration from another saying of Lao Tzu: "A journey of one thousand miles starts with a single step."

The three fundamental systems mentioned above (the archive management system, accounting system and workflow process) provided the bank's day-to-day operations with a standardised system to follow, making ours a method-based management philosophy.

In business management, there are also two other management philosophies: mind-based and people-based.

A mind-based management philosophy is the philosophy of personnel management: the focus is on using the manager's own moral character as the basis of his or her management of a large number of subordinates. Subordinates will be constantly aware of the presence of their superiors, even if they're not there.

A people-based management philosophy teaches subordinates how to accept being managed. It is also about learning how to manage people, teaching people how to manage themselves, and showing concern for subordinates based on moral principles. The objective is to create a truly pleasant environment for them.

Corporate banking customers come in all shapes and sizes. They cover hundreds of different industries, and each company has its own characteristics. As a result, a bank's management needs to have a diverse professional background. A wide array of professionals who were a good fit for the banking industry would be the cornerstone of Bank Central Asia's growth, although recruiting the right people would be a huge challenge.

When it comes to human resources, I have the following standards and principles:

- For management and administrative staff, administrative experience and a sense of morality are most important. Honesty is of particular importance.
- Most important for staff involved in the design of service products is industry and sales experience.
- Business development managers must be professionals with wide-ranging social connections and a focus on local connections. They must possess commercial experience and have good people skills.

The majority of the bank's administrative and management talent was recruited from my old staff. In preparation for the expansion of new branches, the training for these new management and administrative personnel was all about workflows.

For the design of service products, I hired two highly experienced managers who had been working in a foreign bank. For the business development managers, I gave priority to business talent who had personal or local connections—knowing people from their home town in the textile, tobacco, flour processing (food products), building materials, and car and bicycle parts industries. In particular, the managers of the 11 regional service centres had to be local people with the above-mentioned backgrounds.

The main focus of my arrangements for the bank's administration and management was on administrative services, accounting and other internal departments; management of the bank's business fell to others. Everyone worked according to the workflows, dividing their responsibilities and making the most of each other's strong points. Many years of experience had proved that this was the most effective distribution of human resources.

At this point, I wished to introduce a new branch strategy. When selecting branch managers, I hired either local business leaders and highly experienced business people or their relatives. All of them had to be personally trained by me before they could take up a position. First, I taught them how to compile a list of the top 10 customers among cigarette suppliers, fabric merchants, building merchants, food suppliers, automobile traders and bicycle dealers.

Second, I instructed them to record these customers' family backgrounds, interests, assets, moral character and relationship with the bank, including how much they might have borrowed from the bank, and so on. After that, they would be trained at our head office for three months and take part in business meetings, before receiving another month of training at a local branch.

Finally, I drafted a customer loan name list and instructed the relevant branch managers to win the business of the top 10 companies from each of the six industries mentioned above. This would be each branch manager's task for their first six months. Once the training was completed, managers could immediately take up their positions. By training personnel in this way, I was able to successfully develop Bank Central Asia's network.

For the bank to become Indonesia's second clearing bank, we required a large volume of commercial trade, as well as branches and sub-branches in large cities. Only by using these branches and sub-branches to create a powerful bank network could we achieve our aim for Bank Central Asia.

In terms of the distribution of Indonesia's population, the island of Java is Indonesia's most populous. When we were making our plans for the bank's expansion, Java accounted for more than 50 per cent of the country's population (more recent estimates put the figure at 58 per cent). Next came Sumatra, followed by Sulawesi and Kalimantan. About 90 per cent of the population lives on these four large islands.

Based on this population distribution, I planned to create our bank network in three phases. During the first phase, key regional service centres would be set up. They would be established in the six biggest cities in Java, followed by the cities of Medan and Palembang in Sumatra, and then Makassar and Manado in Sulawesi.

In the second phase, based on the flow of trade in each of these centres, bank branches would be opened in commercially important cities. And in the third phase, sub-branches would be opened in the cities where regional service centres were located or in the district-level cities below them. I hoped to have a network of 600 banks within 10 years.

As we were building out the bank network, we gave priority to winning customers in important industries in the clothing, food, housing and transport sectors. Those four sectors covered a multitude of industries, so I first selected the textiles, tobacco, flour processing, construction materials, and automotive and bicycle components industries.

The distinguishing features of these industries were as follows: the textiles industry, from manufacturing and distribution to the wholesale trade, was run by natives of Fuqing, a city just north of Putian in China's Fujian province. The largest cigarette manufacturer was the PT Gudang Garam Tbk., run by Tjoa Ing Hwie, a native of Fuqing. Cloves, a key raw material used in the industry, were supplied under a duopoly that included another son of Fuqing—Sudono Salim. The flour processing industry was also Salim's exclusive preserve while over 50 per cent of the building materials merchants were Fuqing natives. People from Putian accounted for 80 per cent of the automotive and bicycle traders. These characteristics laid the foundation for our completion of the tasks ahead.

We made every effort to establish a nationwide banking network. Prioritising key industries and key customers in the clothing, food, housing and transportation sectors, developing an extensive customer base for Bank Central Asia, and ultimately processing all of the customers' financial transactions through the bank—these were the core objectives of our work.

MERGING BANKS

"Using an 'isolate and freeze' strategy"

T urning Bank Central Asia into a foreign exchange bank, and being able to open more branches, would require a merger of at least three banks, according to Bank Indonesia regulations. It was 1977 and by then we had already acquired Bank Gemari as well as another small bank that was in some difficulty. At that point we had met the central bank's minimum requirement. We kept these operations under the old name of Bank Central Asia, and it was not long before we obtained our foreign exchange license. This made us the country's second private foreign exchange bank, after Panin Bank.

One of the biggest problems with acquisitions can be in dealing with employees. Different companies have different work cultures, habits and attitudes, and it is these discrepancies that can cause problems. This was especially so with Bank Gemari. The bank had originally belonged to a welfare foundation under the Indonesian army, and many of its employees were retired officers.

There was a tremendous discrepancy between the work habits, culture and attitudes arising from their military backgrounds and the actual work habits and ideals of a market economy. Getting these employees to change their habits and attitudes and adapt to the practices of a commercial bank was no easy task. They did not have much experience with commerce and found it extremely difficult to communicate with business people. They failed to understand why it was necessary to be polite and accommodating to customers, and could not grasp why they needed to review accounts and balance the books at the end of the day. They also had little notion of profit and loss.

Their military backgrounds had given them discipline, which was a valuable asset, yet getting them to accept the leadership of business people was extremely hard in the beginning. In order to overcome these difficulties, and after a great deal of thought, I opted for a short and relatively bloodless campaign—an "isolate and freeze" strategy.

First, Bank Gemari had no branches, so I made its head office into a branch—which meant all of the head office job positions became branch positions. However, staff retained the authority that came with their positions. To keep them happy, I brought in an accountant to be the branch's head accountant, while the original head accountant was transferred to the Bank of Central Asia. I also sent a trusted subordinate to be deputy head of Bank Gemari's human resources department.

Second, in the short term, I decided not to take on any new business, putting a freeze on accepting new deposits and the issuance of new loans at the branch. I gave them complete independence when it came to existing business.

Third, every month the branch directors had to attend a symposium in order to help them understand the concept of a market economy and slowly integrate them into this new environment. From this, I could observe their abilities and work attitudes, and then assign them to work in new branches. Slowly but surely their old approach to work was broken down so that they could be incorporated into our bank's family.

After three years, the task of integration was complete.

OFFERING AN EXPRESS
REMITTANCE SERVICE

" An opportunity in backwardness *"*

Following the mergers, regional service centres were set up in 11 large cities in accordance with the strategy we had set out for creating a branch network. Afterwards, branches and sub-branches were opened with a focus on the main markets of the nation's cigarette factories. Our goal was to meet the remittance needs of the cigarette market, as well as those of fabric merchants, food suppliers, building merchants, automobile traders and bicycle dealers.

Prior to 1985, telecommunication services in Indonesia were extremely poor, and owning a telephone was seen as a luxury. However, the quality of the telephone service was dreadful. For international calls you had to go to the telephone exchange and queue up before being connected, and even then the sound quality was so bad that you needn't have bothered.

In those days, sending money could take up to 40 days regardless of the distance, and the service was only offered by national banks. This state of affairs caused huge inconvenience and losses for businesses, especially those in the six industries mentioned above. It put an invisible freeze on capital, resulting in higher capital costs.

I saw a golden opportunity in this state of affairs—one that could help Bank Central Asia to become a clearing house for commercial trade. I carried out detailed research into how to solve the problems customers faced in communications and transferring money. If I could find a way to do that, Bank Central Asia could quickly become the largest bank in Indonesia.

The time bank transfers took to reach their recipient was partly due to Indonesia's outdated telecommunication facilities, and partly because the postal service was extremely inefficient. So I tried to think how Bank Central Asia might offer a next-day remittance service, which would provide great savings in businesses' capital costs and also allow companies to use capital more effectively—two things that were bound to be warmly welcomed by the market.

In fact, providing an express remittance service was very straightforward: each branch would establish its own postal department, and specially appointed staff would be dispatched daily to relay information about payable remittances to the relevant branch. For example, couriers from Jakarta and Surabaya would each take the night train and select a midpoint to exchange documents, before taking them back to their own branch. Payment could then be made to the payee the very next day.

Because bank remittances took around 40 days, banks were earning a considerable amount of interest over the period it took to transfer funds. When Bank Central Asia came up with its express remittance service, several colleagues suggested that we promise that transfers would arrive in seven days. Even that would be far quicker than the other banks. But I had decided that we would provide a next-day service. I wanted to achieve this in one fell swoop, so that it couldn't be copied by other banks. I wanted us to be the only bank offering such a service.

I braced myself to seize the market. We would use our position as the only bank to offer an express remittance service to concentrate all transactions in the downstream, midstream and upstream of every industry utilising Bank Central Asia. In effect, our express remittance service would be the basis by which we would become a clearing bank.

The next-day service caused a sensation throughout the country. It was very well received in the market and had profound repercussions.

Payer and payee could enjoy the benefits of the express service as long as they were both Bank Central Asia customers, and almost every day we had new customers lining up at our branches to open accounts. In just a few months, the number of customers had dramatically increased and bank deposits had risen sharply. After several months, all kinds of businesses were using our service. They couldn't do without it.

I decided to make the most of the situation and offer an "accounts payable financing package". This was a special loan aimed at payments by downstream businesses (wholesalers and retailers) to upstream businesses, and its objective was to help the downstream businesses use cash to purchase goods more cheaply, thus increasing their profits. Then, in relation to upstream businesses, I introduced an "accounts receivable financing package". In this way I could bind downstream, midstream and upstream businesses to the bank, going one step further in making Bank Central Asia the clearing institution for every industry.

Through our innovative next-day remittance service, accounts payable financing package, and accounts receivable financing package services, Bank Central Asia was able to systematically win new customers in the upstream, midstream and downstream sections of every industry. In no time at all, we had become an intercity clearing house for the cigarette, textile, food product, construction materials, and automobile and bicycle component industries.

Within five years, Bank Central Asia had grown into Indonesia's largest privately owned commercial bank, and the country's sixth largest. (The top five were all state-owned.) We also had the largest trading volume, the nation's highest number of daily remittances, and the largest foreign exchange volume. We also became the nation's second clearing bank— alongside Bank Indonesia.

I had saved a struggling bank and turned it into one that boasted the largest trade volume in Indonesia. Along the way, I was helped by the vital support of Sudono Salim with assistance from his sons Anthony Salim and Andree Halim, not to mention the hard work of the directors of the 11 regional service centres.

Bank Central Asia had set up these regional service centres, which were the 11 banks in our Indonesian banking network. As a result of also opening branches and sub-branches in the surrounding secondary cities and counties, we were able to provide a comprehensive service that included a next-day remittance service, an accounts payable financial package, an accounts receivable financial package, other types of loans, the best foreign currency rates, free currency exchanges, traveller's cheques, a Bank Central Asia credit card, Tahapan (the government savings programme) deposit bonuses, a fixed-rate savings account, a current account and commercial credit and other services.

When these services were ready with their hardware requirements in place, I decided to take out advertisements in the local newspapers of all 11 regional centres. Their main message was:

"Bank Central Asia would like to express its appreciation for the support it has received from the public by offering loans with an annual interest rate of X percent and annual deposit interest rates of Y per cent."

The loan annual interest rate we were offering was 1 percentage point lower than Panin Bank and the deposit annual interest rate was 0.5 percentage point higher than Panin Bank. The aim of the advertisements was to encourage more businesses to open accounts at Bank Central Asia, and to force competing banks to pay more interest, thus reducing a significant amount of their income from interest. This left our competitors with a difficult choice: if they hesitated, they could lose customers—ones who would be scooped up by Bank Central Asia. The main objective of this strategy was to hobble our competitors and allow us to quickly get ahead of them.

The facts prove that my strategy was right: business grew rapidly and we overtook all of Indonesia's other banks to become the largest private bank.

WINNING GUDANG GARAM
AS A CUSTOMER

" Striking up friendships *"*

G udang Garam was Indonesia's largest cigarette manufacturer and its products were popular in every corner of the country. I had assumed that the boss, Tjoa Ing Hwie (also known as Surya Wonowidjojo), might be an eager supporter of Bank Central Asia.

But Tjoa had been helped by Bank Negara Indonesia (BNI) when he was first setting up his business, and he put great stock in old friendships and personal loyalty. He had vowed that Gudang Garam would always be a loyal customer of that bank and refused to deal with any others. Though he consented to my request that he open an account with Bank Central Asia, he used it only to buy cloves from Sudono Salim, with all other business activity still conducted through BNI.

I asked Salim to speak to him on my behalf, but Tjoa still stuck to his principles and would not be persuaded. Gudang Garam's business was a vital part of my strategy to become Indonesia's second clearing bank, so I remained positive and persevered in my efforts. It was on my mind day and night, yet I still couldn't think of a solution.

Finally, I decided to open a very impressive branch in Kediri, in East Java where Gudang Garam's head office is located. To manage the branch, I settled on a very socially adept and honest member of our senior staff, and tasked him with striking up friendships with the finance manager and sales manager of Gudang Garam. He was to treat them well, play badminton or tennis with them, frequently invite them to dinner, socialise with their families and even go on holiday with them but on no account was he to discuss business.

After a year or so, the three men had become close friends, and were firmly in each other's confidence. Only then did I instruct the branch manager to mention business.

The key points were quite straightforward. First, he should ask the finance manager to talk about monthly sales figures. Supposing the monthly figure was a hundred billion rupiah, and this money was transferred across the country through BNI, they'd have to wait for 40 days before receiving it, with a hundred billion rupiah lying idle in the bank. At the same time, they would be paying 15 percent interest to the bank on their borrowings. How big were their losses?

Second, he was to point out that Bank Central Asia could shorten the remittance period from 40 days to one day, which would mean a monthly cash flow of a hundred billion rupiah.

Third, he should explain that after receiving remittances from all over the country, Bank Central Asia would immediately transfer them to Gudang Garam's BNI account without delay.

Fourth, he should ask the two men to recommend that their head agent in Jakarta open an account with Bank Central Asia and try out our next-day remittance service by making daily payments between Jakarta and Kediri. This wouldn't violate Tjoa's principles and could also be of huge benefit to Gudang Garam. How could they refuse?

The two managers agreed to ask Gudang Garam's agent to send funds to the company's head office in Kediri via Bank Central Asia's next-day remittance service. After a month or so, they had a sense of the convenience of the service and could appreciate its advantages and benefits. As a result, Gudang Garam officially requested that all of its agents make remittances to its head office through Bank Central Asia. An understanding of *guanxi*—Chinese for connections—was crucial to doing business in Indonesia, the same way it remains vital to business relations in China.

In this way, I patiently persuaded Gudang Garam's agents across Indonesia to become a part of Bank Central Asia's network. I followed it up by asking these agents to introduce their wholesalers all over the country to the bank, and then requested that the wholesalers introduce their retailers. In this way, Gudang Garam's entire business chain (from upstream suppliers to mid and downstream agents—wholesalers and retailers) became customers of Bank Central Asia, and all payments between them were completed through us. Bank Central Asia had well and truly become a clearing house for the entire industry.

1937

1946

1948

1989

1992

1994

1996

1998

2010

2013

2015

2016

Personal archive photos of Dr. Mochtar Riady and Madam Suryawaty Lidya.

With wife Madam Suryawaty Lidya during their courtship days.

Dr. and Mrs. Mochtar Riady renewing their wedding vows
on their 60th wedding anniversary shown here
with Shannon Tjokrorahardjo (left) and Joshua Tandiono in 2010.

Dr. Mochtar Riady (top row second from left) in high school around 16 years of age.

Wedding of Li Zi Wen, nephew of Dr. Mochtar Riady, and members of the extended family in the 1980s.

Dr. and Mrs. Mochtar Riady visiting Dr. Riady's childhood home in Batu. This was Dr. Riady's actual childhood home.

The historical "Nusantara" shop, formerly "Nan Yang" on the main street in Jember, East Java, where Dr. Riady laboured for two years to build a small sleepy shop into the city's then largest as "dowry" paid to his mother-in-law in order to get approval to marry Mrs. May Riady.

Dr. Mochtar Riady flanked by his sons James (right) and Stephen in
Dr. Riady's office.

Dr. Mochtar Riady and son James Riady posing for a photo
while on a visit to Labuan Bajo, May 6, 2016.

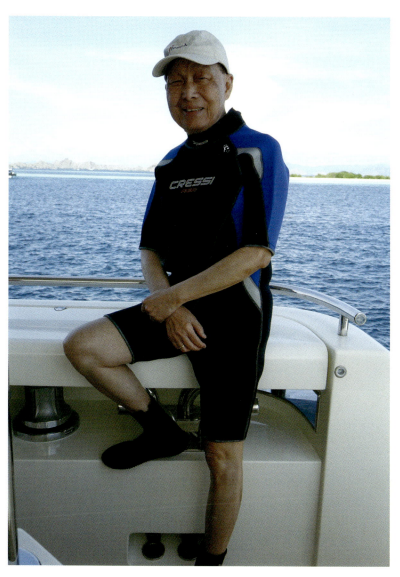

Dr. Mochtar Riady posing for a photo while on a visit to Labuan Bajo, May 6, 2016.

As member of the Board of Trustees of the University of Southern California (USC) together with former USC President, Professor Steven Sample, at the graduation of granddaughter Nita Riady, USA, 1996.

Conferment of the Honorary Doctor of Law degree from Golden Gate
University, USA, April 18, 1996.

Awarded an honorary doctorate by Southeast University President
Mr. Gu Guan Quan, Nanjing, June 6, 2005.

Receiving the Honorary Degree from the Hong Kong Baptist University,
Hong Kong, November 10, 2009.

At the launch of the book "Ancient Philosophy and Modern Management" in Building INTI, December 7, 2008. Previous published works include "Nanotechnology management style: How to heal a company from old illnesses and save a family company", 2004, and "Searching for opportunities amid crisis", 1999.

As Chairman of the Board of Trustees of the University of Indonesia, with the Minister of Education (2004-2009) Prof. Dr. Bambang Sudibyo and members of the Board of Trustees.

Opening ceremony of the Li Wen Zheng (Mochtar Riady) Library in Tsinghua University, April 23, 2011 with then party secretary for Tsinghua University, Dr. and Mrs. Mochtar Riady and Chen Xi, former Dean of Tsinghua University.

At the inauguration of the "Mochtar Riady Plaza Quantum" of the University of Indonesia Faculty of Engineering in Depok, March 10, 2015, witnessed by the Minister of Research, Technology and Higher Education, Prof. H. Muhammad Nasir and Prof. Dr. Ir. Djoko Hartanto.

Dr. Mochtar Riady with Mr. Liem Sioe Liong and other senior management of BCA at the BCA headquarters in Jakarta, June 1975.

Dr. Mochtar Riady giving a presentation to BCA staff, June 1975.

Annual Leadership Meeting of Lippo Bank, 3-5 December 1993.

The Working Meeting on Credit of Lippo Bank, 20 August 1989.

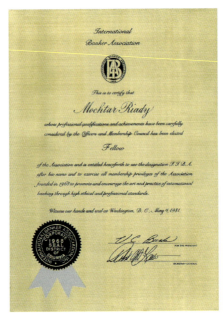

As Fellow of the International Bankers Association,
which Dr. Riady then became Chairman.

Awarded the special Economic Consultant to the provincial government of
Fujian Province, PRC.

Dr. Mochtar Riady receiving the University of Indonesia Dana Abadi (Endowment) Award from Rector Prof. Muhammad Anis in Jakarta in recognition of Dr. Riady's donations and contributions to improve the quality and funding of scholarships on October 22, 2015.
PHOTO: SP Photo/Ruht Semiono.

Recognised as Asia's Most Influential Cover Personality by the then Senior Minister of State for Trade and Industry and National Development Mr. Lee Yi-Shyan, witnessed by the Editor-in-Chief, Fortune Times, Ms. Annie Song at the awards ceremony, Singapore, November 27, 2015.
PHOTO: Fortune Times.

Hosting Governor, Mr. Bill Clinton and Mrs. Bill Clinton on their first visit to Hong Kong.

Dinner with Mr. Jack Stephens and Bill Clinton, Governor of Arkansas, in 1984.

A private moment with President Bill Clinton and Mrs. Clinton during his inauguration as the 42nd President of the United States during the Inauguration Ball on January, 20, 1993.

Dr. Mochtar Riady greeting President Suharto of Indonesia.

Awarded the Bintang Jasa Utama star medal by Indonesian President Joko Widodo for his services and personal contribution to the Republic of Indonesia, at the State Palace, Jakarta, August 13, 2015.

Welcoming People's Republic of China President Xi Jinping on his maiden visit to Indonesia as President at the Presidential Palace on October 1, 2013.

Dr. and Mrs. Mochtar Riady with President Xi Jinping, then Governor of
Fujian Province, taken on November 20, 1993 at Fuzhou Airport, PRC.

Dr. Mochtar Riady and Dr. Stephen Riady with the Fourth Premier of the
People's Republic of China Li Peng.

Meeting with former Chairman of the National Committee
of the Chinese People's Political Consultative Committee
(CCPPC), Jia Qinglin, in Beijing, PRC.

Together with former President of the Republic of Singapore S. R. Nathan as Guest of Honor at the Istana in Singapore, on November 9, 2007.

Dr. Mochtar Riady and Dr. James Riady conferring an Honorary Doctorate degree on President Benigno Aquino III of the Philippines at Universitas Pelita Harapan on March 8, 2011, witnessed by then Minister of Education and Culture, Mohammad Nuh, UPH Rector, Dr. Jonathan Parapak and UPH Vice Chancellor, Professor Gary A. Miller.

The Riady family, from the first to fourth generation, taken March 15, 2016. There will be 98 members of the family by the end of the year.

WINNING
UNILEVER'S CUSTOM

"A month passed, then a quarter, then a year. . ."

U nilever was another key customer we really had to fight for. Unilever manufactures and sells everyday consumables such as soap, washing powder, cleaning agents, toothpaste and tooth-brushes, as well as various cosmetic products. Beloved by the people of Indonesia, its retail network extends into every corner of the country, making it an important potential customer for Bank Central Asia. However, we faced one major difficulty—following a run on private banks in Indonesia in 1967, Unilever's headquarters had ruled that its Indonesian division was not allowed to deal with private banks.

I appointed Andi Buana, a young banker who had worked overseas, to accomplish the important task of winning their business. I told him to follow the same method we had used with Gudang Garam. He would play a round of golf every week with Unilever's general manager and invite him to dinner. They were to become friends before talking about business. This time, however, the strategy did not work. I had no choice but to get involved personally and explain to the general manager the dependability of our operations and the convenience of our services. But it was still to no avail.

My offer of cooperation was politely declined several times, but rather than give up I continued to look for a way to make them a customer.

In the course of one of my visits to the company, one minor aspect of their operations caught my attention: they used telex for communications between the head office and their external offices. I observed that the telex loop used a total of five sheets of paper; the first four were torn off and used by each of the departments, but the final sheet was saved intact.

Every morning the manager had to sign the top of the final telex sheet and make a note of the time and date, and he would repeat this process at the foot of the sheet at end of the day. Every day, the general manager and accountant checked the completed manuscript to verify the day's correspondence and check there were no financial errors entered into the accounts. This served as a security measure, and the manuscript was one of the documents that needed to be checked by head office's audit department.

This gave me an idea: we should send reports to Unilever's Indonesian division using telex. The reports would contain Bank Central Asia's exchange rates for that day, give our cheapest interest rates on loans, and introduce the next-day remittance service. Of these, the exchange rate we quoted would be at cost, and thus more favourable than the one Unilever would be using at the time.

I began telexing this information to Unilever every workday. A month passed, then a quarter, then a year . . . Time was getting on, and everyone had doubts about what I was doing.

Finally, after more than a year, Unilever started to buy a small amount of foreign currency from us. I guessed that the general manager of Unilever Indonesia had grown tired of the auditors at head office always questioning him about why they were buying foreign currency at a price higher than the one offered by Bank Central Asia. He had no choice but to buy a small amount from us to compare the price with other foreign banks.

This gave us an opening, and Unilever made an exception to their rule and started doing business with Bank Central Asia. Soon afterwards, they saw the benefit in using the same-day remittance service and began a full-fledged partnership with us.

Although the small act of sending the reports by telex was not connected directly with our business, it wasn't lost on me how, after all that thinking, it had helped us gain a new customer. Once again, I'd achieved something that had seemed impossible.

It had taken me 10 years, but one by one—from one company to one industry, from one industry to six key industries, and from six key industries to a total of 86 industries—every business (downstream, midstream and upstream) had joined Bank Central Asia's next-day remittance service network.

Bank Central Asia now had the largest customer base in the country and had become, in effect, the centre of banking transactions for Indonesia's entire business community.

THE TABANAS NATIONAL SAVINGS PROGRAMME

"
Drawing inspiration from a lottery mania *"*

I n 1970, the government, with the support of Bank Indonesia, introduced a national savings programme, known as Tabanas. However, after more than 10 years of hard work, the scheme had not achieved its objectives and national savings remained pitifully low. This was due to three reasons. First, the 6 per cent annual equivalent rate (AER) on these accounts was far less than the 12 per cent AER offered on ordinary current accounts. It was a difference that made almost no sense, and was apparently due to the high administration fees involved in handling small savings amounts. Second, the majority of savings were from the urban lower and middle class. Their savings were small and thus they earned very little interest—not even enough to cover the cost of travelling to the bank.Third, because savings were so small, bank staff did not value this business or respect their customers.

These problems had to be fixed so that the Indonesian people's savings could be put back on the right track as soon as possible. The administration of savings needed to be amended by simplifying and automating these accounts to reduce administration costs. Next, savings interest rates had to rise to a level comparable to interest on current accounts. Finally, bank staff had to treat all customers equally and without discrimination, so that lower and middle class customers were given the same respect as anyone else.

Even though all these improvements were made, progress in national savings remained slow. The importance of national savings goes without saying: accumulating capital for a country provides the foundation for its economic development. In addition, teaching people to save more and instilling in them the virtue of industry and thrift as the path to wealth improves the national character. All governments vigorously promote national savings schemes, and every bank should also make a contribution. This was something that I felt strongly about.

One day at home, I heard the household staff excitedly discussing Indonesia's lottery. Both the urban middle and lower classes had been swept up in the lottery frenzy, and there were street stalls everywhere selling tickets. The lottery was held every evening, and during the day no one could focus on work; everyone was too busy checking his or her ticket numbers and waiting for the result to be announced.

It seemed like the whole country was caught up in a gambling craze that was highly detrimental to society. Yet the government overlooked these dangers and continued to grant licences to the lottery industry. It was truly astounding.

I made both the social phenomenon of lottery mania and the national savings scheme the subject of my thoughts. People in the cities were willing to spend money gambling on the lottery, and if they didn't win their money was gone. I came up with a similar way of combining saving with prizes: for every deposit of 20,000 rupiah or more, savers would receive a number, which would be entered into a monthly draw. First prize would be a car, second prize a motorcycle, and there would also be a rich array of other prizes on offer.

Even if they didn't win a prize, the principal in their savings account would still be earning interest. I thought that this savings reward scheme could mitigate much of the harm caused by the lottery, and modify this unhealthy public behaviour. Once I had thought it through, I assembled a team, which prepared a proposal. We then applied to Bank Indonesia for a licence. The scheme was called Tabungan Harapan, or Tahapan for short.

Once all preparations had been made, Bank Central Asia and Lippo Bank (which I discuss in more detail in later chapters) put a great deal of effort into promoting the "Tahapan Savings Prize". It became an instant hit throughout the country, all but displacing the lottery business. Within two months, we'd collected more savings deposits than the government's central bank had managed in 10 years of its Tabanas programme. Once again, I had successfully taken Bank Central Asia to new heights.

Over the next 10 years or so, under my leadership, Bank Central Asia continued to perfect its operating philosophy, unveiling innovative new products, raising service standards, reducing operating costs, and offering high-quality services and real benefits to people throughout society. During this process, other banks had also been forced to change and improve, so in 10 years Indonesia's banking industry had made tremendous progress. I feel very proud to have done something good for the country.

THE BCA CARD, ATMS AND E-BANKING

"Information technology is the future."

Humankind's greatest invention is currency. Before currency, products were exchanged using a barter system, which greatly limited economic development. The emergence of currency invigorated trade, increased production and developed the economy. As a result, life improved.

Some 3,500 years ago, during China's Shang dynasty, shells had already been used as an intermediary form of payment in trading. By the Warring States period (475–221 BCE), the Chinese had mastered the art of metallurgy. Currency began to be cast using copper, gold, silver and other metals, and the value of the currency in circulation was based on the value of the material itself; it had no credit value.

Following emperor Qin Shihuang's unification of China under the Qin dynasty (221–207 BCE), the central government began issuing a unified currency.

By the Song Dynasty (960–1279), China had invented the world's first paper currency. It took various forms, with the earliest of them known as *jiaozi*, and later more sophisticated versions called *jianchao* and *qianyin*. This was the beginning of the use of banknotes, and, in the course of economic development, was the first major revolution in commercial payments.

After the Renaissance in the 14th to 17th centuries, banks that were somewhat like their modern counterparts began operating in Europe. Based on bank credit and bank customer credit, the market began to accept cheques as a form of commercial payment. This was the second major revolution in payment methods.

In the modern era, credit cards have become a new way of paying for goods. People no longer need to carry cash or cheques when buying or selling goods and services. This has been another major innovation in the financial sector, and the third major revolution in commercial payments.

After 1950, we entered the age of information technology, with the US at the leading edge of this revolution. Following several decades of development, we saw the era of e-banking, and people began to use the Internet to buy goods and make electronic payments. This was the fourth major revolution in commercial payments.

Against this backdrop, I believed it was time that Indonesians became acquainted with modern banking and financial services, through which they would learn about information technology. The people of Indonesia needed to move with the times; they needed to understand modern banking services, through which they could learn about IT. I saw this as my responsibility and obligation.

In 1979, I began my research. I wanted to offer a Bank Central Asia (BCA) credit card, digitise the bank's administrative work, make accounting computer-processed and establish an ATM service. I turned to an American electronic consulting company called Systematics for advice, and ultimately decided to begin by offering a credit card service. Based on the principle of tackling the easiest things first, I had made the credit card market my first target.

I wasted no time in recruiting specialists to form a team to prepare this effort. Members of the team were required to understand computers and banking, and I instilled in them two principles: "information technology is the future" and "information technology is essential for progress and for survival". I told them that if they worked hard, we'd be sure to make Bank Central Asia the first bank in Indonesia to offer a credit card, the first to provide ATMs, and the first to have an e-banking service. I made myself chairman of the team so that I could play a direct part in driving forward the bank's digitisation.

After around three years, the BCA card had begun to be widely accepted by the market, and to this day Bank Central Asia remains Indonesia's largest credit-card-issuing bank.

USING FOREIGN CAPITAL

"I succeeded in increasing Bank Central Asia's ability to gain financing."

I n 1969, the Suharto government adopted a policy of economic opening and reform. As a result, the economy showed substantial growth in the following years, yet the nation's accumulated funds were still unable to meet the needs of an expanding economy. In addition to the lack of funds, the banking sector was constrained by the capital adequacy ratio (CAR) requirements set by industry regulators.

This was the first bottleneck in Bank Central Asia's growth, and we needed to find a way through it. After turning it over in my head, I came up with four ways of resolving the situation.

The first method involved raising funds through a stock offer, or initial public offering (IPO). However, Sudono Salim would not agree to this, believing that the timing wasn't right.

The second was to establish a finance company in Hong Kong, and persuade Bank Central Asia customers to accept another form of international financing.

The third option was to purchase a small- or medium-sized American bank, and again persuade Bank Central Asia customers to accept international financing.

The fourth strategy was to invite an international bank to join Bank Central Asia in establishing a joint finance company in Indonesia, in order to make up for the bank's CAR deficiency and allow it to continue to expand.

In light of the strategies above, I established the Central Asia Capital Corporation in Hong Kong. Funded by Hong Kong banks, its main business was to procure financing and open commercial letters of credit for Indonesian businesses, after which it obtained a further six months of commercial financing. Hong Kong had an abundance of capital and interest rates were far lower than in Indonesia. After starting the business, I succeeded in increasing Bank Central Asia's ability to gain financing.

CHAPTER FOUR

EXPANDING BEYOND THE SHORES OF INDONESIA

*" Attempting to buy an American bank,
I made a difficult call to abandon the deal. "*

I n 1976, I began preparations to go to the US to acquire a bank. I travelled to Taiwan to visit Yu Kuo-hwa , the governor of Taiwan's central bank at the time, and he graciously invited me to a dinner party at his home. As luck would have it, I was seated next to Robert B. Anderson, a former US Secretary of the Treasury, and I took advantage of the opportunity to share with him my thoughts about acquiring an American bank.

He replied positively, telling me that it was a workable idea. Not long after, I received a telephone call from Anderson in which he informed me that a 28 per cent stake in the National Bank of Georgia was up for sale. Bert Lance, President Jimmy Carter's budget director, was selling his shares and Jackson T. Stephens—the president and CEO of Stephens Inc., an investment bank in Arkansas—was the broker.

Lance needed to divest his stake in the bank in order to avoid a conflict of interest in his new government position. I was delighted at the chance to own a US bank, and flew to Washington, DC, the very next day. I had an initial meeting with Jackson—who was better known as Jack—and after around five hours of talks, we reached an agreement in principle. However, I requested that I first discuss the bank's future business development policy with its other principal shareholders and the board of directors.

The next day, I met Bert Lance, the bank's other shareholders, and the board of directors. I proposed a direction and strategy for the development of the bank following its purchase, stressing that economic globalisation had elevated Asia's economic and developmental prospects. About 30 per cent of the business of America's 10 largest banks was in Asia, and the region accounted for about 40 per cent of the total profits of these banks.

I hoped that the National Bank of Georgia could play a role in promoting business between the southeastern US and Asia. After answering a few questions, my remarks met with everyone's approval. Jack Stephens was particularly positive about my strategy. He expressed his willingness to support my US business, and said that he hoped we could work together in the future.

Lawyers from both sides worked throughout the night drafting a framework cooperation agreement, in the hope that it could be signed the next morning. At the time I made one special request: that the deal be kept secret for the time being to avoid interference from Indonesian officials. This was accepted and written into the interim cooperation agreement.

Unfortunately, however, the sale was front-page news in the next morning's paper. The article claimed that the Indonesian government had expressly sent Bank Central Asia to purchase Bert Lance's shareholding in order to help the Democratic Party out of a politically embarrassing situation. Mr. Lance eventually was forced to resign from his government post. Although we had already signed an agreement on the sale, he asked if it was acceptable if he backed out of the deal since he no longer had to divest his stake. I agreed, and Jack Stephens promised to find another bank for us to buy. We had failed to buy the National Bank of Georgia but the episode had been very instructive. A simple commercial transaction had become a political football. Soon after, I received a call from the head of Indonesia's Ministry of Finance who had also asked Sudono Salim to discourage my purchase of the bank stake. At that point the deal had already been abandoned but it was clear that it had created political shock waves that were felt far away.

UNION PLANTERS NATIONAL BANK OF MEMPHIS

"The words I had been waiting to hear"

While the planned purchase of the National Bank of Georgia was unsuccessful, it led to a close friendship with Jack Stephens. In 1980 Jack introduced me to a bank in Memphis, Tennessee—the Union Planters National Bank of Memphis. With his help, I managed to quietly acquire a strategic 4.9 per cent shareholding, making me the bank's single largest shareholder.

I arranged a meeting with the bank's management. At first, having little idea where this Oriental man had appeared from, they were not too welcoming. That attitude changed after I offered to introduce them to some major "money centre" banks in New York. They were more than happy to join me on this "get acquainted" visit to the American financial capital. I introduced them to the management of some of America's premier banks at that time: Citibank, Chemical Bank, Bankers Trust, and American Express Bank among others.

In business meetings or at dinner, I asked these major players about what countries and territories their banks' business was spread across. How much of it was conducted on US soil versus abroad? How did profits from these foreign countries and territories rank in terms of overall profits? Because domestic interest rates in the US were around 2 per cent at the time—lower than in many other countries—most banks with international experience focused their business on other parts of the world.

The bankers all responded to my questions in much the same way: most of their business was conducted outside of the US, and the lion's share of profits came from these foreign markets, with the profits from Asia higher than those from Europe. The management delegates of Union Planters National Bank also expressed their agreement with my view on the benefits of finding opportunities in Asia.

I invited the Union Planters' management to visit Asia and see for themselves. I arranged for them to go to Japan first and then Hong Kong, before visiting Singapore and Indonesia. On each of the stops, the delegation saw local central bankers and finance ministry officials in formal meetings or social events.

There was a great deal of pomp and ceremony, and there were extremely productive talks with key people in the financial sector on each of our stops. We had travelled from the US across Asia, and the delegation from Union Planters no longer looked down on this little man from the Far East. They were convinced of my influence in banking circles and had seen that my suggestions were sound. After much discussion with their peers in the industry, they reached a consensus: to grow the bank's business they had to look outside of the US. They chose Asia.

The final stop on our Asia trip was Indonesia, and it was here that the delegates of the Union Planters National Bank expressed a wish to cooperate with me and jointly develop business in Asia. I was delighted as these were precisely the words I had been waiting to hear.

Subsequently, the Bank Central Asia group and the Union Planters National Bank each contributed 50 per cent of the funds required to establish a finance company in Hong Kong, with registered capital of US$3 million. A core management team was appointed with staff from both sides. The Union Planters National Bank's expansion into Asia through the joint venture finance company was able to provide much larger-scale financing to Asian businesses, many of whom were Bank Central Asia's customers.

This resulted in some significant benefits. It helped meet the financing needs of Bank Central Asia's customers, while greatly enhancing the bank's reputation as an international bank. Bank Central Asia was now seen as a regional bank with a Hong Kong presence and the capacity to arrange large-scale financing. This was certainly helpful in accelerating Bank Central Asia's growth domestically, and it empowered Bank Central Asia to eventually set up a branch office in New York.

I became a value-added partner of the Union Planters National Bank, and this helped the US bank diversify internationally. Moreover, the joint finance company in Hong Kong, Stephens Finance Ltd., was a success. This whole synergistic dynamic was achieved with what was in effect a small but influential stake in a bank in Memphis, Tennessee. Sudono Salim described my deal as "extremely strategic". This experience demonstrated what it means to "create something out of nothing", or to "throw out a minnow to catch a whale".

In 1984, Jack Stephens introduced me to another bank in Arkansas called Worthen Bank. Jack and I discussed a possible investment and we agreed to invest up to 30 per cent of the bank's shares. Later on my second eldest son, James, became co-president of the bank. The bank was the state's largest and an underwriter of state government bonds. Because of this business relationship, James became good friends with the man who was governor of the state at the time and a future president of the United States—Bill Clinton. When the president-elect was preparing to take office, James was invited to take part in an economic summit to discuss and advise on key economic issues that the new administration would face.

John Huang, the president of Lippo Bank California, and a community activist, was appointed assistant secretary of the US Department of Commerce, and vice chairman of the Democratic National Committee.

Unfortunately, both James and John Huang were drawn into a politically driven investigation into campaign fund-raising. James voluntarily settled by paying a small fine and agreed that the bank would pay a substantial fine. I was reminded of the old Chinese saying that translates as "Don't mix business with politics".

STANDING ON THE SHOULDERS OF GIANTS

*"*I could now proudly hand over the reins to members of Sudono Salim's family.*"*

I n 1988, the Indonesian government finally began allowing foreign banks to establish financial joint ventures in Indonesia, and these companies could then be upgraded into commercial banks. I promptly responded by inviting the Royal Bank of Scotland, Chemical Bank in New York, Long-Term Credit Bank of Japan and Hong Kong's Jardine Fleming to form a joint venture called Multicor (Multinational Finance Corp).

The first objective in establishing Multicor was to expand Bank Central Asia's financing channels and financing capabilities. The second was to increase public awareness of Bank Central Asia. The third was to strengthen relationships with foreign banks, and the fourth was to learn from the organisational structure and management experience of these same foreign banks.

In the course of my attempted acquisition of the National Bank of Georgia, my stake in Union Planters National Bank, my purchase of shares in Worthen Bank in 1984, and the opening of a Bank Central Asia branch in New York, Bank Central Asia had become a truly global bank—the only one of its kind in Indonesia.

In June of 1975, Bank Central Asia's total assets amounted to Rp998 million. In 1976, this figure had risen to Rp12 billion; in 1977 it reached

Rp24 billion, and in 1980 it stood at Rp100 billion. Total assets were Rp1 trillion in 1986 and Rp7.5 trillion by 1990, making us Indonesia's fifth largest bank. I had also successfully turned Bank Central Asia into the nation's second clearing bank. I could now proudly hand over the reins to members of Sudono Salim's family.

OPENING UP THE FINANCIAL SECTOR AND THE PAKTO 88 RULE

"No limits on expansion"

I ndonesia had gone through a prolonged patch of political and economic instability in the final years under Sukarno. But by 1967, his successor, President Suharto, had consolidated power and the government turned its back on the closed socialist economic model of the past. It adopted an open market economic policy. Against this backdrop, Indonesia's financial industry also had to open up, and the PAKTO 88 rule, also known as the deregulation package of 1988, was introduced. This included a series of measures aimed specifically at the banking industry. One such regulatory change was legislation permitting foreign ownership of up to 99 percent of an Indonesian bank. The banking sector could no longer be dominated by five banks owned by the state.

There were many academics and figures in the financial sector who vigorously opposed the new policy, fearing competition from foreign banks. In an effort to allay these fears, the government organised a research committee. As vice chairman of the Indonesian National Association of Banks and vice chairman of the Indonesian Chamber of Commerce and Industry, I became a member of the committee.

Initially, most of the committee members took a conservative stance and opposed the government measures, primarily because they feared that if foreign banks entered the market, domestic banks would lose out. Much deliberation, however, had led me to believe that monopolies were the primary cause of economic decline and the main reason for the national economy's lack of competitiveness. Businesses must take root and grow under the pressure of free and fair competition. In a fair environment, competition is the driving force behind the growth of enterprises.

But if foreign investment banks entered the Indonesian market, it could result in some areas of unfair competition. Their Indonesian operations would not have to inject capital into the local business, and they could make use of the substantial funds of their overseas organisations. With huge amounts of foreign funds at their disposal, they would be able to engage in large-scale transactions with no capital costs. That would represent unfair competition.

Consequently, I proposed that Indonesia relax the restrictions on the establishment of foreign-owned banks, but on the condition they establish Indonesian subsidiary companies—which would be Indonesian legal entities—and inject capital into them. I further proposed that they be subject to capital adequacy requirements. This, I believed, would create an environment of fair and reasonable competition and I had faith that we could hold our own against foreign-owned banks.

In addition, as Indonesian subsidiaries, these banks would need to bring foreign currency into Indonesia in order to conduct business in the local market. This would increase the amount of foreign exchange in the national treasury. The improved economic environment would, in turn, attract foreign investment into the country, which would ultimately result in the introduction of new technology and management techniques. Indonesia was sorely in need of foreign funds, as well as skills and technology to accompany its shift towards a global economy.

After more than two years of discussion and debate, the committee finally agreed to open up the financial markets—a decision that was the antecedent of the 1988 PAKTO reform measures. PAKTO 88 went much further than anyone had imagined, however, by lifting the restrictions on the number of branches that banks could open. I was delighted, because this meant that Bank Central Asia now had no limits on its expansion. That said, for the banking industry overall, too little regulation would lead to a lack of control—something I was convinced the government would eventually realise and address by revising the reforms.

ESTABLISHING
150 NEW BRANCHES
IN 12 MONTHS

*"*Sudono was my closest confidant.*"*

T he PAKTO 88 financial reforms were a once-in-a-lifetime opportunity, and I decided to establish another 150 branches within
12 months to further consolidate Bank Central Asia's national
network. To this end, I took personal charge of the new branch preparation
team and divided it into four sub-groups, each of which was given the following responsibilities:

1. Selecting branch locations and purchasing (or renting) premises.
   The exterior of branches would be standardised. Contractors
   would be sourced to carry out the work, and branch managers
   given the task of finding suitable locations for purchase or rental
   within 60 days.

2. Establishing branch organisational structure, personnel standards, and recruitment and training procedures.

   The organisational structure was to be basically divided
   into two groups: sales managers and administrative managers.

   For sales managers, staff at our key regional centres would
   recruit prominent figures from the local business community; in
   addition, together with the branch managers (we already had over

100 branches by that time), these same staff could also make wider recommendations that would be subject to my final approval.

For administrative managers, each branch would recommend three members of staff, who would each undertake an initial in-branch internship, followed by a three-month head office internship. From this we would be able to determine whether they had the right character and abilities for the new position.

3. Branch furnishings and office equipment.

The layout and office equipment, customer counters, furnishings, etc., would be standardised and contractors would carry out the work. For example, counters would be pre-assembled with dimensions of 200 cm x 80 cm centimetres and then sent to the branches for installation. Other fixtures and fittings would be ready-made; once head office had calculated how many items were needed, they would be bought in bulk and distributed to each branch for installation.

4. Formulation of a branch-opening budget.

The cost of the three tasks above would need to be calculated and a budget drawn up. Costs would also need to be controlled while the 150 branches were being set up.

At that time bank administration had yet to be automated, so each branch needed around 40 staff—which equalled a total of 6,000 staff for 150 branches. Poaching such an enormous number of qualified personnel from other banks wasn't feasible, so we had no choice but to train new staff.

But how do you train 6,000 new staff for 150 branches? The training procedures were based on the "workflow" functions I had formulated during the early days of Bank Central Asia's development. A new staff member at a branch would only require an hour of training before starting work.

I also introduced the digitalisation of accounting and the use of budgets. For each branch, we compiled a loan list based on pre-prepared information about prospective customers. Branch managers were then given a work programme that included using these lists to win new customers and issue loans.

Thanks to these measures, all 150 branches were turning a profit and growing rapidly within six months of opening, proving that the quickly reproducible mechanisms I had established for Bank Central Asia worked, and that the standardisation and systemisation of the bank's operations were also an effective strategy. Bank Central Asia's position as Indonesia's second clearing bank had been further solidified, and there was no other bank that could replace us.

The rapid growth of Bank Central Asia was the result of the diligence and concerted efforts of the entire staff, in particular, the managers of the key regional centres.

The bank's success also reflected the strong support of the shareholders, and the credit here belongs to Sudono Salim. Without his faith and assistance it would have been impossible to open all those branches in such a short period of time. In my 15 years at the bank, there had never been any misunderstandings between us—in fact, I never heard Sudono utter a bad word about anyone. He had always been modest, kind, and understanding when things went wrong. He was my closest confidant and I will forever cherish his memory.

OPENING A BANK CENTRAL ASIA BRANCH IN NEW YORK

" No reason to feel we weren't up to the task. "

As early as 1980, I had dreamed of opening a branch in New York. When I told Sudono of my ambition, he said he thought we were still too small and wouldn't be able to compete with the American banks. I, however, was of a different view. America had nearly 18,000 banks of all sizes; admittedly, several of those were as large and as powerful as countries, but many of them were smaller than us. If they could survive, then so could we. The key would be targeting the right customers and fulfilling their needs.

Bank Central Asia's American branch would be positioned as a bridge between the two sides of the Pacific Basin. With the Chinese diaspora as our customer base, I believed we could accomplish great things and had no reason to feel we were not up to the task.

After enlisting the support and guidance of Jack Stephens, and after a great deal of effort, in 1985 Bank Central Asia was given approval to open a branch in New York. We would be the first Indonesian bank ever to do so.

At that time, my son James was head of Worthen Bank, so he took responsibility for all of the preparatory work for the new branch—from choosing a location to renting the premises and fitting it out, as well as recruiting staff. When we were ready to open the branch, I invited Sudono, his wife, and their sons, to take part in the opening ceremony in New York. The ceremony was simple but dignified, graced by many distinguished guests. I was delighted.

The branch's customers were mostly ethnic Chinese, many of them from Vietnam, along with a handful of Taiwanese. They were hard-working, had been bold enough to come to America to seek their fortune, and were prudent with their money. As such, they made great customers. I encouraged them to open grocery stores and we set up specialist desks to help them open usance lines of credit, so that they could purchase goods from Hong Kong, Taiwan, and China.

With our support, these grocery stores became very successful, and naturally the bank shared in that success as its own business grew.

SUDONO SALIM AND I PART COMPANY

"Despite the risks, I decided to go ahead with heart bypass surgery. "

Flights back to Indonesia stopped in Los Angeles, and on one occasion, Sudono arranged for us to have some tests in a hospital there. The hospital offered an excellent physical examination service and the doctors were very conscientious.

Sudono's test results were all very good, but mine showed a small abnormality in the vessels of my heart, and the doctor advised me to have another check-up in Indonesia in six months.

In 1989, a doctor examined me and informed me there had been some fairly significant hardening of my arteries. He advised me to see a heart specialist, Victor Cheng, who was in Sydney, for a heart catheterisation procedure. The test revealed severe blockages in three blood vessels. I needed to have a heart bypass.

A heart bypass is a major procedure, and in those days the technique had yet to be perfected. The risks were high. After a great deal of consideration, I decided to go ahead with the surgery. With the outcome uncertain, however, I needed to clear all of my debts, credits, and open accounts, and leave all of my affairs at the bank in good order.

Together with Sudono, I also went over all the joint accounts we held, and asked for his consent as to how to divide up our partnership if the surgery didn't go well. For this, I drafted an agreement, which—after reassuring me and telling me not to worry about the surgery—Sudono signed unconditionally. Our discussions took no more than a couple of hours and were very amicable. I was very grateful to him for his understanding. Later on, Sudono and I referred to this agreement when we actually parted ways.

In July of 1975, I had entered into partnership with Sudono to develop Bank Central Asia, and, as first in command, I strictly adhered to the principles of that partnership.

When I had opportunities to buy Bank Perniagaan Indonesia, Bank Umum Asia, Worthen Bank, the Union Planters National Bank, National Bank of Georgia, Stephens Finance Hong Kong, Hong Kong Chinese Bank, and others, rather than acting on my own I always invited Sudono to become a joint shareholder. I believed that was the way to keep to the spirit of our partnership.

I would also immediately inform Sudono whenever President Suharto asked to meet me. After the meeting I would relate what we had discussed so as to avoid any misunderstandings. I believed it was the right thing to do to maintain good relations, and it was one of the main reasons for the success of our 16-year partnership.

Sudono was a kind and affable man. He would often say: "I don't understand banking—Mochtar's the one for that."

There were two questions he would always ask me: "What is the plan for next year?" and "How much will business grow by next year?" He also told his two sons who were involved in banking (Anthony and Andree) to regard me as their teacher. Salim's playful manner belied great wisdom, and I was fortunate to have had the chance to work with him. He was blessed with sons who are a lot like their father. After 16 years, Anthony and Andree had learned all they could from me and were ready to take over the reins of Bank Central Asia. Meanwhile, I felt that it was time for me to devote more of my efforts to building my own family's business. I was getting older and should have been spending more time working with my own children. Ultimately, I felt that I had to end my partnership with Sudono so I would have time for my family. Initially, Sudono wouldn't agree: he hoped that our arrangement could continue, and said there was no need for us to go our separate ways. However, after much discussion, he finally agreed to my request.

We began discussing how to divide things up. Our partnership covered a wide array of business interests and we held cross-shareholdings in a number of companies. How were we to value and distribute them?

I suggested leaving it up to Sudono, but he insisted that I decide. Since he wouldn't be persuaded otherwise, I proposed that there be no revaluation of the assets of any enterprise, there should be a cash-free exchange of shares between Bank Central Asia and Lippo Bank and that joint shareholdings in other enterprises should remain unchanged.

When he heard my proposal, Sudono promptly agreed and suggested that our sons Anthony and James handle the share transfer formalities. From start to finish, the entire process of ending our business partnership took less than two hours.

CHAPTER FIVE

THE RISE OF LIPPO BANK

"A six-year wait for an answer"

A t this point, I would like to back up a bit to describe the events that led to the creation of what became Lippo Bank. In June of 1975, one day after I signed the cooperative agreement with Sudono Salim to develop Bank Central Asia, I was invited to lunch by Hashim Ning—a politician, social activist, chairman of the Indonesian Chamber of Commerce and Industry (Kamar Dagang dan Industri, or KADIN), founder and owner of Bank Perniagaan Indonesia, and one of Indonesia's wealthiest businessmen. He extended the invitation through Professor Peng Lai-kim, a well-known economist whom I knew and respected. During our meal, I was asked about the future prospects of Indonesia's banks (in particular, banks that focused on indigenous Indonesian customers) and their strategies for growth.

I replied that the Indonesian economy was still in the process of reform, and in the early stages of moving from President Sukarno's socialist planned economy to President Suharto's capitalist market economy. The foundations of the economy were weak, there was a lack of capital, bank regulations remained inadequate, and the standard of bank services lagged far behind those of Western banks.

Indonesia's banking sector was still in its infancy. This was a weakness but also an opportunity, and I believed that Indonesia's banks had a bright future. In my personal view, this was the industry with the most potential.

Indonesia's banks back then fell into three categories. First, there were the state-owned banks, which enjoyed dedicated national support and were more akin to monopolies.

Second, there were Indonesian banks that focused on indigenous Indonesian customers. These banks were more idealistic. The scale of these companies, however, was small, and they were incapable of fulfilling all of their customer's needs. As a result, these banks were like plants that had not bloomed and were already withering.

Third, there were banks aimed at Indonesia's Chinese population. Many Chinese Indonesians own their own businesses, and these companies often have extensive trading networks. The banks that focused on this segment of the market usually performed well as soon as they opened. But although they did a thriving trade, they lack roots. These banks often had a very narrow business outlook, so they were like plants that have bloomed but wither before bearing fruit.

The latter two categories of banks lacked the conditions necessary for adequate development. In my view, the correct development strategy was to appeal to a broad mass of people in attracting deposits and making loans. In terms of how capital should be used—given that the only capital available was short-term—these banks needed to use their funds for short-term loans. Long-term lending should account for only a small part of their business.

This, I believed, was the right strategy for the Indonesian banking industry at the time. In terms of the customers they served, merchant banks focusing on both indigenous and Chinese customers should be more open-minded, rather than limiting their customer base and therefore chances of success. If they took the whole of Indonesia's economy into consideration when thinking about growth, then Indonesia's banking industry would have unlimited potential.

We spent a long time discussing these ideas before Hashim Ning unexpectedly invited me to join Bank Perniagaan Indonesia. I could decide how big a share I wanted, and the bank's assets could be priced according to their book value. There was one condition: that Bank Perniagaan Indonesia must soon catch up with Panin Bank, which at the time was the country's largest private bank. I certainly was interested in his offer. At the time, Bank Perniagaan Indonesia's assets were more than 50 times greater than those of Bank Central Asia and it was managed by what was then America's third largest banking institution, Chase Manhattan Bank.

Bank Perniagaan Indonesia had an excellent reputation and was in an entirely different league from Bank Central Asia. Had my decision been based only on economic considerations, I would have chosen Bank Perniagaan Indonesia over Bank Central Asia. However, given that I had already entered into a partnership with Sudono Salim, I had no choice but to state frankly that I had only a day earlier signed a cooperative agreement related to Bank Central Asia, and would be unable to accept his kind offer.

Hashim suggested that I become a shareholder in both banks, but I knew that I was only capable of developing one bank at a time. I apologised once more and promised that if he still wished me to become a shareholder, I would be willing to do so after I had successfully developed Bank Central Asia. Afterwards, Hashim asked Professor Peng to bear witness to my promise. It was then that we became firm friends.

Six years later, in 1981, Hashim invited me to dinner, once again through Professor Peng. He wasted no time in telling me that he had waited for me for six years. Bank Central Asia had grown into Indonesia's fifth largest bank and its largest private bank, so it was time that I became a shareholder and helped develop his bank. He hoped to overtake Panin Bank within three years.

This time I accepted his offer. As before, his terms were very favourable, and I suggested a 49 per cent share, with Hashim retaining the remaining 51 per cent. I told Sudono Salim about the deal and invited him to take an equal stake in my 49 per cent shareholding (with exactly the same favourable terms). As his partner, I felt that this was a moral principle by which I should abide. Sudono agreed and we appointed my son James to take charge of the bank.

At this point, I need to mention how I became a shareholder at Bank Bumi Bahari, as this was part of an eventual merger with Bank Perniagaan Indonesia and therefore important in the subsequent renaming of the combined institution as Lippo Bank.

The Marine Corps welfare foundation owned Bank Bumi Bahari. Its CEO was Colonel Nuryono, an honourable and widely respected man, who was also chairman of Indonesia's National Banking Association (Perbanas). Colonel Nuryono attended the Perbanas annual meeting and I was one of the principal speakers. I gave a talk on "banking commodities and functions". (See speech in this section).

Nuryono seemed quite taken with my talk and arranged to meet me, primarily because he wished to invite me to become a shareholder in Bank Bumi Bahari and direct its future growth. I was touched by his sincerity, but I had no experience in working with the military. Additionally, I was in the process of developing Bank Central Asia.

Not wishing to overextend myself, I had to decline his offer. But the colonel was insistent, and asked me again several times during the following months. He finally asked the navy's commander-in-chief to lobby me. Eventually, I agreed to take a 50 per cent share and I appointed Dr. Li Yulong, a colleague of mine, to head that bank.

THE POSITIONING OF LIPPO GROUP

"A source of strength"

W
hen I was trying to grow the business of Bank Central Asia, my objective was to make it Indonesia's second clearing bank. After I took my stake in Bank Perniagaan, I was also looking for a suitable way to position that bank – which eventually would be rebranded as Lippo Bank – so that the two institutions would complement one another rather than be in direct competition.

At this time I was also gradually building up a collection of domestic and offshore operations in finance, property and manufacturing. Ultimately, this group would include the banking operations built around Bank Perniagaan and Bank Bumi Bahari, which would be combined and rebranded as the Lippo Bank in 1989. All of these companies would eventually come under the Lippo banner. I envisioned Lippo as a "source of capital" and its name would reflect that concept. In Chinese, the name is 力宝 (pronounced "Li bao" in Mandarin). *Li* means power or strength while *bao* can mean treasure or source. In the financial sector, capital is strength, so taken together the name suggests financial strength.

America was the world's financial and economic centre and Hong Kong was Asia's financial centre. Any influential financial institution needed a presence in those capital markets—and that was how I planned to position Lippo Group.

Later in this chapter I will discuss my plans for the overhaul of Bank Perniagaan Indonesia and how that led to the creation of Lippo Bank. But first I want to give readers a sense of my global vision for this bank and how I planned to achieve it. I have already touched on the need to gain a foothold in the key international financial markets. In order to break into the US financial industry, for example, you need to "ride a horse to catch a horse", which means first finding a dependable associate or partner in America whose connections would make it easier for your business to grow and gain credibility. Before finding a suitable partner, you need to understand the economic environment in the US; only then would it be possible to correctly position your business.

To this end, I recruited a Chinese Indonesian in the US named Adam Wen to set up an office in San Francisco.

There are very specific qualities associated with the dominant players in the US market. The US is a huge country in which the development of the national economy has been relatively even. Given the vast size of the country, commercial organisations often could not develop their own independent sales network. Instead, many companies relied on thousands of sales representatives across the US to sell products on their behalf. Sales reps engage in three types of business: selling goods on behalf of their clients on a commission basis; acting as agents under the accounts receivable insurance system; and acting as agents under the discounted accounts payable system.

These businesses might not seem like much, but in a country as large as the US, they serve as the county's basic economic driving force. What's more, many of these businesses have cultivated ties with the legal profession and media organisations, as they understand that these links are crucial. We would need to bear all of this in mind if we were going to establish ourselves in the US. There was much to learn. How would we adapt to the wider economic environment? What kind of strategies should we employ? These were all topics that deserved in-depth research.

CHINESE AMERICANS AS POTENTIAL BANK CUSTOMERS

" We should fund small groceries and general stores. "

If we were to engage in commercial banking in the US we would naturally look to the Chinese community, and we identified this group as a potential source of individual and small-business customers. Chinese Americans come from many different places and make their living in a variety of ways. Many immigrants from south China's Cantonese-speaking community live in the "Chinatowns" of bigger cities around the country. Many of them run restaurants, though their descendants have integrated with the local community to a greater extent. Immigrants from Hong Kong are extremely good at adapting to US culture as Hong Kong has a long history of ties with the West. Taiwanese often go on to higher education in the US and decide to settle there instead of returning to Taiwan. But the ones who stood out as potential customers, in my opinion, were those Chinese originally from Vietnam. Most of these people came to the US as refugees. They tended to be highly ambitious, thought little of hardship, and proved adaptable to changing circumstances. With no possibility of returning to Vietnam, they were forced to sever ties with their home country and put down roots in the US. They worked hard and without complaint.

I came to the conclusion that if I were going to run a commercial bank in the US, then we should focus on these Chinese from Vietnam as our customers. We would fund them in opening small grocery and general stores that predominantly sold Asian goods. We could become a bridge between the merchants of the two continents. My sixth sense told me that these people would one day occupy prominent positions in US business.

TIES TO STEPHENS INC.

" I'd rather miss out on 100 investments than make one bad one. "

S tephens Inc. is one of the largest investment banks outside of Wall Street. Jack Stephens was the company's chairman and CEO. He was a very prescient and insightful strategist, and his son Warren succeeded him in the top job in 1986.

Through guidance and restructuring provided by Stephens Inc., many firms, both large and small, successfully raised funds in the capital markets and went on to build corporate empires. Walmart (the world's largest supermarket chain), Tyson Foods (one of the world's largest processors and marketers of meat) and JB Hunt (one of the largest overland freight transportation companies in North America) are three such examples. All headquartered in Arkansas, they were able to raise funds on the capital markets during their early years thanks to strategic restructuring by Stephens Inc.

Ultimately, all three have become top global enterprises. As an investment banker, Jack had the Midas touch, and he and his brother have long been among the wealthiest Americans, according to Forbes magazine's rich list.

Jack loved to say: "I'd rather miss out on 100 investments than make one bad one." His approach to investing and making strategic judgements was one of cautious deliberation. He always studied the strategic potential of an enterprise before making any changes to the way it was run. It is an approach that I greatly admire and have tried to emulate.

I sent my son James to work at Stephens Inc. for over a year, and later on, James also sent his oldest son, John, to work there for two years. Jack and I had a friendship that spanned three generations. Through him, I began my business expansion into the US with the Union Planters National Bank of Memphis, Worthen Bank and others. Jack Stephens was also involved with Stephens Finance Hong Kong, as well as the purchase of Seng Heng Bank in Macau and the Hongkong Chinese Bank. (I will describe these ventures in a later chapter.) In these investments, Jack gave me full operational control, and even appointed James to take charge of Worthen Bank in Arkansas. A large part of our business dealings were interrelated.

As I mentioned earlier, it was because of my attempted acquisition of National Bank of Georgia that I was lucky enough to meet Jack. Back then, when he asked me about my thoughts and plans for the acquisition of the bank, I told him of my belief that the United States was the world's economic and financial centre, and that we needed a presence in this key market. I also introduced him to Lao Tzu's philosophy and how it related to my own conviction that in the world's economic and financial centre, one had to start small. If the strategic principles were the right ones, then through diligence and thrift, a small business would become a great one.

When I shared my thoughts with him about how we might find a path to success in the big US market, he agreed. Together we devised a strategy whereby commercial banking would serve as the root system of our business while investment banking would be the trunk.

PREPARING TO MOVE INTO THE HONG KONG MARKET

"I needed to ride a horse to catch a horse."

L i Ka-shing is an outstanding businessman who built up a huge conglomerate, starting from practically nothing. His achievements far exceed mine. He is someone I greatly respect, and I am of the firm belief that you have to know him if you want to do business in Hong Kong. When I was a newcomer to Hong Kong, I needed someone to help me get my business off the ground—I needed to "ride a horse to catch a horse". The person I thought best suited for that was Li Ka-shing.

I have a friend whose name is Huang Qingbo. One of his acquaintances was a man named Huang Keli, who was then a vice president of the Hong Kong-based Overseas Trust Bank. He was a leader in the Fujian community and an investment expert. He was also a good friend of Li Ka-shing.

I first asked Huang Qingbo to introduce me to Huang Keli. After a year, we had become friends and I asked Huang Keli to be my advisor. I explained my expansion strategy for our banks in Indonesia, as well as my future plans for an international finance business. He was of an older generation, but we became good friends even though I was around 15 years his junior. It was through Huang Keli that I finally became acquainted with Li Ka-shing in 1991.

Each time I went to Hong Kong, I would be sure to visit Li Ka-shing and ask for his advice. On one particular occasion, he invited me to afternoon tea. We chatted about the capital markets, and he appeared to appreciate my insight. We became good friends and he provided me with a great deal of support for my Hong Kong business. My acquisition of the Ambassador Hotel in Kowloon and Lippo Centre in Admiralty on Hong Kong Island were both the result of his help. He has been the driving force behind the development of my business in the financial centre that is Hong Kong.

THE THREE STAGES OF BUSINESS GLOBALISATION

" Lippo Group is Indonesia's most globalised business. *"*

I have already talked about the irresistible trend towards globalisation. This trend convinced me that Lippo Group needed to be a worldwide business and one that could take advantage of globalisation.

One person who was particularly helpful in gaining an understanding of the implications of globalisation was Peng Lai-kim, the same economist who delivered the key lunch invitation from Hashim Ning. The renowned professor gave me a great deal of guidance on what to expect as markets around the world became more closely integrated. My task was then to examine the practical significance of his conclusions and apply them to the real business world. After much research, I decided to adopt a three-step approach in order to make Lippo Group a global company:

First, I recruited several American experts in finance and capital markets in order to standardise, modernise and restructure Lippo Group's business. This was the globalisation of human resources.

Second, following the restructuring of Lippo Group, I instructed the financial team to work towards taking Lippo Bank public. This was the globalisation of capital.

Third, armed with the funds from the initial public offering (IPO), I called on management to look for business in Singapore, Hong Kong, the United States, and elsewhere. This was the globalisation of business.

All of Lippo Group's other companies were eventually taken public. This was also followed by successive listings of Lippo Group businesses in Hong Kong and Singapore. In this, Lippo Group became the first of Indonesia's major corporations to be listed on international markets and to use capital from international markets in its expansion.

The two speeches that follow represent my understanding of the banking industry and my views on banking developments in the Pacific Basin. They also contain my principal thoughts and ideas about the expansion of the Lippo Group. The first speech was given in 1981 and the second at Harvard University in 1984.

Bank Commodities and Functions: Speech Given at the Annual Meeting of the Indonesian National Banking Association, 1981

It has always been my dream to be a banker. But to be a good banker, one must have an in-depth understanding of a bank's commodities, and so I would often research the banking industry. What kind of industry was it? What kind of commodities did it trade in? Many people said to me that a bank deals in currency, that a bank's commodity is "money".

However, after extensive inquiries, I came to a realisation: banks are not places where currency is bought and sold; they are, in fact, places where "credit" is bought and sold. For example, if you were to deposit a million rupiah in a bank, the bank would give you a receipt, which shows that you have deposited a million rupiah. You have sufficient faith in the bank to hand over a million rupiah. With this sum, you have purchased the bank's credit.

(continued)

Similarly, if a bank loans someone a million rupiah to buy a house, and the borrower leases the property out to a third party for 100 years and collects 100 years' rent, this touches on issues of property ownership and usage rights. The borrower pledges the ownership of the property to the bank, but retains the usage rights and can lease the property and keep the profits. In other words, the property itself holds no value for the bank; the bank, upon granting a 100-year mortgage to the customer, is in effect buying his trust. Hence, a bank's true commodity is not money but credit.

What, in addition, is a bank's function? In my view, it is credit expansion. The real value of one dollar in the hands of someone who doesn't know how to use it is only 50 cents; however, in a bank, with its credit function, how much more credit can this dollar be turned into?

I'll give you another example: a 100-seat passenger plane doesn't need to allocate 100 washrooms; three would be sufficient to satisfy passengers' needs. A school with 1,000 pupils would probably only require around 30 washrooms. What does this tell us? When taking turns to use the washrooms, 1,000 people do not require 1,000 washrooms.

The same applies to banks: suppose I have a bank with 100 customers, and I pledge to loan each customer one dollar, making a total pledge of 100 dollars. All 100 of these customers will not use their loans at the same time; in reality, only around 20 per cent will. Therefore, the bank can pledge to loan five times that amount of capital, a total loan amount of 500 dollars.

In addition, if a bank pledges to loan to 100 customers, and 80 do not use it, then under normal circumstances that money will be deposited in the bank. If we suppose that those 80 customers each deposit 50 dollars, then the bank can pledge to expand loans to the value of five times 20 per cent of that amount. The credit expansion function of banks is quite extraordinary; banks with a large customer base in particular have a great capacity for credit expansion.

Banks also function as a customer-base clearing house (each industry's upstream, midstream and downstream customer base). This is a bank's most important and profitable function.

This function can be further extended to become a globalised currency credit expansion function, as we have seen in the past with the British pound, and currently with the US dollar. Both were used as valuation currencies for world trade, and as such served as global clearing houses.

In the Bretton Woods system, the US currency was tied to the gold standard. In 1971, after President Nixon withdrew from the Bretton Woods system and the US dollar became an unsubstantiated gold or silver reserve currency—essentially a fiat currency—the wealth of the world was centralised in the US dollar, by means of a piece of paper.

The US dollar is universally acknowledged as the world's commodity valuation currency, and from this it derives pricing power. As we all know, the price of oil is calculated using the US dollar; regardless of the country, the base price of oil takes the US dollar as its standard, and this is precisely because the US dollar has become the unit of commodity valuation. Market prices in the United States can have a strong influence on the price of commodities worldwide, through futures derivatives and other functions.

But what effect does a commodity valuation function have? Because both buyer and seller adopt the US dollar as their

(continued)

standard, both parties must open US dollar accounts. For example, a buyer buys a barrel of crude oil from the seller, for say 100 dollars. The buyer must deposit 100 dollars in an American bank account in advance, and then transfer the money to the seller at the time of the transaction. Similarly, the seller cannot deposit the money in his own country; he must also deposit in an American bank.

Hence, global commodity transactions are made entirely within American banks, which is analogous to money being moved from America's left pocket to its right pocket, at no time leaving the American banking system. One can imagine the annual volume of commodity trading: most likely several trillion US dollars, all of which is deposited in the American banking system at no cost.

The US dollar had become, then, the clearing currency for international trade, futures currency, debt currency and securities currency. All of the world's central banks need to deposit a portion of their capital in the American banking system as national reserves. With the US dollar as the global clearing currency, the United States has become the world's central bank, with control over vast sums of interest-free capital; consequently, it possesses unlimited powers of global financial control.

If the US dollar, then, has such major functions, what is the confidence in the currency based on?

First, the huge amounts of US tax; second, the United States' vast GDP; and third, the country's influence over commodities prices derived from international trade. Based on these three factors, the US dollar is a globally trusted currency.

There is another important issue: the United States' usurping of oil trade diplomacy. What is this based on? First, the nation's powerful financial control; second, its military strength; and third, its use of unregulated futures derivatives to control the world oil market. Because of these three factors, the country's currency and financial market expansion has been propelled to a whole new level.

However, if the issue of currency and unchecked development of futures derivatives is not controlled, like a business, if the balance sheet and profits are unsound, then decline and bankruptcy may be the result.

With regard to the banking credit system and functions I have mentioned, all banks, from small local banks to national central banks, have credit system and credit expansion functions. Consequently, in discussing bank development, we must first understand what is intrinsic to credit. Then we can study how it is used. How is credit packaged so that it is beneficial for customer service products? And what self-controls does it have to mitigate business risk? The answers to these questions are precisely the measures and means used to develop a bank.

Finally, I would like to stress once again that Indonesia's economy is in the early stages of development, and that this is an opportune time for the growth of the banking industry. It is an opportunity that should be grasped. I wish you all a prosperous future.

Thank you.

Future Development and Trends in the Pacific Basin: Speech Given at the East Asia Conference, Harvard University, Cambridge, Massachusetts, 1984

When discussing the development of banking during the 1990s in the Pacific Basin, it is very important to first have an understanding of the changes in the political, economic and commercial structure of the region. At present, it is possible to pinpoint three major changes:

First, there is the emergence of the Pacific Basin as a new world economic centre; second, there are changes over the last 20 years in the economic structure of the United States; and third, there are changes in the pattern and mode of international trade and commerce.

To begin, I would like to take a look at the first of these changes: the emergence of the Pacific Basin as a new world economic centre.

In the 18th century, the invention of the steam engine heralded the Industrial Revolution, and the Europeans, vastly superior to the rest of the world in terms of scientific and technological development, wielded almost total control over world politics and the world's economy. As a result, the economy around the Atlantic Basin developed into the world's first and foremost economic centre, including on its periphery the eastern seaboard and the United States. Hence, it became known as the Atlantic Basin economic centre.

At the conclusion of World War II, Japan, which had learned a bitter lesson from its defeat, set about reconstructing itself and implementing a democratic political system. For the next three and a half decades, with the assistance of the United States, the Japanese people made an enormous effort to develop the country's economy, and today Japan has grown to be the major driving force behind all economic development in Asia.

During the 1950s, Japan put a great deal of effort into developing its textile industry, which subsequently took up a dominant position in the world textile trade. During the 1960s, Japan put its muscle behind its iron, steel and shipbuilding industries, and very soon Japan found itself once again in a leading position, thereby gaining a firm grip on iron, steel and shipbuilding markets all over the world.

The 1970s saw Japan tackle the automotive and consumer electronics industries and even today, the country still enjoys a dominant position in the world markets for cars and consumer electronic products. Now, in the 1980s, we see Japan forging ahead with development in high technology, computer and robotics industries. Once again, Japan's aim is to lead the world in these fields and secure a firm grip on world markets.

When we look at the development of Japanese industry, as I have briefly outlined, it would appear that Japan has put all its energy into developing one particular strategic industry every 10 years and, having succeeded, then went on to harness world markets in this industry.

As this process continues, every decade sees another strategic industry no longer suitable to the changing environmental conditions at home. Consequently, the industries are obliged to relocate to neighbouring countries more suitable for those industries. These neighbouring countries primarily include South Korea, Taiwan, Hong Kong and Singapore, and from those

(continued)

countries, the extension continues outward to other countries in Southeast Asia, such as Malaysia, Thailand, the Philippines and Indonesia.

As a result of the ripple effect on the above industry-relocation process, these various countries have achieved significant economic growth, along with the independence they gained at the end of World War II. Over the last 20 years, Japan, South Korea, Taiwan, Hong Kong and Singapore have registered some of the highest economic growth rates in the world. It is for this reason that the world-wide press has referred to these countries as "Asia's dragon economies".

I feel that this name is very appropriate, and it reflects realistically the situation that exists in this region. For it must be remembered, the dragon is an important symbol in Oriental culture, a mythological creature in Chinese tradition and, of course, the seal of the emperor in ancient times. Ask the people of these countries to write the word "dragon" in their own language and they will all produce a similar character or word. It is this, perhaps, that best illustrates the enormous influence that Chinese culture has had on the five countries.

This influence has its origins in ancient Chinese Confucianism, which advocated high moral principles and the so-called doctrine of the mean. As a result, relations between labour and management in the five countries tend to be harmonious and coordinated, in stark contrast to the sharp confrontation between labour and management in the modern Western world. This is perhaps one of the most important factors that have contributed to the fast economic and industrial growth in the Pacific Basin. Another important factor is that the people of these regions boast a very ancient cultural heritage and have had to adapt to many changes over time and innovate for progress. Hence they are able to absorb modern science and technology relatively easily.

In addition to the dragon economies, it should not be forgotten that large numbers of ethnic Chinese are involved in economic activities in almost all other countries in Southeast Asia, and thus they, too, have to a certain extent been influenced by elements of the "dragons".

The Pacific Basin has, therefore, become the world's second economic centre and has the best potential for continued and sustained growth. When one looks at the commercial and economic activities that exist between this region and the western seaboard of the United States, one can see that there is a relationship of mutual benefit of each supplying what is needed by the other. This relationship is becoming increasingly close. It is very important to understand that the enormous developments in science, technology and industry in the United States and the resultant improvements in the standard of living sent wages soaring, which brought about continual increases in the manufacturing costs of light and labour-intensive industries.

High labour costs in light and labour-intensive industries in the United States were a great disadvantage for the United States in competing with various Asian countries. This led the Asian countries to establish light and labour-intensive industries for export to the United States, to take advantage of the low labour costs in Asian countries. On the other hand, the United States, being superior in technology and abundant in agricultural products, exported these types of products to Asia to take advantage of Asia's new-found purchasing power.

Thus, trade between the two Pacific coasts became more and more frequent, with each side filling the other's gaps.

(continued)

Eventually, the entire Pacific Basin developed into an economic centre. In another sense this process may also be seen as a move on the part of Asia-Pacific countries to expand outward, breaking their former isolation.

At this point, I would like to take a look at the second set of changes that I cited at the beginning of my paper: that is, the changes in the economic structure of the United States.

Being Asian, I'm less qualified to speak on the US economy to this, largely US audience. However, it is meaningless to look at the Pacific Basin economic centre without discussing the US economy. Consequently, I will try my best to discuss this subject with the distinguished guests and experts in this field.

During World War II, the Soviet Union sustained massive damage from the conflict but it also reaped considerable benefits. When the war ended, it used its influence to spread communism throughout many regions that had been left in a vacuum as a result of the war. The United States did not suffer as much destruction on its own soil during the war as some other Western countries did. Thus it fell to the United States to maintain and protect the stability of capitalism and balance it against the activities of the Soviet Union. The United States became the international policeman of the free world.

As a consequence of this responsibility, the United States became involved in both the Korean War and the Vietnam War. US participation in both these wars resulted in considerable military expenditure. If the US government of the day had been tackling these two wars with a war economy, instead of a peacetime economy, then perhaps it might have greatly lessened present-day US economic problems.

I would now like to briefly run through the effects of the changes in the structure of the US economy.

The first change is the weakening of the US dollar, which forced the US to abandon the gold standard and adopt a floating currency system.

After World War II, the US dollar was the most powerful and influential currency in the world; it also became the standard monetary unit for all international trade and, consequently, an internationally accepted currency. The change of the US dollar to a floating currency system has created enormous repercussions throughout the world economy.

Extremely fierce competition and confrontation have developed throughout global trade and finance. For example, in order to strengthen the sales of Japanese goods to overseas markets and prevent imports from entering the Japanese market, all Japan has to do is depreciate the Japanese yen.

On the other hand, if the United States found itself burdened with financial and economic problems, it could of course raise interest rates, but such a move would affect economic conditions in other countries throughout the world. Therefore, this first change is the precursor to the second change: that is, the internationalisation of the US economy. Let's now focus on this second change.

In its role as guardian of capitalism and in the implementation of policies aimed at opposing the Soviet Union, the United States has been obliged to provide support for other countries in the world so as to balance and limit the spread of communism. Witness, for example, South Korea, Japan and Taiwan in Asia, and West Germany in Western Europe. Furthermore, the United States has to support various developing countries in

(continued)

order to ensure that they, too, are not dominated by communism. What this means is that the entire spectrum of financial and economic measures implemented by the United States government requires consideration of political factors.

The implication is that the United States' economy is becoming increasingly internationalised. The consequence of internationalisation has been that US industry and commerce, which previously only had to reckon with domestic factors in making key decisions, now also has to take into consideration overseas factors and, in addition, the financial and economic measures adopted by the governments of other countries.

Let me cite an example. In the past, the Ford Motor Company only had to consider competition from domestic automotive companies. Today, it is forced to assess the strategies and tactics of all Japanese automotive companies as well as its competitors in Western Europe. A similar change has now been reached in which all financial and economic policies drawn up by the US government are subject to obstruction, interference or coercion from numerous other countries of the world. In other words, the US economy has now become truly internationalised.

The deregulation of the banking industry is the third change in the US economic structure. In recent years, the US government has adopted policies toward deregulating economic activities in the United States. The aim has been to reduce or eliminate protectionism and encourage free competition. One of the main areas of deregulation has been in the banking industry.

In the past, US banking laws severely limited the expansion of American banks beyond their home state. In some cases, there were even restrictions prohibiting the establishment of branches in different counties within the same state. The effect of these stringent laws was an expansion by most major banks—not domestically, but internationally. This international expansion abroad left a huge vacuum in the domestic US market.

If those restrictive laws were completely abolished today, I believe the major American banks would almost certainly realign their attention, concentration and efforts towards domestic expansion, thereby filling the vacuum just mentioned. This trend is already taking place and US bankers are asking themselves what the effects will be. Therefore, we have discussed the second of the three changes that were brought about by the change to the floating currency system in the US, the internationalisation of the US economy and the deregulation of the banking industry. I add here that this second group of changes is characterised by the concept of a "point-to-pan-regional" structure, which is the basis of my discussion of the third change.

The third of three major changes in the Pacific Basin is the change in the pattern and mode of international trade and commerce.

It is necessary to examine this change in light of related factors such as the United States' role as international protector or policeman. Furthermore, it is important to take into account the country's unprecedented post-war increases in productivity, resulting from tremendous advancements in science and techology. Coupled with this development were, of course, corresponding increases in the standards of living. However, labour-intensive industries, faced with increases in wages at home, looked overseas for investment opportunities offering cheaper labour in order to remain competitive in world markets. Such a shift of investments, in a way, strengthened the economies

(continued)

of developing countries. Most major American companies, then, set about organising multinational corporations.

They built factories abroad and set up marketing and distribution networks. Large Western European countries soon imitated this model. Such changes or shifts in industrial and marketing development are important structural changes in trade relations and patterns. Previously, trade relations had been between two local points, or what I refer to as "point-to-point" relationships, but now there is evidence of a shift towards a relationship between a localised point and a pan-regional, or a more embracing target.

In other words, whereas previously trade relations had been between an exporter or producer in one country and an importer in another, they were now developing towards the present-day set-up in which the exporter directly establishes a marketing and distribution network in the target country and markets his or her products through his or her own sales network. This, then, is what I mean by structural change in international trade relations and patterns from a "point-to-point" relationship to a "point-to-regional" network concept.

In other words, modern trading requires a network and organisation in the target market area or countries. A salesman with a suitcase is no longer effective. To succeed in today's trading environment, the trading house must be international, with a network all over the world that can mobilise people power, information and financial resources rapidly, prior or in response to market changes and competition.

Now I come to the conclusion that I feel can be drawn from the three important changes in the Pacific Basin scenario.

It is vital that we correctly understand the emergence of the Pacific Basin as the world's second economic centre.

As a new economic centre, the Pacific Basin can be divided into four different categories of countries, with unique and specific needs and characteristics.

The first category is identifiable in that the countries are generally small in size, with no natural resources and a high population density. The countries possess an industrial base with highly developed technology. This category includes the five dragons: South Korea, Japan, Taiwan, Hong Kong and Singapore.

The second category includes large countries with an abundance of natural resources and a large population but with a weak industrial base. China, Indonesia and Malaysia fall into this category.

The third category comprises countries that are relatively small in size, not too rich in natural resources and with a weak base of industry and technology. Thailand and the Philippines are examples.

Finally, the fourth category embraces those countries of a large size, which are rich in resources, blessed with a reasonably sized population, and with a highly developed industrial and agricultural base, such as Canada, the United States and Australia.

Clearly, the countries in each of these four categories have different needs and, hence, with each one supplying the other's needs, international trade between them will increase and relationships will become more interdependent. In the coming years, as the economies of the region grow, each country will be able to develop its own advantage.

(continued)

As this happens, it seems very probable that at some point in the future, Japan and those in the first category will become suppliers of machinery and technological services for the region, while China and Indonesia of the second category will become suppliers of industrial raw material and labour for the region. Countries in the third category, such as Thailand and the Philippines, will become suppliers of labour-intensive light industrial products. The countries of the fourth category, such as Canada, the United States and Australia, will become suppliers of high technology and agricultural products, as well as being the largest consumer markets in the entire region.

By understanding exactly the economic changes that I have outlined, we are able to make far more accurate decisions concerning the direction that banking development should take in this region. In doing so, we are sure that banks will achieve greater results and benefits by playing the right roles. In view of the major economic changes in the Pacific Basin, I firmly believe that bankers have a duty to educate and encourage their clients to understand the changes more clearly and improve their management quality accordingly.

In general, banks in the Pacific Basin, with the possible exceptions of the United States and Japan, should pay more attention to the "point-to-pan-regional" trend and find appropriate methods to overcome the ever-increasing fierce competition.

The "pan-regional" network concept that I just mentioned is essentially a business network. The sphere of banking services has already spread to just about every layer of society. Banks have now become agents for the financial activities of both individuals and institutions, and intermediaries for industrial, commercial and economic exchanges. Furthermore, they act as investment consultants for both individuals and institutions.

Banks will play an ever-increasing role for both individuals and institutions in the Pacific Basin in the near future. In view of the rapid advancement of computer technology in banking, home banking will become a reality in the not too distant future. As for institutions, nearly all business transactions will go through the banking system no matter whether they are small transactions in villages, middle-size transactions in cities or at state level, large transactions within the country, or the largest transactions internationally.

Consequently, to serve the business community well, banks must adapt themselves to the new changes in the Pacific Basin by expanding and strengthening their network within the Pacific Basin to cover the region, the countries, the states and the cities, as I just mentioned.

The construction of such banking networks can be done in three different ways: first, by directly establishing representative offices and/or branches in key regions; second, by entering into cooperation or joint venture business relationships with banks already operating in the key region so as to create a relationship of mutual supply to each other's needs; and third, by purchasing existing banks in key regions as a means of expansion.

Ladies and gentlemen, when trying to predict the future development and trends of banking in the Pacific Basin, we must always be aware of the ever-changing political, economic, regulatory and technological environment that we are dealing with. Nevertheless, I feel the development and trends I have outlined, in particular the trend towards the "pan-regional" network strategy, will be one that will be more and more evident in the future.

Thank you.

A PLAN TO REFORM BANK PERNIAGAAN INDONESIA

"Helping customers helps you"

L et me now return to describing how we redirected the operations of Bank Perniagaan Indonesia, and how this in turn led to the bank being renamed Lippo Bank. At that time, the bank focused on indigenous Indonesian customers and this meant it enjoyed favourable treatment from the Indonesian government. Its founder and owner, Hashim Ning, was a respected and far-sighted business leader. He had very enlightened ideas when it came to operational strategy, and had no qualms about inviting Chase Manhattan Bank to run and manage his bank for him. As a result, the administration of Bank Perniagaan Indonesia was extremely systematic, and all of its managers were trained professionals. With such a strong foundation, common sense would dictate that the bank should be doing very well.

After three months of finding out everything I could about Bank Perniagaan Indonesia, I discovered that, although its assets were in good condition, it had issues with its positioning. The bank saw itself as a corporate bank and a bank for indigenous Indonesians, which caused two problems. The bank's capital didn't fit its positioning as a "corporate bank", and this prevented it from achieving healthy growth. Additionally, by only serving indigenous Indonesian customers, it had confined itself to a small segment of the market. Without a broad customer base, it had a limited lending capacity and was unable to meet "corporate" requirements.

Its staff, however, consisted of highly paid professionals who were in many cases overqualified for their jobs. Costs were high and there was a lot of waste, yet there was no way for the business to expand. This was the crux of why it wasn't doing well. After doing some research, I put forward a proposal to Hashim Ning to turn his business around:

- The bank's positioning had to be changed. Instead of just limiting itself to corporate banking, it should be more agile; in this, we would start small and then go onto bigger things.
- The bank shouldn't just limit itself to being a bank for indigenous Indonesians. It should transform itself into a bank for everyone in Indonesia.
- It should try to win customers in the upstream and downstream segments of Indonesia's auto parts, bicycle parts, motorcycle parts, general merchandising, and the textiles and garment sectors— becoming a clearing house and intermediary bank for these six industries.
- It should provide import financing for these six industries.
- It should also recommend and introduce parts manufacturers in Taiwan, South Korea, Japan and China to customers in these six industries in Indonesia.
- It should provide re-export services to these industries from Hong Kong and Singapore.
- It should provide Indonesia's most convenient domestic and international money transfer services.
- It should offer its customers the best rates on foreign exchange.
- It should set up branches (300 of them) to serve the business networks in these key industries.

- Training should be in line with the kind of operational staff needed to serve these industries, and the sales staff should be required to promote the bank's foreign exchange services.
- Some of the highly paid but underperforming staff should be dismissed.
- Budgets should be revised to reduce expenditure and boost efficiency.
- The bank's capital should be increased to give it more financing capacity, allowing it to meet the needs of the six industries.
- It should aim to be outperforming Panin Bank within four years.
- Lippo Ltd's operations in Hong Kong and Singapore needed to be bolstered in order to support all of its trade and foreign exchange-related activities. The bank should also try to procure more import and export financing. This would enable it to become a bridge connecting its customers in these six industries to their interests overseas, and would provide them with services that they couldn't find at any other banks.
- The bank should introduce a new slogan: "Helping customers helps you".

After a detailed explanation of my ideas, Hashim Ning proved extremely receptive to this ambitious plan, and vowed to give it his full support. He agreed to appoint James as Bank Perniagaan Indonesia's CEO, and gave him full authority to implement the reforms.

RAISING AN 'ARMY'

" We focus on six key sectors. *"*

O nce the plan had been established, the main task was to reorganise Bank Perniagaan Indonesia so that it could adapt to the new reforms in the banking sector. We also had to work out how to find the right professional talent to cater to the business development needs of the six sectors. I proposed several principles that could serve as a guide to staff structure:

Focus on six sectors: auto parts, bicycle parts, motorcycle parts (mainly run by natives of Putian), general merchandising (dominated by people from various parts of Fujian); textiles (mainly run by people from Fuqing and southern Fujian), and garments (dominated by people from Fuqing and other parts of Fujian).

That meant that the bank, when trying to recruit talent, should look for people with operational experience in these six sectors, or else professionals who already had connections in these areas.

The bank's business would cover an extremely wide range of operations, and for this it needed mutually complementary teams with a broad mix of talent.

Since James had already been appointed as Bank Perniagaan Indonesia's CEO, it would be best if he were in charge of putting together the new teams, through which he would be able to create his own platform. This would be a good learning experience for him, and would allow him to create a dynamic and effective staff based on the major principles given above.

Hashim Ning was very appreciative and supportive of James's work, and it all went smoothly. Observing from the sidelines, I was pleased to see that James had put together a highly capable staff. I was confident that he would be able to implement the development plan.

Inside, I prayed that his first time doing business on his own would go well, that he would learn interpersonal skills and how to handle different stakeholders, and that he would figure out how to take a balanced approach to personnel issues.

THE BANK GOES DIGITAL

"The software needed for growth"

One part of the development plan concerned the creation of a network of branches, which would provide the "hardware" for the bank's growth. However, smooth communication and cooperation between these branches could not be achieved without the digitalisation of their operations and accounting—this would be the "software" of the bank's growth and was a prerequisite for the rapid opening of new branches.

I previously described in detail how workflows were established and how operational and accounting procedures were digitalised when we set up new bank branches, so I won't go into that again here.

But in the 1980s, information engineering was an emerging science that was also very costly. Particularly in Indonesia, it was a very foreign concept. IT talent was difficult to find, even at a high price. As a result, digitalisation was hard to achieve. After several forays that had to be abandoned halfway, I turned to Jack Stephens for help. He had a software and information engineering company called Systematics to which Stephens Inc. outsourced all IT work for its subsidiaries. In addition to the group itself, Systematics also provided IT services to external companies. It was a great business concept, and one that I decided to emulate.

I acquired PT Multipolar, little more than a shell company, to undertake this task. I asked Systematics to provide technical cooperation. PT

Multipolar grew very quickly. It undertook IT projects for Bank Central Asia, Bank Perniagaan Indonesia, and Lippo Life Insurance Co., after which it did the same for other external banks.

Today, PT Multipolar is one of Indonesia's three largest software companies and is listed on the Indonesian Stock Exchange.

LIPPO BANK OPENS 100 BRANCHES IN 12 MONTHS

"Management had doubts about my plan."

Earlier, I described the government's intent to deregulate the banking sector via the PAKTO 88 reforms so banks could become much more effective in financing Indonesia's growth story. It became obvious by the end of 1987 that a bold and massive deregulation in the banking sector was about to take place given my participation in those discussions in my capacity as a banker and a board member of the Indonesian bankers association. By that time, my son James had taken temporary leave to be in the US to develop our group's East and West coast beachheads, so I told him to come back in anticipation of the changes and opportunities that were coming. He returned in August 1988 and the government announced the massive PAKTO 88 in October.

BPI had developed well over the eight and a half years, becoming the largest non-foreign exchange bank and the eighth largest private bank in Indonesia. Prior to expansion, I wanted to remedy another handicap of BPI: the bank was living in the shadow of the much larger and well known Lippo Group; it was always seen as just one of Lippo's many businesses. Hence, the decision was made to rebrand and rename the bank into Lippo Bank and at the same time merge Bank Bahari to create a broader platform in 1989. The move was also made in anticipation of the IPO which was soon to come.

I had decided to open 150 new Bank Central Asia branches within 12 months, and I also wanted to open 100 Lippo Bank branches over the same period. When I revealed my plan to my partner Hashim Ning and what was by then the management of the Lippo Bank, there was a great deal of scepticism. As I understood it, the concerns were as follows:

1. Branch locations would be difficult to find.
2. Equipping the branches would be difficult.
3. Funds were limited.
4. We had insufficient qualified personnel.
5. There would be losses to bear for the initial period after the branches had opened.

I had an answer for each of my colleagues' misgivings:

1. The PAKTO 88 reforms of Bank Indonesia and the Ministry of Finance were not perfect, and would certainly be revised. As a result, we had to make the most of the time we had to open new branches; opportunities like this didn't come along often and it would be even more difficult in the future if the regulations on opening new branches became more restrictive.
2. Fitting out the branches would be simplified, modernised and standardised, and would involve pre-assembly of many components. Several contractors could get started on it at once.
3. At the time, the economy was still in recession and there were many empty shops that could be either leased or bought. If there were no empty units in busy downtown areas, we could temporarily lease ones in relatively downmarket areas; we'd improvise as we went along. Since many people who owned these units would be in rather difficult financial positions, they would lease it at a

much lower price, and therefore we would be able to more fully leverage our limited funds.

4. Qualified personnel could be divided into sales talent and administrative talent. For sales talent, we could hire the children and relatives of successful local business people. They just needed to know people in local business circles and be able to create strong business relationships with them. The sales talent would receive six months' training in banking concepts, but didn't need to have any administrative skills. For administrative personnel, existing staff could be sent to the branches to gradually polish their skills. In addition, we could recruit university graduates who would take up their position in the branch after 11 months of training; they would make up for the lack of existing staff. For low-level staff, workflows could be used to explain their role and tasks. In fact, given that their tasks were relatively simple, they only needed a senior high school education and could be taught using workflows in an hour. The efficiency of this approach had already been proven, so there was no cause for concern.

5. With regard to the branches losing money in the initial stages due to insufficient business, that was indeed a possibility. But Lippo Bank was already making progress in its business development and it had some very attractive services. There was no question of winning new customers. These young bankers were eager to put our plan into action. Working day and night we managed to open 106 new branches in 12 months, establishing Lippo Bank's position in Indonesia. Confidence at the bank soared.

LIPPO GOES PUBLIC

"
Making my dream come true.
"

I have already described the three aspects of capital markets and three stages of globalisation. Going public was the best way for banks to raise money and had long been an aspiration of mine. When in 1988 the Indonesian government issued the PAKTO 88 reforms, it gave me the chance to make my dream a reality.

I told Sudono Salim and Hashim Ning at the same time of my plan to take Bank Central Asia and Lippo Bank public. Hashim agreed to the plan unconditionally, but Sudono believed that the time wasn't right for Bank Central Asia, and wanted to delay any public offering of shares. Other colleagues were of the same opinion: raising funds by going public was, without doubt, a good thing, but it also would lead to problems.

Most importantly, it would increase our tax burden, and after going public, we would be subject to a huge amount of regulation, which would increase our legal fees. Being tied up in so much regulation would be a great inconvenience, and there were fears that it would hold back the bank's future growth.

Another concern was that major shareholders would lose their control over the bank. Moreover, there would be a lot of preparatory work in the run-up to the IPO, which would take a colossal amount of time and effort.

None of this was untrue, but those who objected to going public were only worrying about the negative aspects of the regulatory burden without recognising the benefits. The same regulations would help make a company's operations more systematic and that in turn would help avoid risk.

Furthermore, there were no limits to how much we could raise from the market in order to expand the bank. Without access to the capital market we would lack the funds needed for our ambitious plans. In addition, the capital markets would reduce the unchecked influence of large individual shareholders, which would make the bank's growth healthier and more secure. We could also use this as an opportunity to separate the bank's ownership and management, which would increase professionalism at the bank.

In the end, everyone agreed to my plan to take Lippo Bank public. After a year of hard work by Lippo Bank's entire management and board of directors, we managed to put together all the necessary data and make our way through a mountain of legal documents.

Having overcome numerous obstacles, Lippo Bank became the first bank to be listed on Indonesia's capital market and the first Indonesian bank ever to go public successfully. It caused a national sensation, and people were eager to buy Lippo shares. In a short period of time, Lippo's market value almost doubled. My dream had come true.

ENVY AND RESENTMENT

"A tall tree catches much wind."

A tall tree, however, catches much wind, and the success of Lippo Bank's listing also caused envy and resentment among some people. Intellectuals and financial commentators wrote articles attacking me for having "prettied up" Lippo Bank and swindling the public out of money, while others criticised the bank for having a share price that was far higher than the actual value of its assets, and so on.

Among them was one highly influential commentator, Kwik Kian Gie, who achieved considerable fame thanks to an article criticising Lippo Bank's listing. Later, President Megawati Sukarnoputri appointed him as National Development Planning minister. After taking up this position, he commissioned an exhaustive investigation into Lippo Bank. It lasted about a year, and ended when the investigators were unable to find any evidence to corroborate their accusations.

On one occasion, senior central bank official Juanda invited Nyoman Moena, chairman of Perbanas, to join me (I was vice-chairman of Perbanas at the time) in a televised interview in the Indonesian media. The topic was: "The pros and cons of the PAKTO 88 financial reforms".

After the interview, Kwik remained on the set, and insisted that I go on air for a debate about the dispute over Lippo Bank's public offering. He really put me in an awkward position. In front of Juanda and Nyoman Moena, I had no choice but to be honest with Kwik. We were acquaintances, and also colleagues in the Prasetiya Mulya Foundation, the educational foundation that set up the Prasetiya Mulya University, a leading business school. He was one of the few Chinese Indonesians admired by indigenous Indonesians—and one of the first Chinese cabinet ministers in Indonesia—something that I was also proud of given our shared cultural heritage. He was someone who should be celebrated, and I was extremely reluctant to confront him so publicly because I would end up having to attack him. I felt that instead, we should maintain our dignity.

But Kwik kept pressing for an on-air debate. In the end, with no way to convince him that it was a bad idea, I suggested that we invite Juanda and Moena to act as adjudicators and first have a debate off camera. If I lost, I was willing to go on stage and do the debate publicly; if Kwik lost, for the sake of his reputation, we would cancel the TV debate.

When everyone agreed, the debate began. I asked Kwik to state his case. Right from the beginning, he aggressively accused me of having no business ethics, of deceiving people, and of selling worthless bank shares to the public.

I waited for him to finish, then asked if he understood the listing process. He replied that he did. I invited him to explain how it worked. He said that he understood that companies wishing to go public were required to hire an independent accounting firm, independent lawyers and an independent foreign investment bank. The results of the financial and legal audit, as well as the underwriting contract for the issue price of shares and their number (agreed upon by several well-respected international investment banks), were compiled into a prospectus. If the prospectus contained untrue statements, this could lead to criminal proceedings.

I applauded Kwik's erudition and familiarity with the listings process. What he' said showed that, in fact, Lippo's shares were first sold to investment banks, after which they were sold on to the public in Indonesia and abroad. The reason why these investment banks dared to underwrite our shares at a higher price was because, over the last 30 years, I had taken four small banks on the brink of crisis—Bank Buana, Panin Bank, Bank Central Asia, and Bank Perniagaan Indonesia —and transformed them into highly profitable, large-scale financial institutions within two or three years. What the investment banks were buying was the creditworthiness, banking acumen and the brand of Mochtar Riady.

It was the same principle whereby people of wealth and status are willing to pay a premium to buy a Rolex watch, or why smoking aficionados bought expensive Gudang Garam cigarettes. This was one of the most basic principles of business—that a product's value included many intangibles of which the reputation of and trust in a brand factored greatly. Furthermore, deceiving people meant selling a black cat in a bag as a white cat, and required misrepresentation of fact. If everything recorded in Lippo Bank's prospectus was true, and Kwik had been unable to come up with any evidence to the contrary, exactly which part of it was imprecise?

With no way of proving he was right using the theory of capital markets, Kwik then launched into an unfounded personal attack on me. In the end, on the advice of the two adjudicators, I cancelled the TV debate with him, realising that he was less interested in having a factual debate and more interested in unjustifiably shaming me. Luckily, the outstanding performance of Lippo shares showed that the markets and the public were on my side, for which I was very grateful. In the unpredictable arena of doing business, naysayers can present themselves in all shapes and forms. I have learnt that the best policy to defuse such attacks is using patience and grace. Over time, the truth will be revealed. This is exactly what happened after we listed our shares. To this day, Lippo continues to thrive and remains a trusted name both domestically and globally.

MARKET OPENING
HELPS LOCAL BANKS

" I sensed new opportunities. "

I n addition to helping domestic banks, the PAKTO 88 financial reforms also opened up the market to foreign banks by allowing them to establish joint ventures with Indonesian partners.

This had three benefits for Indonesian banks. First, partnering with foreign banks would improve their reputation (both at home and abroad). Second, they could learn new operating techniques and management expertise from the foreign banks. Third, they could use the foreign banks to improve their financing capacity.

Intuitively, I sensed that this was a good opportunity. Using my connections, I sought out a 50-50 joint venture with Japan's Tokai Bank and another 50-50 joint venture with France's Banque Nationale de Paris. Following protracted negotiations, we were finally successful in creating two joint-venture banks: PT Tokai Lippo Bank and PT Bank BNP Lippo.

Everyone at Lippo Bank understood that earning money was not our primary aim in working with these institutions; much more important was that we would be able to interact with them, learn new skills, and endeavour to make them our correspondent banks abroad, which would support our business in commercial credit instruments. The point of this was to make Lippo Bank's transfers quicker than those of other banks, so that we could become a leader in this field among Indonesian banks. That was our true objective, and in this my colleagues at Lippo Bank were very successful.

CHAPTER SIX

ACQUIRING
NEW ASSETS

"
Lippo Life had helped to reform
Indonesia's life insurance industry. "

In 1980, we obtained a licence to operate as a life insurance company under the name of Lippo Life. Back then, however, the average income in Indonesia was less than US$1,000 a year, which meant that most people had no money to invest in life insurance. As a result, we didn't put a lot of effort into developing this business. Our strategy at the time was to hold on to the licence and wait until it could be of greater use. In the meantime, we'd train up talent and accumulate experience.

By 1988, the average annual salary in Indonesia had reached US$2,000, and I estimated that this figure was as high as US$3,000 in the cities of Jakarta, Surabaya, Bandung, and Medan. At that level of income, a section of the population would have enough money to invest in life insurance. It was the right time to take a closer look at the market and prepare to go on the offensive.

Indonesia's largest life insurance company in 1988 was PT Jiwasraya, which was a legacy of the Dutch colonial era. It had a 100-year history and had become a state-owned company. PT Jiwasraya had accumulated significant assets, but was not performing well.

The second largest life insurance company was an indigenous Indonesian life insurer called PT Asuransi Jiwa Bumiputera. It, too, had a lot of assets, but likewise its performance was mediocre at best. In addition to these two companies, almost every bank had a life insurance subsidiary, but not one of them was a success.

Sudono Salim also had his own Bank Central Asia life insurance arm. It had been in operation for over 30 years and was supported by several banks, including Bank Central Asia and Bank Windu Kentjana. Sudono had repeatedly held strategy sessions in which he called on each bank to give more support to the life insurance business. The branch managers repeatedly expressed their support for the business, but they'd always fail to come up with any new customers.

I found this curious. It might have been that the average income was still too low, but more likely it was due to an insufficiently focused business plan and a lack of clarity in marketing and the distribution of commissions. But I still couldn't come up with a way to kick-start our life insurance sales. I decided I would have to start my research from the very beginning. For example, what exactly was the life insurance product we were trying to sell? What products were most needed by our potential customers? What level of insurance premium could customers afford? The product name was also extremely important: it should be instantly understandable, pleasing to the ear, and have no connotations of death. There were also commissions and bonuses for the insurance agents, and we needed an advertising campaign.

After a comprehensive business plan was worked out, we would need a budget. Only then would we have an idea of the potential profits or losses for the next several years. We also had to select the right management team. As with our other operations, there would be two sides to the team directing this project: one would be marketing and the other would have professional and operational skills.

I thought that if we got these things right, we'd have a chance of developing our life insurance business. It was important to come up with a good name for our product. I called it Warisan, which actually just means "heritage", and the product proved very popular with the public. The rest was rudimentary work, and I won't go into it here. However, the key strategy was mobilising the entire Lippo Bank staff to advise customers to buy our Warisan life insurance. If they devoted themselves to the task, we could easily gain a million new customers and create a solid customer base for our life insurance business. What's more, we'd overtake the two long-established insurance companies in the market.

I approached the senior managers of several insurance companies and asked them why bank staff didn't actively promote their life insurance products. They replied that life insurance companies and banks were two separate legal entities, and neither of them had any control over the other. Why should bank staff work for free on behalf of the life insurance company? So in most cases people would say, "Yes, we'll do it!" in front of their boss, but as soon as they left the meeting room they forgot their promise and went off to fight their own battles. Without regulations, it wasn't anyone's responsibility, and there was no way of promoting meaningful cooperation.

After a lot of thought, I called a joint meeting between the senior staff of every Lippo branch and the management of Lippo Life. First, I announced that the head of Lippo Bank branches, Billy Sindoro, would become the managing director of Lippo Life for one year, and would also serve as a consultant to Lippo Bank's Branch Management Office. After a year, he would return to his original post and continue managing Lippo Bank's branches. Second, I proposed a bonus system for Lippo Bank staff who recommended our life insurance products to customers. Third, I arranged for Lippo Life to have offices in every Lippo branch that would be responsible for running insurance operations. At the beginning, I temporarily placed the head of Lippo Bank's human resources department in charge of these offices.

In this way, Lippo Bank and Lippo Life each had legitimate interests in the other's progress. Most crucial of all was that Billy Sindoro still held on to the prestige of managing all of Lippo Bank's branches, and that we could motivate Lippo Bank's branch managers to put their heart into promoting our life insurance business. At the same time, everyone understood that if Lippo Life's business grew, this would also increase Lippo Bank's customer deposits; in effect, we had added another service product that would help Lippo Bank.

After detailed arrangements and some careful detective work, the life insurance products proved highly popular and the business took off.

Incidentally, most insurance companies rely on a large sales force to promote their products. The condition demanded by the salespeople is that for every policy they sell, they receive the first year's premium. Only after the first year does the premium go to the insurance company. This means that in some cases, if there is a claim, the life insurance company has to make the payout without ever having collected any premium from the customer. This puts companies that have just entered the market at a real disadvantage and is one of their biggest burdens.

After carrying out in-depth research, I put aside US$40 million in preparation for these losses. We put a lot of effort into recruiting high-performing professional salespeople to expand our insurance business, and also held a "performance bonus" prize draw every month. Event advertising also helped to build our brand.

After three years of hard work, Lippo Life had already overtaken the other two long-standing insurance companies to become the industry leader. We had also become the new model for life insurance in Indonesia, and other Indonesian insurers all vied to emulate our growth model. Lippo Life had invisibly helped reform Indonesia's life insurance industry.

The growing number of people buying insurance meant that our risk was increasingly small, and the ratio of payouts to total premiums was also becoming increasingly favourable; in the end, we didn't need to use the

US$40 million that had been put aside. The decisions I'd made had set the stage for our success but it was the hard work of Billy Sindoro and the dedicated staff at Lippo Bank and Lippo Life that allowed us to achieve that success.

From the 1970s to the 1990s, Indonesia's economy was in the early stages of its development and still relatively small. Public wealth was limited, which meant that the level of bank deposits from individual customers was low. Private banks had yet to become foreign exchange banks, and were unable to issue commercial letters of credit for their customers. Additionally, they possessed only a small amount of capital and were subject to strict limits on their capital adequacy ratio.

This left them with no way of providing large-scale financing for their customers. Consequently, many Indonesian importers opened letters of credit with Singaporean agents to buy goods from Japan, Taiwan, South Korea, and Hong Kong. At the time, there were over 100 Singaporean companies re-exporting to Indonesia, and their business was booming.

These were the circumstances that I faced at the start of my banking career. As a result, in around 1971, I also opened a company on Shenton Way in Singapore called Lippo Ltd, which specialised in the re-export business. My main customers were auto parts dealers, bicycle parts dealers, sewing machine dealers, and grocers who were natives of the Putian area of Fujian. In the beginning, Lippo Ltd had registered capital of only S$100,000, but after several years of operation, Lippo Ltd was able to make use of bank letters of credit worth several hundred million Singapore dollars. Business was expanding.

At the time, I invited a business associate and an elder from my church named Chen Qinghai to be the general manager of this Singapore operation. Lippo Ltd helped Bank Buana, Panin Bank, and Bank Perniagaan Indonesia solve their problem of a shortage of foreign currency. It also helped them become some of the liveliest foreign currency traders. It was a successful example of using foreign (Singaporean) capital to make up for the Indonesian banks' lack of funds.

Later, I applied the example of the Singaporean Lippo Ltd to Hong Kong, where I opened another arm of Lippo Ltd. The Hong Kong operation of Lippo Ltd was the predecessor of Stephens Finance Ltd (which I set up in Hong Kong), as well as Seng Heng Bank in Macau and Hongkong Chinese Bank. I used this strategy to solve the problem of funding bottlenecks at my banks in Indonesia.

INFORMATION TECHNOLOGY AND PT MULTIPOLAR

"At the core of the Lippo Group"

L ooking at economic development around the world, we see that major breakthroughs have been closely related to motive, power and speed.

In the earliest times, humankind learned to use manpower to develop the economy, after which came other forms of power, such as ox or horse power, and eventually wind, thermal and hydropower. In the 18th century, the British made major improvements to the steam engine and in the 19th century, the Americans further developed the same technology. In the 20th century, the US developed microelectronics, from which digital technology is derived.

Digital technology then led to the birth of computers, the foundation of which is the binary system. Computers are able to read electric charges that are either positive or negative, and they use 0s or 1s to process a string of binary numbers and express ostensibly simple things such as a capital "A", which is represented by 01000001; a small "a", meanwhile, is represented by 01100001.

These strings of numbers become a machine language, which is written using any number of other "languages"—including Basic, C++, Java, and so on. This language is then understood by the computer. In other words, computers simplify everything into numbers; each letter on the screen is composed of either a 0 or a 1.

To manage computers, a completely man-made digital language was invented to allow computers to process all the data they receive. As such, the function of computers is to be able to control and quantify all data, so that music, films, and written text can be simplified into numbers. Computers also provide a unique way of viewing reason.

They do have their limitations. Computers can only handle things expressed in binary code. They can play music, but they can't compose it, or say what makes it beautiful. They can save poetry, but they can't interpret its significance or the feelings it inspires. Computers can't do everything that humans can; they are, after all, only tools used by humans.

But the use of this tool to process, store and examine data can be incredibly impressive and powerful. In 1990, US President Bill Clinton officially launched the Human Genome Project. The project took the world's scientists almost 13 years to complete. A computer can now do the same thing in a matter of hours.

Today, almost everything relies on computers; whether it be travelling to the moon, diving to the bottom of the ocean, geological exploration, finding out more about the human body, administrative management, military operations, TV broadcasting or transferring data—computers have become ever-present and all-powerful, and are an indispensable tool in our lives.

Computers and smartphones have also become integrated and astonishingly widespread. Their speed and capacity are increasing daily, making them even more indispensable in our lives.

Back in the 1980s, I already had a sense of some of the important changes that would be driven by computers. I looked into the possibility of setting up an independent IT company to start digitalising the operations of Bank Perniagaan Indonesia, Bank Umum Asia, Bank Central Asia, Bank Bumi Bahari, Lippo Life and their numerous subsidiaries. Outsourcing the automation and digitalisation to this company would be far more economical than having each bank set up its own individual IT department.

Furthermore, the company could also take on IT work for other banking institutions. To achieve this, I decided to acquire PT Multipolar.

Industries derived from IT can be divided into four major sectors: software, hardware, networks and content. The software and hardware industries are evolving rapidly, and product life cycles are becoming shorter and shorter. They are both challenging industries.

The networking segment is more stable; for example, people use the information highway every day, and the greater the prevalence of mobile phones, the more important networks become. As a result, I felt that it offered the best prospects and should be our focus.

Next is the content industry, which generally spans three main areas: information flows, fund flows, and product flows. Information flows include media, television, information transmission and cloud computing (cloud storage). Fund flows refer to fund transfers, online payments and online banking. Product flows include online purchases and online market places, which have partly replaced brick-and-mortar shops.

I believed that the most vibrant industries were the networking industry and online marketplaces with the latter combining flows of information, funds and products. These industries would become the business direction and focus of PT Multipolar's efforts. They should also be one of the core industries of Lippo Group.

After decades of hard work and diligence, Lippo Group owns the following today: a cable network, a 4G wireless network and a communications satellite, as well as associated cable, terrestrial and satellite television operations.

We also own print media outlets (such as daily newspapers and monthly publications), cinema chains, online banks, and an online marketplace that is currently in development. It is my profound belief that this will be a multibillion-dollar business for us, and it is one of our core businesses.

The information technology revolution has been the single greatest revolution in economic productivity during the last 5,000 years. It has yielded an increase in major economic forces and has brought about massive changes in people's lifestyles. I believe the Indonesian people should do all we can to be a part of this huge change, and should spare no effort in promoting progress and revitalising the nation's economy. This is both our mission and our responsibility.

THE STORY OF
MACAU'S SENG HENG BANK

"

Using a peaceful and amicable approach to solve our problem. *"*

I n Macau, there was a bank called Seng Heng Bank, whose shareholders consisted of well-known Hong Kong businessman Cheng Yu-tung, renowned Macau banker Ho Yim, and Lu Daohe—Cheng's brother-in-law. Lu was also director of the Seng Heng Bank. It was 1983, there were concerns over the local economy, and the bank's shareholders were looking to divest. After being introduced by a friend, I met Lu several times and eventually agreed to buy all the bank's shares for the sum of MOP (Macau patacas) 50 million (about 50 million Hong Kong dollars).

I then hired attorneys and an accounting firm from Hong Kong to carry out due diligence on the bank and, several months later, the deal officially went through. I invited my close American friend Jack Stephens to become a shareholder, with each of us having a 50 per cent stake. Jack and I would be the bank's trustees and we would each nominate a director to run the bank. At the time, owning a bank in Macau was a huge achievement, and I was very excited.

However, after carrying out an in-depth investigation of the bank's operations, I discovered that 80 per cent of the bank's loans were associated with Lu. Many had incomplete legal documentation for the collateral, or else were unsecured loans without any collateral. Overall, these loans amounted to approximately MOP 300 million. It was a big shock that spelled disaster for us. I couldn't understand why the accounting firm had failed to notice these loans; was it oversight, or had they colluded with the bank?

Jack's representative was furious and suggested that we immediately file a lawsuit against the shareholders and the Hong Kong accounting firm. I advised him against such a course of action: the reliance on gambling to drive the economy had seriously distorted the way business was conducted in Macau, and the territory's legal system and bureaucracy weren't as impartial as the institutions in Hong Kong. A lawsuit would be tricky.

However, I discovered that the Ho family did a lot of business with mainland China and had strong connections with the Chinese government. Here was a ray of hope. I was certain that filing a lawsuit would be costly and time-consuming, and that it would be better to solve this problem through Bank of China's Hong Kong office. I immediately got in touch with the bank's head, Huang Diyan. I explained our problem and asked him to approach Cheng Yu-tung and Ho Yim about resolving this issue.

After mediation by Huang and his deputy Lin Guangzhao, the sellers said they were willing to cooperate in three areas: first, they would supply all the missing legal documentation for the collateral; second, they would add collateral for the unsecured loans; and third, Ho would have his son, Edmund (Ho Hau Wah), help sort out the collateral for the unsecured loans.

After around five months of negotiations, I agreed to accept just under MOP 300 million of real estate (which included Macau property and two hectares of empty land in the Chinatown area of Los Angeles) to clear the bad debts. Essentially, I'd ended up buying not just a Macau bank, but also MOP 300 million of real estate. At the time, however, the real estate was actually of little use as the economy was in recession, and no one was interested in buying it. But it was a better option than going to court. I was confident that we could make the bank a success, so it was worth making some concessions in order to reach our goal.

I am eternally grateful to Huang and Lin at the Bank of China for their help in resolving this difficult issue. I also was pleasantly surprised by the straightforward and sensible approach taken by Edmund Ho in settling this dispute. His talents were apparently noticed by others. He later went on to become the first chief executive of Macau after the Portuguese-run territory was returned to China.

After a year, Macau's economy had begun to improve and the property sector started to come back to life. My real estate unexpectedly doubled in value, and I took advantage of this opportunity to sell it off. What I had originally thought would be a loss ended up making some money. In the end, I'd got Seng Heng Bank practically for free and all parties had come out satisfied. I was happy that I'd once more made the right move by using an amicable approach to solve a dispute. It is not always wise to drag your opponent into court. Pursuing another course is often the easiest way to reach your objectives.

I picked a very able and enthusiastic team for the bank, and in less than two years, we transformed it from a teetering bank into a profitable financial institution.

THE STORY OF
HONGKONG CHINESE BANK

" It is better to repair the house before
it rains. *"*

I n 1984, China and the UK reached an agreement on returning sovereignty over Hong Kong to the mainland. The discussions had been
protracted and there was a major currency crisis amid sagging confidence the year before the deal was finally put in place.

Many people were panicking, clamouring to sell off their assets—
regardless of the price —and rushed to emigrate to countries such as the US
or Canada. It was an earth-shaking human tide. Real estate that had just
shaken off global concerns and regained its value plummeted once again.

My sixth sense told me that this was a great opportunity. I immediately set off for Hong Kong to visit every friend I had there. I asked them to
recommend anything good for sale, particularly banks. I wanted to develop
a financial business in Hong Kong, and this was a once-in-a-lifetime
opportunity.

An opportunity soon presented itself. One of my friends informed
me that Hongkong Chinese Bank (HKCB) was looking for a buyer. Its
owner, a Chinese Malaysian businessman named Chang Ming Thien,
whom I had been friends with in the past, had just passed away and the
management of the bank had been taken over by his son Patrick Chang.
I immediately sought out Patrick to ask about buying the bank.

He confirmed that they were currently looking for a buyer, and we began serious discussions about the conditions of sale.

After about a week, both sides had arrived at the terms: the price would be HK$300 million. The bank's total assets were worth approximately HK$600 million; and if bad debts were discovered, the seller would take responsibility for them. The bank had its own office building and branch. I immediately hired a renowned law firm and an accounting firm to perform due diligence, and requested that they be vigilant in ensuring we did not repeat the mistakes that were made with Seng Heng Bank.

Everything went well, and all that remained to deal with were several potential bad debts with a total value of HK$80 million. Soon after, however, HKCB's parent company, Overseas Trust Bank (which had also been Chang Ming Thien's bank) found itself in financial trouble due to the turmoil following the owner's death. The government had to step in and take control of the company. As a result, the HK$80 million of bad debt turned into a dispute with the government.

Several months of negotiations between the bank's management and the government failed to produce any results and led to the mistaken belief that HKCB was in arrears to Overseas Trust Bank. In the end, I had no choice but to handle the negotiations personally. I told the director of Overseas Trust Bank that I had bought HKCB from Overseas Trust Bank, and explained that Overseas Trust Bank was responsible for compensating HKCB for any bad debts.

If Overseas Trust Bank didn't settle this debt, then HKCB might have to close its doors, and ultimately the government would be responsible for providing compensation. The director understood that confidence in the financial system was at stake and arranged for both sides to sign the minutes of the meeting. Afterwards, he immediately transferred HK$80 million to HKCB. With that, the acquisition was officially concluded.

I used the same growth model and management techniques that I had employed with Bank Central Asia to turn HKCB around. Under the new management team, the bank prospered. After two years, the bank's total assets had grown from HK$600 million to HK$4 billion, and it had gone from making a loss to turning a profit. In the same two years, we also increased the number of branches from one to seven.

As the saying goes, it is better to repair the house before it rains. The incident with Overseas Trust Bank made me think about how I should react if governmental or economic unrest in Hong Kong caused closures or bank runs. After giving it a lot of thought, I paid a visit to Huang Diyan at the Hong Kong and Macau office of the Bank of China. I requested that Bank of China become a shareholder in HKCB.

Huang very sincerely explained that Bank of China was currently unable to become a shareholder in any other bank, but suggested that I approach China Resources Group, a big state-run conglomerate, with the same offer. He then arranged for me to meet with the group's chairperson and managing director, Zhu Youlan, to talk about her company becoming a shareholder in HKCB. Zhu agreed to purchase a 50 per cent share, and in this way, HKCB became a "pink" Chinese enterprise—or one that had a mainland connection—thereby boosting its reputation and status in Hong Kong. Business thrived.

CHINA REGAINS SOVEREIGNTY OVER HONG KONG

"When one door closes, another opens."

I had gone on the offensive in Hong Kong, seeing new opportunities in the transfer of sovereignty to China. This was a matter of "when one door closes, another opens". The British were withdrawing but China would be in charge in the future. And it was a new and different kind of China that was eager to push ahead with long-delayed development. My actions piqued the interest of several of my friends in the US banking sector, who all asked my reasons for doing so. I gave them the following answers:

- I had observed that China's pragmatic leader Deng Xiaoping was committed to economic reform and opening China to foreign trade.
- I was also convinced that Deng Xiaoping's position in China was secure.
- I had observed that economic reform had been successful in Shenzhen, the testing ground for these reform policies.
- I had seen that the Shenzhen model was being introduced in other cities (Zhuhai, Shantou and Xiamen).
- The above-mentioned cities were being opened up according to the Hong Kong economic model.

Since mainland China was trying to learn from Hong Kong, it made no sense that, following the transfer of sovereignty, Beijing would try to change Hong Kong's economy and way of life to make it more like the mainland's.

I had invested a total of HK$300 million in acquiring HKCB. In one or two years, when things had returned to normal, I was able to sell the bank's building for HK$200 million. As a result, I had in effect invested about HK$100 million.

From 1984, there were still 13 years to go before the transfer of sovereignty—a long time, during which there was money to be made. If I had no way of earning back HK$100 million during this time, then I wasn't fit to be a businessman.

Even if I didn't earn back HK$100 million during these 13 years, the deal would still have been worth it: I could present HKCB as a present to the People's Republic of China following the transfer of sovereignty.

These are the reasons why I went into business in Hong Kong when I did. In short, I believed that, in terms of its policy direction, China was committed to economic reform and opening up to foreign trade. Moreover, I was confident that the wisdom of the people of China would allow them to achieve these economic reforms. There was no doubt that the country had a bright future and I was certain it would achieve great success.

THE STORY OF
THE LIPPO CENTRE
IN HONG KONG

"I will never forget Li Ka-shing's generosity."

E ver since my youth, I have dreamed of owning an iconic building in each of five major cities either side of the Pacific: Jakarta, Singapore, Hong Kong, Shanghai, and Los Angeles.

The Sino-British accord on the return of Hong Kong to Chinese rule helped set the stage for my purchase of one such building in the territory that eventually became a Special Administrative Region of China. China had gone through some difficult periods and many people in Hong Kong had seen the destructive policies of the Communist Party in the past. They were understandably fearful of the future under Beijing's rule and wanted to get out at any cost. Even years after the agreement was signed, the concerns over Hong Kong's future under Chinese rule were very much alive. I, however, took a different view and remained optimistic.

Someone informed me that there was a unique building on offer in central Hong Kong called the Bond Centre. It was one of Hong Kong's iconic buildings and had a truly magnificent design. The owner was Japanese and had mortgaged it to the Long-Term Credit Bank of Japan. As it happened, I was a consultant to this bank, so I could enquire about buying the building directly. Unfortunately, the day before I could ask about buying the building, it was sold to the renowned Hong Kong tycoon Li Ka-shing. The purchase procedures, however, had yet to go ahead.

After some serious thought, I gathered up the nerve to call Li and ask him if he'd give up on the building and sell it to me. If I wanted to establish myself in Hong Kong, I needed my own building. He replied point-blank that I could have it as long as I gave him the third floor in Building B to establish a financial subsidiary. Building B would also bear the company's name. I hadn't expected Li to make it so easy. In this way in July 1992, I achieved my dream of owning an iconic building in Hong Kong, and we called it the Lippo Centre. I will never forget Li Ka-shing's generosity.

THE FOURTH PERIOD
1991–2010

CHAPTER SEVEN

THE CHALLENGE OF CHINA AND THE CHINESE CENTURY

" Its economy will probably overtake the United States in the not-too-distant future, and its expanding geopolitical clout has already shaken the world order. "

M uch has been written about the rise of China. Its emergence as a global power has been so swift and so dramatic that it cannot fail to impress even the nation's harshest critics. It has gone from a relatively backward country at the beginning of the reform period in 1978 to the world's second largest economy today. In the process it has raised living standards, extended life spans and absorbed major technical innovations. China has become the world's leading exporter overall and the biggest importer of energy. It boasts the biggest auto market, the most Internet users and the most mobile phones. It has built the world's largest airport in Beijing and has invested heavily in roads, railways and better housing for its people. Along the way it has also amassed a world-beating US$3 trillion in foreign exchange reserves. Its economy will probably overtake the United States in the not-too-distant future, and its expanding geopolitical clout has already shaken the world order.

While its economic growth rate has slowed from the double digit levels of not so long ago, China is still a force to be reckoned with, and other countries around the world will need to adjust to this new political power.

My views may be coloured by the fact that China is my second home. But I have seen China from up close as a child in the chaos of the warlord period and later as a young man in the final years of the Nationalist government. I have had numerous occasions to return since then and participate in the nation's economic development. And I have also been privileged to know some of those who have been responsible for setting the agenda in this modernisation drive.

In this chapter I would like to recount some of my personal experiences in the early days of the reform period to illustrate the problems that had to be overcome to bring China to its current stage of development. I also hope to show how this affected Indonesia and the global economy— and how I hope my country will respond to the developments in China in the future.

PRELUDE TO REVOLUTION

"A moment of great hope."

D uring my years as a youth in China, I observed the many short-comings of the Kuomintang (Nationalist Party) government. It was a regime that was incapable of dealing with a wide range of political and economic problems—not all of them of its own making. It struggled unsuccessfully to break the grip of local warlords and it was una-ble to end its unpopular reliance on an unjust landlord class. It was also faced with the humiliating loss of territory under an occupation by Japan. Add to that its own corruption and economic mismanagement and it is no wonder that it lost popular support and was unable to stop advancing com-munist armies. On October 1, 1949, Mao Zedong proclaimed the founding of the People's Republic of China. For Chinese around the world this was a moment of great hope.

Mao was an idealist who hoped to remould Chinese society. He launched a series of mass movements aimed at rooting out the vestiges of feudalism. He was ruthless at times and some of his methods led to great political chaos. In 1966 he launched the Cultural Revolution—perhaps his most disastrous mistake. It was meant to create a renewed revolutionary fervour in the nation he was building. It was in fact a decade of political turmoil marked by factional fighting in the streets, massive damage to the economy and the disruption of countless lives.

But Mao's death in 1976 and the gradual rise of the pragmatic Chinese leader Deng Xiaoping cleared the way for a major policy shift. It was that policy shift that laid the foundation for the emerging superpower that is China today.

Deng was a visionary who saw that it was economic development that would make China strong. He was willing to experiment with ideas such as private enterprise, monetary incentives and even stock markets if they succeeded in achieving his development goals. Deng famously said: "To get rich, is glorious". This made it clear to all that after years of shared poverty it was now politically acceptable to strive to become rich. Deng also had some unique advantages in getting the economy moving in a short period of time. As land belonged to the state, the government could decide how to exploit it. It could also draw upon the country's large pool of cheap labour to do the work needed to lift the country out of poverty. It was a development opportunity without precedent anywhere in the world. China was on a course of rapid economic development that would make the world sit up and take notice.

China's economic opening began just as the "little dragon" economies of South Korea, Taiwan, Hong Kong and Singapore were entering the information age and exporting their labour-intensive manufacturing industries to developing countries with abundant labour resources. China was one such country. The opening and reform programme matched the needs of a shifting global economy and the structural changes taking place in these four fast-growing export economies. It was my firm belief at the time that these four "little dragons" were the China of tomorrow, and that tomorrow wasn't far off.

China had a vast population and its people had a keen desire for reform and improved living conditions. Once proper economic incentives were in place, the nation could tap into a strong work ethic.

I was convinced that we were witnessing the rise of China, and it would produce positive effects for the rest of the world. The country would become a leading power in the Asia-Pacific region, and the new century starting from the year 2000 would be the Chinese century.

The emergence of China had also coincided with an economic recovery in Southeast Asia. Aided by the solid growth of the American economy, the Pacific Basin was about to become the world's economic centre. How to make the most of this rise of the Pacific Basin is an issue that deserves close attention.

THE FIVE IMBALANCES
OF THE CHINESE ECONOMY

" Deng's sayings were in simple,
understandable language but they had
profound significance. "

I n 1966, just as China was headed into the trauma of its Cultural
Revolution, diplomatic relations between Indonesia and China were
suspended. This followed the destruction of the Communist Party of
Indonesia (Partai Komunis Indonesia, PKI), which had close links to
Beijing. From that time onwards, trade between the two countries could
only be conducted through Singapore or Hong Kong.

But two decades after the break in normal relations, China was clearly
changing and Indonesia needed some kind of rapprochement. On the
Indonesian side, the mistrust was deep. President Suharto was staunchly
anti-communist. But with Deng Xiaoping moving China in a new and less
ideological direction, the question was, how could we make an overture to
Beijing? No one dared to broach this idea with Suharto.

I discussed the issue with Sudono Salim, who was one of the president's close confidants. Only he could raise so sensitive a subject. I asked if
he could use his influence to persuade the president that a policy change
was in Indonesia's interest. I suggested he mention some of Deng's more
widely quoted sayings to demonstrate Beijing's more pragmatic policy
direction. One was the famous line that whether a cat is black or white isn't

important—what is important is whether it catches mice. The other was Deng's pronouncement that "getting rich was glorious". These sayings were in simple, understandable language but they had profound significance. Moreover, Deng was there to stay, and China would not return to the bad old days.

Salim's efforts started to bear fruit. In 1986, at the behest of Suharto and under the leadership of Sukamdani Sahid Gitosardjono, general chairman of the Indonesian Chamber of Commerce and Industry (KADIN), talks began with the China Council for the Promotion of International Trade concerning the resumption of direct trade between Indonesia and China. I was part of those talks.

BANKING AGREEMENT

"An important first step in Sino-Indonesian relations."

A key topic of the talks was a bank remittance agreement, and in the end, Bank Central Asia and the Bank of China were chosen as the correspondent banks for the two countries.

In 1986, I travelled to Beijing in the capacity of managing director of Bank Central Asia to facilitate the signing of the Correspondent Bank Agreement with the Bank of China. Indonesia would still need nearly four years to restore formal diplomatic relations with China but this was an important first step. It was also the first time that I'd set foot in the country since leaving it 36 years earlier. It was a very emotional occasion.

At the time, Beijing had only one hotel that came close to international standards. But even there, guests had to return to the hotel to eat at the appointed time and would have to go hungry if they were late. That's because it was still a centrally planned economy with little thought for the convenience of guests. It was impossible to eat elsewhere since food and other essential commodities were rationed. Without a ration ticket there was no way to buy ingredients. Money alone couldn't buy a meal.

On the streets of Beijing, you could see thousands upon thousands of bicycles jostling for space alongside rickety old buses. There were no taxis, so foreigners had to book a car in advance. In the evenings, the street lamps were dimly lit and the pavements deserted. It was a depressing scene.

On my second day in the capital, I received an unexpected invitation from General Ye Fei, who was vice chairman of the Standing Committee of the National People's Congress, China's parliament. General Ye was born in the Philippines but his family was from Fujian. He had come to China to join the communist cause and had risen through the ranks of the army. He welcomed me at a dinner at the Great Hall of the People, the huge building used for official meetings and ceremonies in the heart of Beijing. He began by addressing me as his *xiangqin* (a term used to refer to people of the same area; in this case, Fujian Province).

Ye was a soft-spoken but congenial man, and the dinner had a very pleasant atmosphere. During the meal, he asked me my thoughts about the opening and reform of China's economy. Perhaps, because of the friendly attitude of my host, I didn't hold back in telling him the following:

- There was an imbalance between the value of goods and the price of goods.
- There was an imbalance between the price of goods and the value of labour.
- There was an imbalance between the value of mental labour and physical labour.
- There was an imbalance between the value of the renminbi, China's currency, and the price of the renminbi. (The official exchange rate was set too high.)
- There was an imbalance in China's rules and regulations.

I told him frankly that the imbalances would be a stumbling block in the development of China's economy, that the "imbalance" in its rules and regulations would hinder its opening up. The reform and opening needed to focus on these shortcomings.

After listening to my remarks, Ye's demeanour suddenly turned very serious. I felt a little regretful, and fretted that the Chinese economy at that time was still unable to accept free market concepts. I feared I might have been too direct and spent the evening unable to sleep.

Early the next morning the phone rang. It was Ye's adjutant, inviting me on his behalf to go and meet him. He told me that a car was already waiting outside the hotel. With no way to decline, I set off with no idea of where I was going. On the way, I worried that I might be taken into custody.

After a long drive, we arrived at the destination: not the public security bureau, but Peking University. Ye and the university dean at the time, Luo Haoqiang, personally came out to meet me and took me to a conference room filled with 20 or so other guests. Only when I saw that they all looked like academics did I finally start to relax.

After introducing me, Ye handed the meeting over to Luo, who asked if I could repeat the five points I had made the previous evening.

In view of the circumstances, I adjusted the order of the five points I had made to General Ye. I began by talking of the separation between the value of mental labour and physical labour, since this was the viewpoint that Karl Marx had put forward in *Das Kapital*. I thought that, since China was a country that officially believed in Marxism, it would be prudent to start from this point.

I then quoted Friedrich Engels to explain my example. There was a textile mill in London where the machinery had broken. After five days of trying to fix the equipment, the workers in the mill still hadn't succeeded in making the repairs. In the end, they had to invite a skilled worker from the outside to sort out the problem. It took him an hour, and the machinery started running again to the delight of all.

But there was another problem: the skilled worker demanded £5 in payment, which the factory refused, insisting it was the equivalent of a month's wages for a factory worker. It was absurd that he had only worked an hour for the same £5. But the skilled worker replied to the factory owner that none of the workers who earned £5 a month could fix the machinery. And how much money did the factory lose from a five-day halt in production? The skilled worker had got the factory up and running again in just an hour. Didn't the benefits outweigh his £5 fee?

In the end, the factory owner agreed to give him the £5. This example perfectly explained why the value of mental labour should be higher than that of physical labour: only in this way can productivity be liberated. If you treat these two forms of labour as equals, then that's a distortion.

For the imbalance of the price of goods and the value of labour, I gave the example of workers in Shenzhen and Hong Kong. A worker in Shenzhen on the border with Hong Kong had to work for 39 months to be able to afford a 12-inch black and white TV set at that time. If the same worker were to get a job across the border in Hong Kong, he or she would be able to buy a 12-inch colour television with just one month's wages. Chinese wages were too low and needed adjusting.

As for the imbalance between the value of goods versus the price of goods: if bread was cheaper than flour, then this was the result of the planned economy not taking cost into account, which contravened the laws of the market.

For the imbalance between the value and price of the renminbi, a simple example was the foreign exchange certificates that foreigners had to use to purchase things in China. The two parallel systems showed that the price of the renminbi had been set too high, which was neither conducive to the exchange of goods between China and other countries, nor was it advantageous to Chinese exports. The imbalance between the value and price of the renminbi also contravened the laws of the market economy.

My last point concerned the imbalance in China's laws and regulations. The "laws" I was referring to were the unwritten rules that ensured that everyone wore the same drab clothing and ate the same poor quality food. To have more than someone else was frowned upon in this egalitarian society. I felt that this was against human nature and contravened the laws of a market economy.

I gave a simple summary in which I said that these five discrepancies and imbalances would hinder the opening and reform of China's economy. Everyone kept nodding and it looked as if they all agreed. After I had replied to a few questions, the meeting came to an end. It was only after a few people had introduced themselves that I learned this was the economic reform think tank of Premier Zhao Ziyang. Zhao was an enthusiastic backer of economic reform and would soon become head of the Communist Party. His hold on that job would be short-lived, however. Zhao was ousted ahead of the crackdown on a student protest movement in 1989.

The year after that first visit, I was invited back to Peking University for another exchange of ideas. I felt extremely pleased to have the chance to offer a few suggestions to help develop China's economy. Talking to this group also made me realise that the Chinese were eager to develop their economy. I was convinced that China was on the right track.

WITNESSING CHINA'S REFORMS BY INVESTING IN THE MEIZHOU BAY POWER PLANT

"I had contributed to building the economy of my native town."

After concluding my official business in Beijing, I accepted an invitation to visit Fujian and meet the province's Communist Party leader, Secretary Chen Guangyi, and Deputy Secretary Jia Qinglin. I was received with the utmost courtesy and on the second day of my stay, Secretary Chen personally accompanied me to Putian to visit my grandparents' tomb.

After that, we were treated to lunch with Putian's party secretary, Xu Kairui, and he used the occasion to introduce a plan to develop Putian's economy. One of the key points of the plan was to invite me to invest in my native town. Sudono Salim had already invested in the Rongqiao Industrial Area in Fuqing in northern Fujian, and Chen Zongcai, a Chinese businessman from the Philippines, had led investment in industrial areas in southern Fujian. The government hoped that I could invest in an industrial area in central Fujian.

After two days of visits and discussions, I had come to the following conclusions:

- There was still a lot of room for growth in northern and southern Fujian, and the geographic conditions and economic base there were more favourable than in Putian. For the moment, it wasn't Putian's turn.
- The highways to Putian from Xiamen and Fuzhou hadn't been repaired in years, which made transport difficult. Putian also did not have electricity, water, or a port, so it met none of the conditions for development.
- Nearby Meizhou Bay, however, was a natural harbour and thus, should be given priority in economic development. It should be turned into a base for southern China's petrochemical, steel, and shipbuilding industries, and a centre for storing and supplying liquefied natural gas. Before anything else, a power plant and waterworks should be built in Meizhou Bay.

Secretary Chen Guangyi wholeheartedly agreed with my suggestions, and after returning to Fuzhou, he invited Deputy Secretary Jia Qinglin to hold a meeting with me for an in-depth discussion about ideas for developing Meizhou Bay's economy. At the end of the meeting, I agreed to consider investing a total of about US$2.5 billion in a 30-million-kilowatt power plant.

Since Chinese foreign exchange reserves were only several hundred million US dollars at the time, this was an astronomical figure, and Jia asked me if I was really serious about this. I told him that I didn't have that much capital of my own, but I did have the ability to bring others into a project like this. If the government's project was seen as feasible, I would be able to find the needed investors and financial institutions. After signing a letter of intent to build the Meizhou Bay power plant with the Fujian provincial government, I arranged to meet a senior official at the Asian Development Bank in Manila. We first exchanged views about China's economic opening and reform. I asked whether the Asian Development Bank would be willing to lend its support if I had the opportunity to partake in developing China's infrastructure—such support would mean that the Asian Development Bank would become a shareholder and spearhead the organisation of an investment group. The bank agreed, and I was confident that we'd be able to quickly put together a team to begin preparing for construction of the power plant.

After the discussions, we settled on the following work programme:

- Push for the signing of a cooperation agreement with the Asian Development Bank
- Have the Asian Development Bank invite investors
- Hire a Hong Kong law firm to negotiate the construction contract with the Chinese government
- Hire an experienced power plant engineering firm to draw up construction blueprints and draft a feasibility study report
- Put together a power plant construction preparation committee to set a budget
- Select a work location for the committee
- Select a location for the power plant.

After the work programme and personnel arrangements had been completed for the construction preparation committee, I wasted no time and took the group to Manila to visit the Asian Development Bank, so that we could officially begin discussions on the financing plan and on the incorporated company for the construction of the power plant. The discussions went very smoothly.

The Asian Development Bank's initial suggestion was to invite US firms InterGen and Bechtel, Singapore investment company Temasek, and World Bank affiliate the International Finance Corporation to become shareholders alongside the Asian Development Bank and the Lippo Group. Lippo Group would form the backbone of the consortium. The Asian Development Bank's feedback on this was very positive, which was a source of great encouragement to me.

To boost everyone's confidence, I accepted a 51 per cent share in the project. US firm InterGen took a 30 per cent share, and the remaining shares were divided up among the other parties. The Asian Development Bank, meanwhile, had already taken the preliminary steps to establish a syndicate with 39 other banks across the globe to provide long-term financing covering 70 per cent of the power plant's needs. The whole enterprise was starting to take shape.

There were changes in the shareholdings during the preparation phase; InterGen increased its ownership to 75 per cent and Lippo took 25 per cent. Once construction had been completed, InterGen sold a percentage of its shares to an American power company, El Paso Corp. By the end, the share structure was as follows: Lippo–25 per cent, InterGen–45 per cent, El Paso–24.8 percent, and the Asian Development Bank–5.2 per cent.

The first-phase power capacity was 7 million kilowatts, achieved with a total investment of US$756 million. The Asian Development Bank had taken the lead with financing of US$567 million, and the shareholders had put in US$189 million. The Asian Development Bank sent a senior staff member to join the construction preparation committee.

Since the Meizhou Bay power plant was being built so early in the reform programme, there were no precedents for the Chinese government and the foreign investors to use as guidance. It was a case of what Deng Xiaoping described as "crossing the river by feeling the stones". We had to figure things out as we went along.

For the sake of the project, China had to create special legislation, and this was a laborious process. By the time legislation for the project was ready, two years had passed. We'd also spent close to US$10 million in preparation fees, and all the documents covering negotiations would have filled several large boxes. But in the end, my long-awaited dream came true. I had done something important for my native town.

The Fujian provincial government was very active in facilitating construction of the power plant, but at the time, the provincial economy was still very weak. A lot of heavy machinery had to be brought in from outside the province to help with construction. Officials from the provincial government's electric power department suggested using Japanese power-generation machinery, hoping that the Meizhou Bay power plant would become China's most advanced power plant and a model for others across the country. I had initially hoped to use Chinese-made equipment, but in the end I agreed to the officials' suggestions.

My aim was to turn Meizhou Bay into a petrochemical, steel, and shipbuilding base for southern China. Several major industries would support the construction of Meizhou Bay's economy, so at the time, Putian Secretary Xu Kairui agreed to allot approximately 60 square kilometres of the Zhongmen Peninsula for the Harbour Economic Zone.

People from Putian called the peninsula "beyond the pale" because it was such a barren, wretched area. In the old days, people from Putian would often tell children that if they were naughty, they'd be sent to the peninsula. The land was so short of water that even sweet potatoes wouldn't grow there, but I was confident that it could be developed into a major industrial complex.

When he first saw the underdeveloped conditions in Zhongmen, my second son, James, asked me why I did not choose a city like Shenzhen, Xiamen, or Shanghai for an investment project. I told him it was because when I was young, I'd drunk the water and eaten the local food in this undeveloped area, and I felt I had to give something back. I could still remember my grandmother's words: "You must go away in order to come back."

Four years later, construction of the power plant began. The location chosen was a piece of land I'd bought earlier that bordered the deep sea. After discussions between all parties, it was decided that this land would be sold to the power plant at a 20 per cent discount. The money I earned from the sale of this land significantly reduced the cost of my investment in the project.

As I mentioned earlier, I ended up with a minority 25 per cent stake in the project. I had acquired that share without having invested much money, but more importantly, I had contributed to building the economy of my native town, about which I felt extremely pleased.

I've made special mention of the investment process of the power plant because I want to show just how determined China was in its pursuit of the reforms and economic opening. In the search for investment, Fujian Party Secretary Chen Guangyi had been willing to make the difficult journey to visit Putian with me, and had accompanied me on a visit to the tombs of my grandparents. For the sake of developing Meizhou Bay's economy, Deputy Secretary Jia Qinglin had also come to Indonesia three times to enlist my help, and officials from Fujian had worked hard to build the local economy.

The Chinese people involved in the project worked for over 10 hours every day, and never took time off during national holidays or on the weekend. At times, they'd even work throughout the night. I concluded that if others were willing to work like this, over the next 25 years, China would be able to achieve what would have taken 75 years in the West. I saw that China's economy was about to take off, and could really sense what people have called the "China factor".

I often remind my Indonesian friends that they should pay attention to the rise of China, and adapt to changes in the new international economic and political situation.

From 1960 up to the present, Asia's economic landscape has undergone three major transformations:

- Japan took on America's labour-intensive industries, which, after 15 years, were then transferred to South Korea, Taiwan, Hong Kong and Singapore.
- The economies of these four countries and territories grew into Asia's four "little dragons", which then transferred their labour-intensive industries to low-cost centres, including China.
- Ultimately, the technology wave arrived in China and the country did its best to welcome it.

UNIQUE CHALLENGES

" A problem for China is a problem
for the world. *"*

C hina is facing some unique challenges now. Its economic growth is slowing, its wages have risen to levels that make it less suitable for labour-intensive manufacturing and it has seen rapid out-flows of foreign exchange as confidence in the nation's economic management wavers.

Some economists like to say that China is headed for what they call the "middle income trap"—meaning it will lose its low-cost advantages without being able to rise into higher value production. Moreover, with its ageing population and thanks to its years of enforcing a one-child policy, it may get old before it gets rich.

But Beijing is using two methods to ensure its future competitiveness. It is rapidly shifting away from low-cost production like toys and textiles and moving into higher technology products. Its high-speed railway prowess is attracting global attention while its mobile communications products have taken market share from more established Western competitors. And as a country that has mastered manned spaceflight, China has definitely moved up the technology chain.

At the same time, China is encouraging its companies to move offshore as part of its "going out" strategy. This means that some low-cost production will move to lower-cost areas—such as Southeast Asia—while some companies are investing in foreign markets to ensure market share and acquire more advanced technology.

More recently, Beijing has relaxed its one-child policy in the face of a decline in the size of its labour force and the need to support a growing number of retirees. It is unclear whether young families will respond as life-styles change and the cost of raising children climbs. But it is an important issue that policy makers hope to address.

Some people ask whether China's leaders are up to the task of steering the economy through a difficult period. They note serious swings in the Chinese stock markets, sudden bouts of weakness in the Chinese currency and a failure on the part of the government to fully explain its policies to the markets. They note that a problem for China is a problem for the world.

Years ago, when Chinese President Xi Jinping was still an official in the Fujian provincial government, I had several opportunities to meet him and assess his operating style. He never lobbied me to make fresh investments in Fujian. Instead he was focused on finding ways to get things done. He asked questions such as how best to push ahead with development and how to get needed financing. He never let on whether he agreed with my views, but he was certainly a student of economic development.

China's development path—and the methods of its president—have been closely watched in this part of the world and elsewhere. I recall a conversation with Indonesian President Joko Widodo who told me that in terms of development, Indonesia needed to look to China. And in terms of political strategy, the president saw much to learn from Xi Jinping—a politician who has consolidated power in a very short period of time and outflanked some serious rivals with a surprising display of political toughness in a prolonged anti-corruption campaign.

With its diligence, dynamism and embrace of technology, China is already becoming a powerhouse in the information age.

Indonesia, however, has heedlessly let opportunities slip amid the major economic shifts of recent years. No one has paid much attention to Indonesia; it has always been left by the wayside by other Asian countries and the rest of the world. Its neighbours have clearly never viewed it as a rival. This needs to change.

I've always had the following philosophy: there is no greater threat in this world than your own incompetence and lack of a sense of urgency. Today, China's population of approximately 1.35 billion is building its own markets, and these domestic markets are enormous, with ample room for growth.

Indonesia has a young population of around 250 million and is also in the process of creating its own markets. It also has huge potential for growth. As such, if both countries can identify their own strengths and weaknesses and be mutually complementary to each other, the potential for synergistic growth is enormous.

Today, the world has become a global village, and it's inevitable that countries will be affected by each other. We should face the rise of China head on, look for mutual opportunities, and adapt to the new international environment. If we do, great things lie ahead.

CHAPTER EIGHT

THE LIPPO GROUP EXPANDS INTO NEW TERRITORY

" These three barren plots of land were far from the city and had a total area of 70 square kilometres. How were we going to make use of them? "

By 1990, after 20 years of economic prosperity, Indonesia began entering a phase of sharp cyclical adjustment. As the central bank tightened monetary policy in response, increasing interest rates, a large number of companies found themselves in financial difficulty, which directly affected the banking sector. There was a steep rise in bad debts at a number of banks.

In this adverse economic climate, Lippo Bank had no choice but to accept three large plots of land, which had been used as collateral on loans that could not be repaid. The plots were all outside Jakarta. Cikarang was 45 kilometres east of the city and Karawang 59 kilometres east of the city. Both were barren, grassless pieces of land used for baking tiles. The plot to the west—Karawaci—was also a piece of barren land 25 kilometres from the city, and had only about 100 trees on its 13 square-kilometre site. Back then, anywhere further than five kilometres from the Semanggi city centre was rural countryside. These three barren plots were far from the city and had a total area of 70 square kilometres. How were we going to make use of them? It was a real problem.

To come up with a development plan for the land, I visited Singapore, Kuala Lumpur, Manila, Taipei and Shenzhen in south China to look around the emergent residential communities in those areas. I wanted to learn from their experiences and examine the various business models for developing land. In the end, inspiration came from Shenzhen's development model: I realised that the positioning of the land's use was key.

The real estate developments in Taipei, Manila and Kuala Lumpur were all an extension of the greater city, rather than being entirely new communities. Lippo's three plots of land were far away from Jakarta and suffered from poor transport; as a result, it would not be possible to adopt the models from Taipei, Manila or Kuala Lumpur. Shenzhen's model, however, was worth emulating.

The Chinese government had originally positioned Shenzhen as a satellite of Hong Kong, and the aim was clear: to embrace the transfer of Hong Kong's labour-intensive industries. As a result, the entire direction and process of development had been prepared in support of this positioning. Shenzhen's development model fitted with the development direction of our three plots of land, so we employed it in our analysis of their potential uses. In effect, we had to decide how to position them.

We carried out a detailed study of the surrounding area of Karawaci, which was the plot to the west of Jakarta. We learned that since the economic reforms of the Suharto era, industrial development had been concentrated in an area 50 kilometres to the west of the capital. Because there had been no long-term planning, factories were scattered over a large area, without any proper housing to accompany them. Senior executives at these plants had to make long and time-consuming commutes, leaving home early in the morning and returning late at night. Heavy traffic congestion added to their headaches.

After completing our research, we viewed Karawaci as a good location for housing that would support the industrial area, as well as luxury accommodation for the west of Jakarta.

With Karawaci positioned as a community for west Jakarta's middle and upper classes, I now asked myself what kind of facilities and criteria would they demand. The results of my research showed that the following features would be important for Karawaci:

— Prices should not be too cheap, because price reflects status
— The environment should be attractive
— Additionally, there should be a top-quality school
— a top-quality hospital
— an exclusive golf course
— a luxury club
— a shopping supercentre
— high-grade offices.

These premium facilities would, in fact, become the economic driver of the community. Communities without such an economic driver are less likely to retain their residents.

Next, we had to put the plan into action. The first building was an international primary and middle school with lessons taught in both Indonesian and English.

For its faculty, we hired over 100 qualified American teachers and more than 100 English-speaking local teachers. A teacher-student ratio of 1:10 meant that each student received a lot of attention. The school embraced a teaching philosophy in which moral and intellectual development were given equal importance.

The school's name was Sekolah Pelita Harapan (ray of hope). With its construction, we filled a vacuum in Indonesia for good primary and middle schools, since until then wealthy families had no choice but to send their children to international schools in Singapore. We made establishing the school our top priority, and construction began on it before anything else. As soon as enrolment started, people were extremely eager to sign their children up. The level of interest exceeded our most optimistic forecasts—we'd been right on the mark in our positioning.

The second building was a state-of-the-art hospital. We hired Singapore's Gleneagles Hospital to run it, since that was where all of the Indonesian executives went for treatment. Joint Commission International, a global health care accreditation agency, certified our hospital, giving Indonesia's middle and upper classes confidence in the quality of our services.

The third building was a 200,000-square-metre modern shopping plaza, which in addition to a department store and supermarket, also boasted a children's play area with a roller-coaster and video games, as well as a cinema and a full complement of restaurants. It also had a wide range of shops and services.

We built an exclusive golf course, leaving the land around it for premium apartments, and also a luxury club equipped with a range of exercise and dining facilities.

An ambitious project of planting 80,000 trees helped make the surroundings look more attractive, and we proceeded with the construction of five high-end apartment buildings and two office buildings.

Finally, a road encircling the community was built, ensuring easy access.

These eight projects were essentially all undertaken at about the same time. The project's visionary planning, as well as massive scale and novel business philosophy, created an instant sensation throughout Jakarta. Lippo Karawaci gained considerable media attention, and that served as free advertising for us. To boost the public's faith in the development, I moved my own home and Lippo's offices to Karawaci.

From the initial cost of US$10 per square metre, the price of the land had risen to US$300 per square metre in just four years. Today, that figure has increased to US$2,500. After many years of planting trees and landscaping, the community is also the most picturesque place to live in Jakarta's suburbs.

Construction on the land required a substantial amount of capital, and the best way to get it was to tap the stock market with a share offer. To achieve this, I offered small stakes to China Resources Group and Hong Kong tycoon Li Ka-shing in order to drum up interest—yet another example of riding a horse to catch a horse.

DEVELOPING LIPPO CIKARANG INTO INDONESIA'S MOST IMPORTANT INDUSTRIAL PARK

"Correct positioning is the foundation for success."

C ikarang was once a slum area where tiles were baked, and its previous owner had positioned it as an industrial park. But the wrong marketing approach had led to operational difficulties.

After detailed research, we decided to first select 1,200 hectares to divide into four different parks. For the first park, we went into partnership with Sumitomo Corporation of Japan. The Japanese company held a 51 per cent stake and was in charge of finding Japanese investors willing to set up factories there.

The second park was a partnership with South Korea's Hyundai Group, and the land was sold to them at cost. The South Korean company held a 51 per cent stake and was in charge of finding South Korean manufacturers to invest in setting up factories. The third was sold at cost to a Taiwanese manufacturer to attract Taiwan investment, while Lippo Group operated the fourth. We focused on finding local Indonesian companies to build factories.

Dividing up the responsibilities like this was advantageous to everyone and each park developed smoothly. In just two years, the entire

1,200-hectare plot was covered with all kinds of new factories and facilities. It was thriving.

To make the park even more convenient for the business community, we donated land to the government so that it could relocate its district administrative offices there. We also built a residential complex with an international school on the site—the school was better than most national primary and middle schools—and provided a hospital, hotel, club, modern shopping plaza, waterworks, and water treatment plant.

The whole complex's landscaping was also coordinated. Before long, Lippo Cikarang had become the entire region's administrative, commercial and residential centre, in addition to being the largest and highest quality industrial park in Indonesia. Today, the price of residential property within the complex has risen to US$500 per square metre.

Because many of Cikarang's industrial plants come from Japan, there are many Japanese working there. Together with the Japanese trading company, Mitsui & Co., we are in the process of looking for a partner to develop a large-scale urban complex, which we refer to as "Little Tokyo". Positioned to meet the needs of the park's executives and their families, it will cover an area of 500,000 square metres and feature a Japanese department store, supermarket, restaurants, hotel and apartments. There will even be a Japanese-language primary and middle school. Currently, the plan has been met with an enthusiastic response from the market and it looks like it is going to be a success.

Developing Lippo Cikarang taught me that correct market positioning is the foundation for success.

A DIFFERENT KIND
OF CEMETERY

" *Resources should be used in a way that
adds maximum value.* *"*

T he third plot of land covered an area of 500 hectares and was
located in Karawang district, about 14 kilometres east of
Cikarang. It was more remote than the other two plots, and like
the others it too had been used for baking tiles. It lacked water and trees, but
rolling hills made it very beautiful. However, the land was neither suitable
for residential development, nor could it be transformed into an industrial
park. I was really at a loss as to what to do with it.

One year, during the Qingming Festival (Tomb-Sweeping Day), the
day that Chinese traditionally tidy up the graves of their ancestors, I travelled to Malang to sweep the tomb of my mother and father. Their tomb
was in a 10-hectare cemetery, which had fallen into neglect. It had become
overgrown with weeds and infested with snakes. Security was poor and
grave robbers were all too common. I thought about moving my parents'
tomb somewhere else.

After returning to Jakarta, I visited other cemeteries, but found the
situation to be more or less the same. After the landowner had sold the
tomb plot, the responsibility for its upkeep would shift to the new owner.
Each family tended to its own plot and no one bothered with the common
areas. Things were quite chaotic. I figured that in a few years, they'd be as

bad as the tombs in Malang. This gave me the idea of developing the 500 hectares in Karawang into a cemetery.

I had previously visited Rose Hills Memorial Park in the US, a cemetery that had been designed to resemble a huge garden. Inside, the park featured bed after bed of roses, lawns that were like carpets, winding paths that led to quiet, secluded areas and neat rows of trees of varying heights. Each grave was neat and tidy. The whole place was very solemn and dignified. In addition, it had its own chapel and restaurant. I thought to myself that this model was right for Indonesia. I flew back to California to experience it again. At the same time, I hired people to draw up designs and begin preparatory work.

What I hadn't taken into consideration, however, was that many of the people living around the Karawang plot were Muslims who opposed turning the land into a Buddhist and Christian cemetery. We needed to be patient as we made long and detailed explanations of what the project would entail. It took us 10 years to win their trust and gain all of the necessary government approvals. Eventually, the project moved forward.

With its naturally rolling hills, only a small amount of construction work was required. The lower part was excavated to create a man-made lake. Along the shore, we planted pines and other specially selected trees. The remaining ground was covered with grass and all sorts of flowers. In a suitable place, we built a chapel, a shop and even a swimming pool.

Looking down from the top of the hill, the whole cemetery now resembles an idyllic landscape painting. I believe it is Southeast Asia's most beautiful memorial park, and on national holidays it teems with visitors. It has become popular with young couples as a lush backdrop for their wedding photos and it has become one of Jakarta's many attractions.

The memorial park was a further testament to how land resources should be used in a way that adds the most value.

THE BUSINESS OF DEVELOPING LAND RESOURCES

" We'd been forced to go into the land development business by Indonesia's steep economic downturn. "

MY experiences developing these three plots of land led me to a conclusion: fundamentally, all land development involves determining the grade of land use. Or, to put it another way, it is about deciding how to enhance the grade of land use; the higher the grade, the greater the added value. Of course, the higher the grade, so too the greater the requirements for related facilities. It is never a good idea to open a first-rate restaurant at a second-rate location with a third-rate cooking staff and fourth-rate prices. An incoherent business model like this will result in a restaurant that is neither one thing nor the other. Ultimately, it will fail.

I mentioned earlier that the price of land and fees can't be too low, because price is a measure of status. Karawang's tombs, for example, were positioned as tombs for the wealthy. In addition to providing some facilities, it was important to set the price of the tombs high as an expression of respect as well as status. In my experience, the more expensive the tombs, the greater the demand.

We'd been forced into the land development business by Indonesia's steep economic downturn. We weren't just positioning real estate; we were determining a market position for the development of land resources.

Among our many challenges we needed to consider how we would turn wasteland into agricultural land, how we could turn agricultural land into industrial land and how we could turn industrial land into commercial and residential land. Commercial and residential land had low-end, mid-range, and high-end uses. With every increase in the grade of land use, there was a corresponding increase in price. The profits of the developers followed this increase.

Thanks to our successful experience in developing these three plots of land, Lippo Group established an enviable reputation for itself in the real estate sector—one that has led to more and more people asking us to develop their land. Among them are a seven-square-kilometre development zone in Makassar and 36 square kilometers in Sentul in Indonesia, as well as a three-square kilometre plot in Incheon in South Korea. Under our painstaking management efforts, every square metre of land has been correctly positioned, and every project has become a development success. Our projects have been much sought after in the market.

OPPORTUNITY IN CRISIS

" Mature plots are the ones that really turn a profit. "

Experience told me that land development offered limitless opportunities and should be Lippo Group's core business. It also gave us ownership over the educational and medical facilities, shopping plazas, as well as the department stores, supermarkets, cinemas and other businesses within these shopping plazas—all of which would form huge industry clusters that would also be part of Lippo Group's core business. This is the new aim for Lippo Group in its future development.

I once carried out a study of two development firms in Jakarta. Their business was booming, but they weren't making a lot of money. Analysis showed that they were always selling plots as soon as they were completed and then buying up new land. They didn't own any mature plots, yet mature plots are the ones that really turn a profit because they have so much more room for appreciation.

When I was developing Lippo Karawaci at the beginning of the 1990s, I decided to hold on to around 400 hectares of land right at the very centre of the project. It was used initially as a small square as well as a playground and orchard. It is a scenic spot, and the rent covers its upkeep. My real aim was to wait until this land had matured, and then develop it in order to substantially increase its value.

If we calculate using 60 per cent buildable area and five times the floor area ratio, then the gross floor area could be as high as 12 million square metres. At a price of US$2,000 per square metre, that puts the total value of the plot at no less than US$24 billion. If we build and sell 500,000 square metres every year, the whole project will be completed after 24 years. That's the business model of turning "new" land into mature land. In the Cikarang industrial park to the east of Jakarta, I have also retained 700 hectares of land that I am waiting to develop and sell off once it has matured.

In 1991, the Indonesian economic crisis caused an unexpected adjustment in Lippo Group's business direction that led to its entry into the land resource development sector. It was an experience that taught us that in every crisis, there is always an opportunity.

THE SEPARATION OF OPERATING RIGHTS AND OWNERSHIP RIGHTS

" Responsible bankers must tread carefully and not cause losses to their country. "

The biggest risks and threats in banking come from rumours in the market, political upheaval, financial turmoil, economic downturns and currency depreciation. In developing economies, these are routine occurrences; they can erupt at any time and are extremely difficult to anticipate. During my 49-year banking career, I have experienced a number of bank runs. I have seen many bankers come to an unfortunate end, and when their banks go under they also take their large customer base with them, meaning that the government has to step in and assume responsibility for the bank's debts.

I came to the conclusion that the government was ultimately responsible for banks. However, responsible bankers must tread carefully and not cause losses to depositors. They must not treat their bank as their private cash machine. Banks play a key role in maintaining social stability. This is especially so when there is no deposit insurance—as was the case in past years in Indonesia. Banks must be open, above board and subject to public scrutiny—only then can they enjoy lasting public confidence.

I believe that the only way to keep a bank's operations in the open is to go public, so that there is a separation between management rights and ownership rights. What's more, banking regulations also disperse the equity of a single shareholder, thus preventing one large individual shareholder from having executive control over the bank. Only in this way can operational failings be eradicated and rumours be dispelled.

Although we made it safely through all of the bank runs we experienced, I'd never been able to get rid of that feeling of unease—it cast a shadow over my life and added stress to my work. How could we improve the bank so that it would be worthy of its shareholders, clients and the country as a whole? It was a problem that often troubled me deeply.

In 1991, I parted ways with Sudono Salim. After a share swap had been completed, I became the largest shareholder in Lippo Bank. Ever since the bank was founded, my son James had held the position of president, which meant that after I became the chief shareholder, the bank's ownership and management rights were both concentrated in the hands of family members. I was now responsible for James's position, and I had to make a choice about whether to put the theory of separating ownership and operating rights into practice.

After a lot of thought, and for the sake of both the public's and James's interests, I decided to honour my commitment to maintaining this clear separation. I turned to Markus Permadi, a senior bank executive, to replace James as the bank's president, and brought in respected banker Hashim Ning to replace me as chairman. With this, I kept Lippo Bank's operations out in the open.

THE BANK RUN OF 1995

"One of the greatest risks and threats to banks comes from rumours."

I previously mentioned that one of the greatest threats to banks comes from rumours, which can undermine public trust and lead to a bank run. In the spring of 1995, Lippo Bank was hit by a devastating rumour. Before I describe what happened, let me first relate how the rumour came about.

The west and east of Jakarta are flatlands, the north faces onto the sea and the south backs onto mountains. In the foothills of these mountains is a small town called Sentul, which lies around 40 kilometres from the capital. At the time, the Jakarta-Bogor highway passed by it but there was no exit, so to get to Sentul from the capital you had to take small roads through the countryside.

On the way, you'd pass through many crowded open-air markets and sections of road unrepaired for many years. This meant that the 40-plus-kilometre trip could take two hours. The scenery, nonetheless, was stunning, and upon arrival at Sentul you'd feel like you were a million miles away from the city. The air was cool and fresh, the natural environment was virtually untouched, and the views were breathtaking. The people, too, were good honest folk who led peaceful, contented lives. It was like a paradise compared to Jakarta. There was no better place to live this close to the capital, and it had great development prospects.

President Suharto's third son, Hutomo Mandala Putra (widely known as Tommy), had bought several thousand hectares of land in Sentul. There had been talk that he wanted to move the capital there, and he had made several fruitless attempts at developing a residential complex in the area. Afterwards, having seen Lippo's success in developing Karawaci and Cikarang, he sent someone to invite me to become a shareholder in the development of Sentul.

I had always advocated the separation of politics and business, and so I politely declined. At the time, the State Secretary was a man called Moerdiono. He had a great understanding of how to wield bureaucratic power, and had a close relationship with the president, often acting on the president's behalf. In Jakarta, officials and businessmen alike were wary of offending him. Tommy sent Moerdiono to ask us to become shareholders in the Sentul project. He made me an offer I couldn't refuse. I tried to limit my exposure to the project but in the end I agreed to contribute enough to give me a 25 per cent stake. I also ended up with the responsibility of supervising the project.

My assessment was that Sentul's location had clear advantages and could be developed into a leisure destination for Jakarta. However, we had to buy a two-kilometre tract of land that would connect the development area to the highway. This would solve the difficulty of getting there from Jakarta and reduce the journey time from two hours to 40 minutes. After tough negotiations with a large number of landowners, we were finally able to buy up this tract of land and connect the development to the highway. With our biggest challenge out of the way, success was in sight.

Next, as with previous projects, we first built an international school, golf course, five-star hotel, and shopping centre in Sentul. We also carried out landscaping: planting flowers and trees, creating a lake and improving the overall environment of the town. After that, housing was constructed and sold. In this way, we made the development a success.

Yet before long, the unexpected happened. There was a scandal involving the financial manager of the Sentul project. This news spread and other rumours followed.

Even though our bank was witnessing early withdrawals by some of its major clients, this failed to set off any alarm bells. It was only after the withdrawals continued for two weeks and we saw long lines of people waiting to take out their savings that we realised we had a bank run on our hands. We heard that the source of the problem was a rumour related to the Sentul project. This finally triggered an investigation, which revealed the problems with the project's financial manager. But by then the rumours were so widespread that it was too late to stop the bank run.

Having experienced many such bank runs, I had always insisted on holding 30 per cent of customer deposits in reserve. As a result, after the run had gone on for over a month, the bank's liquidity was still secure. There were, however, long lines of customers at Lippo Bank branches across the country almost every day.

I had already called on Bank Indonesia to publicly state that we were in good shape but they had not responded. Finally, under these desperate circumstances, I had no choice but to write a letter to the bank, the gist of which was: "Just three months ago, the central bank carried out an annual inspection of Lippo Bank, the results of which were very good. Lippo Bank has now been subjected to two months of rumours. It has twice requested that Bank Indonesia step in to dispel these rumours. Bank Indonesia, however, has provided no response. Now, it is estimated that Lippo Bank's deposits can only last for another two days. We once more request that Bank Indonesia refute these rumours. If Bank Indonesia is unwilling to do so tomorrow, we will have no choice but to issue an announcement in the newspaper saying that we are closing our doors, and will be handing control over to Bank Indonesia so they can resolve the problem."

I personally handed this letter, together with a key symbolising the authority over Lippo Bank, to the governor of Bank Indonesia. The governor very coolly advised me not to panic, and then sent me on my way. I left Bank Indonesia burning with emotion.

After returning to Lippo Bank, I could do nothing but wait. Suddenly, the telephone began ringing: it was Sudono Salim, inviting me to go and see him right away at his office at Bank Central Asia. Upon arrival, I saw that Sudono was already waiting for me in the guest suite together with the heads of Indonesia's other key private banks—Bank International Indonesia, Bank Danamon, Bank Bali, and Bank Danang Nasional Indonesia.

After exchanging pleasantries, everyone began asking what was happening at Lippo Bank. I calmly reported the bank's situation, saying I firmly believed that Lippo Bank was healthy and had enough funds to cover its debts. But I told them that we had decided to close the bank the next day. It would be handed over to the central bank and they'd have to deal with the aftermath. I could only apologise to them: if Lippo closed tomorrow, it would no doubt have a small knock-on effect on each of their banks, for which I asked for their forgiveness.

They looked surprisingly calm after hearing this. They pledged their support and asked how much money I needed. I replied that Lippo Bank was currently in the midst of a bank run—for any institution facing a bank run, there was nothing that cash could do to restore confidence. Shaken trust among customers could be a fatal and irremediable blow to a bank. Not wanting to delay them any longer, I declined their offer of assistance. They were all taken aback by my attitude.

In the end, Sudono told me that they were here at the behest of the governor of the central bank. Bank Indonesia was not willing to come out and support Lippo Bank directly because it had recently allowed another Indonesian bank to go under without doing anything to save it. As such, the central bank was unwilling to publicly assist Lippo Bank, and had instead specially arranged for these five privately run banks to lend their support.

Now that I knew the underlying reason, I was truly grateful to Bank Indonesia and my five peers for their concern and assistance, but I told them: Lippo's real problem was these banks' very own branch managers. To win more business, each day the managers related these rumours to customers. This was natural, and I didn't blame them for it, but the ones who could really save Lippo Bank were these same branch managers. As such, I immediately composed a letter for the board of directors of the five banks to issue to their branch managers. The gist of it was as follows:

Dear branch managers,

The boards of our five banks have collectively reviewed the operations of Lippo Bank and determined that Lippo is a healthy and trustworthy institution. Given this, we five banks have decided jointly to support Lippo Bank, and hope that each branch will do the same.

Board of Directors (of all five banks)

I requested that my five associates agree to send out the letter and then help me prepare three to five days' worth of operating capital. If we did that, all my problems could be resolved. They agreed to my request, and immediately got to work.

As expected, the day after the letter was sent out, the news spread that these five Indonesian banks were standing behind Lippo Bank because it was a healthy and trustworthy institution. Lippo customers began returning their deposits. Their trust in the bank had been restored, and business began to pick up again. This once again proved my view that a bank's foundation is credit, and that rumours are the enemy of credit.

The 1995 bank run was another reminder that, at all times, we had to keep the bank healthy and continue to develop it. There was the need for a comprehensive examination of the bank as well as a one-off streamlining of its operations in order to further ensure it remained in good financial health.

Perhaps, then, this crisis and its challenges had been a blessing in disguise.

A COMPANY HEALTH CHECK

"The reforms were that simple."

W hen I looked at our financial reports during the run on Lippo Bank, I discovered that a large number of borrowing and lending accounts had been suspended for no apparent reason. It was time to carry out a review to locate the source of this problem and make proper adjustments.

To this end, I made an unscheduled visit to Lippo Bank and called for a meeting with all the managers. I asked the finance managers to explain the reason for these suspended accounts and how they were dealing with them. But no one was able to tell me the reason. For over a year, there had been many occasions when they had to cut off an old account and re-record it later on. Yet, for reasons that remained unclear, many of the re-recorded accounts contained errors, and with no way to clear them, they had to be suspended.

As I saw it, suspending the accounts was like using a rubbish bin. Accounts that couldn't be sorted out would be tossed into this rubbish bin to temporarily balance the books. This was a form of self-deception and a major taboo in accounting. It was also the origin of corruption and fraud. It was a potential disaster—something that could not be taken lightly.

After hearing the managers' reports, I took a close look at the financial statements and their accompanying documents for the last few days. I saw that most of the suspended accounts operated either between internal positions in branches, between branches, or between branches and the head office. The managers acknowledged that it had become a serious problem, but they placed the blame on the computerised accounting system.

At this point I could begin to guess the possible sources of the account suspension problems. I immediately called up the managers of our Medan, Bandung and Surabaya branches and posed the same questions to each of them:

- Has your branch ever submitted a completely perfect financial statement, without any suspended accounts? Or do the statements always contain defects?
- Are the same accounts always being suspended, or does it alternate between different ones on a daily basis?
- Do the branch's computers often go offline?

The three branches all came back with the same answers:

- Suspended accounts didn't occur every day; sometimes there were no defects.
- The same accounts were not always being suspended; it alternated between different ones.
- The computers hadn't gone offline.

After hearing the branch managers' answers, my first conclusion was that there were no issues with the computer system. There were four parts to the computer system—the hardware, software, operating system and network—and if there was a fault with the computer system, it would have to occur at a fixed point rather than alternating between different points.

In other words, the suspended accounts were alternating between different positions and, therefore, the fault could only be caused by human error. To find the real reason for these suspended accounts, I'd have to start by observing staff operations. The next morning, I went to the head office sales department and chose a place from where I could monitor each staff member. I observed them one by one to see whether each of them was following work procedures properly.

I watched from the start of business right up until the end of business at 5.00 p.m., and I had seen nothing out of the ordinary. Everything seemed in order, so where was the problem coming from? It was really perplexing.

I was beginning to get frustrated, but then something surprising happened: as soon as the clock struck five, the whole staff immediately cleared their desks and headed home, branch managers included. I asked these branch managers in astonishment why the staff didn't go over their accounting work before leaving? If they didn't, then who did?

I was told that the regional centre did the checking as it wasn't the branch's responsibility.

I immediately realised why the suspended accounts had been appearing. It was because the checking should have been carried out personally by the individual who had done the accounting in the first place. They had to assume legal liability by checking each transaction, and if there was an error, they would not have fulfilled their legal responsibility until it had been rectified. If someone else did the checking, that person wouldn't know anything about the transaction, and if they found an error, they wouldn't know whom to ask about it. In the end, they'd have to suspend the account. I had finally identified the real reason behind these suspended accounts.

The following day, I called a meeting with branch managers from across the country and announced that I would be dissolving the regional centres with immediate effect. In addition, each staff member in every branch would be responsible for checking that day's transactions before leaving for home. If there were mistakes, the person who discovered it had to immediately send a message to the culprit and request a correction. If that was not done, the person who discovered the error was to immediately notify the compliance officer at the head office. After establishing the truth, the compliance officer would issue a warning to the culprit: if a similar incident happened again, that person would be immediately dismissed. The way to solve the suspended accounts was to take a zero-tolerance approach.

The reforms were that simple. When accounts were squared at the end of the next working day, there were no suspended accounts. I kept an eye on it every day and everything went smoothly. Lippo Bank was once more operating in a healthy and normal manner.

I also took this as an opportunity to amend Lippo Bank's work procedures to make them more streamlined. This allowed us to provide better services to our customers and it meant another step forward for Lippo Bank.

STREAMLINING LIPPO BANK

"A bank's major customers are more sensitive to bad news than its smaller customers."

Five bank runs led me to a conclusion: a bank's major customers are more sensitive to bad news than its smaller customers.

As soon as major customers heard a rumour about a bank, regardless of whether it was true or false, they'd all rush to withdraw their deposits. They even used bank runs as an opportunity to defer repayments. Their philosophy was to ensure their own safety by erring on the side of caution. By doing this, these major customers compounded the problem instead of helping to alleviate it. It was, however, also human nature, and thus not at all surprising.

The experiences of the past taught me that in order to avoid a bank run, it was necessary to maintain a 30 per cent risk reserve. The last bank run had shown that a 30 per cent reserve was enough to see us through for 60 days, but there was still room for improvement. The structure of the reserves should be based on that of the bank's deposits, which would help rationalise the reserves and improve their performance. At the same time, attention should be paid to the value and liquidity of the reserves.

I decided that we should concentrate on four things.

- First, fixed-term deposits should be in direct proportion to loan terms to prevent short-term deposits being used to fund long-term loans.

- Second, more attention should be paid to liquidity and the proportion of our funds from non-fixed-term deposits shouldn't be too large.
- Third, particularly large non-fixed-term deposits should all be deposited in interest-bearing accounts at the central bank.
- Fourth, 30 per cent of the risk reserves should be used to buy short-term treasury debt as well as other short-term debt instruments.

To help streamline Lippo Bank's operations, I also believed it was necessary to call in some large loans to reduce the pressure on the bank's liquidity.

INDONESIA AND THE 1997–1998 ASIAN FINANCIAL CRISIS

" Like riding a tiger—it's very difficult
to get off. *"*

Asia's economies made four great leaps forward during the 40 years from 1960–2000.

The first leap was the export of labour-intensive industries from the US to Japan and the associated transfer of technology. Next, these labour-intensive industries shifted from Japan to South Korea, Taiwan, Hong Kong and Singapore, transforming them into the "four little dragons". After that, these industries moved to Thailand, the Philippines, Malaysia, and Indonesia; these four countries, however, were much less successful.

By 1990, China was carrying out an opening and reform of its economy, and did all it could to welcome the great wave of industrial transfers. Thanks to timely reforms in its economic system and corresponding changes in education, China achieved brilliant results. It has eclipsed the "four little dragons" and its economy is now even bigger than Japan's.

Indonesia had heedlessly allowed the first two industrial shifts to pass it by as a result of the anti-Western ideology of its government. It was only in 1975, when the Suharto regime felt genuinely secure, that Indonesia officially accepted the liberal economic model of the West, and began to welcome the tide of industry transfers. Unfortunately, it was a case of too little, too late, and when the Asian financial crisis hit in 1997–1998, the whole economy collapsed. Other countries around Southeast Asia fared a little better during the same period, and the crisis proved extremely beneficial to China.

The origins of the Asian financial crisis lay in part in rumours from Wall Street about Asian financial risk. As I have previously mentioned, nothing is more dangerous to a bank than rumours: they threaten credit, which is the lifeblood of a bank. In some severe cases, they can pose a similar threat to a national economy.

During the financial crisis, some Wall Street speculators and investment banks used derivatives and the immense leverage of the US financial industry to sell down the currencies of Asian countries. The central banks tried to halt these attacks on their currency but eventually their foreign exchange reserves were exhausted. Rumours about these countries' central banks began to circulate, undermining their banking systems. As a result, the rupiah plunged in value from about Rp2,000 to Rp18,000 to the dollar in just 40 days. Consequently, in Indonesia there was widespread panic buying of foreign currency. This further drained Bank Indonesia of its dollar reserves.

Interest rates leapt to 70 per cent overnight, and it was impossible to get a loan. Food prices also shot up and the economy was practically paralysed. The capital markets had completely collapsed, stocks were in free fall, and banks went under one after the other. Public order disintegrated, and political instability began to rear its head. What had been a perfectly functioning economy was plunged into chaos largely due to rumours. Many people took refuge by moving their families to Singapore.

In the end, Indonesia had no recourse but to accept unconditionally the debt arrangements of the International Monetary Fund and the World Bank. Controlled by Western countries, these financial organisations quickly exerted their influence and enforced draconian terms on these struggling economies. The West's aversion to authoritarian military rulers ultimately caused the downfall of the Suharto regime.

As soon as it was announced that the IMF and the World Bank had reached a financing agreement with the Indonesian government, the rumours ceased. Despite the tough terms of the aid programme, people's minds were put at rest and the rupiah began to regain its value. The bank runs ended and the markets returned to normal. By virtue of a simple agreement, the storms of the financial crisis had been quelled. This is the value of confidence: it is the foundation of a bank's credit, and credit drives everything.

The 40-day financial crisis severely affected Bank Central Asia (owned by Sudono Salim), Bank International Indonesia (owned by Eka Tjipta Widjaja), Bank Danamon (owned by Rao Yaowu), Bank Dagang Nasional Indonesia (owned by Lin Dexiang) and Bank Bali (owned by Rudy Ramli). These five of Indonesia's eight largest banks had to be bailed out, and were put under government management. Only Lippo Bank, Panin Bank, and Bank Buana survived the crisis, and remained in private hands.

We were able to survive the crisis as a result of our structural resilience, likely due to the streamlining we had carried out after the bank run in 1995.

Though the bank runs were over, the economic fallout was considerable. The depreciation of the rupiah led to the insolvency and subsequent bankruptcy of many companies, which in turn left banks with a huge amount of bad debt. Other loans were uncollectable because companies were unable to make repayments on high interest borrowings, and this translated into underperforming assets for the banks. This was a potentially life-threatening challenge to Lippo Bank.

We had only two choices. One was putting Lippo Bank into administration and surrendering our equity to Bank Indonesia. The second was increasing capital to cover non-performing assets. In the end, I chose to increase our capital. I sold 70 per cent of Lippo Life to American International Group (AIG) for US$310 million and used the funds to shore up the capital of Lippo Bank. This solved the problem of Lippo Bank's underperforming assets, though it still left Lippo Bank with a lot of real estate. Lippo Group had gone unofficially from being a financial company to a real estate company.

I might point out that at this time, the Malaysian government acted very decisively in responding to the Asian financial crisis. At the first sign of trouble, the government immediately announced currency controls, introduced fixed exchange rates, temporarily closed the capital markets and announced its full support of commercial banks. Indonesia didn't adopt these measures and, as a result, emerged from the crisis a lot worse off than Malaysia.

The conclusion that can be drawn from these painful experiences is that risks are everywhere when you run a financial business in a developing country. Political instability can lead to a bank run, economic turmoil can lead to a bank run, natural disasters can lead to a bank run, and little rumours can lead to a bank run. It's exhausting and exasperating but, as the saying goes about riding a tiger, it is always hard to get off.

Because of Indonesia's political and economic instability, the regulatory authorities in Hong Kong and other markets did not treat Lippo Group's banking divisions in the same way as non-Indonesian banks. Whereas other banks were subject to an 8 per cent capital adequacy ratio, ours was 15 per cent. How could we compete when our capital costs were almost double? Exceptionally strict supervision made things even worse. Every day, we had to reply to endless questions through our law firm, and the lawyers' fees were breathtakingly high.

Although the Asian financial crisis had passed, its after-effects lingered. The central bank dispatched teams to review the bank's financial documents almost on a daily basis and every month we had to convene a board meeting to question managers about their operations. We even had to ask for consent from the central bank before issuing any loans. It was exhausting and demoralising, and it lasted for six years.

I started to wonder whether I should place such an onerous burden on the next generation of my family.

Growing In Stewardship
Transforming Lives

AMBITIOUS PROJECTS   **Lippo Village**
The Incomparable City

The Lippo Group has gained a reputation for undertaking ambitious projects, among them the construction of integrated townships that have become models of urban planning. One such project is Lippo Karawaci – now a dynamic community of 250,000 people in a once-sleepy district west of Jakarta. Lippo invested heavily in basic infrastructure, building homes, schools, healthcare facilities and shopping centres.

A key attraction at Lippo Karawaci is Imperial Klub Golf, one of Jakarta's premier golf courses. The 18-hole, 6,486-metre championship course was designed by the late British golf course architect Desmond Muirhead.

Landscaped gardens surround modern homes in a leafy and sustainable living environment. Lippo Group planted more than 80,000 trees as part of its Karawaci project.

The Riady family and the Lippo Group take social responsibility seriously. Bringing schools and hospitals to remote parts of the country is part of their important social mission.

Preparing the next generation of Indonesia's leaders is a key objective of the Riady family and the Pelita Harapan Educational Foundation. The emphasis is on providing a holistic education that challenges students intellectually, physically, emotionally, and spiritually.

Schools are designed to address different linguistic and educational needs in Indonesian society. Pelita Harapan schools offer academic excellence on a par with the best K-12 schools in the US, where most of their teachers and staff are trained.

Universitas Pelita Harapan is Indonesia's top private university. While valuing academic excellence, UPH grooms graduates who will give back to society. The Teacher's College and Faculty of Nursing offer full scholarship programs aimed at training teachers and nurses to meet growing demand in these two critical areas.

WILL BE THE TRUE AMBASSADORS OF UPH

EDUCATION, THE CORNERSTONE OF PROGRESS UPH

The Lippo Group's world class hospitals provide Indonesians with holistic care and the highest level of clinical excellence through a network of world-class hospitals across the Indonesian archipelago. More than 3 million patients were treated over the past year.

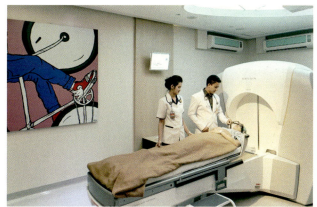

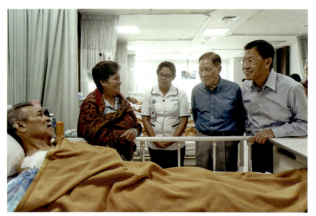

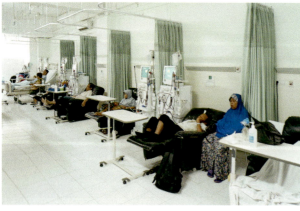

The Lippo Group's Rumah Sakit Umum Siloam (or Siloam General Hospital) provides services to those who would otherwise be unable to afford professional healthcare. The Lippo Group believes it has an obligation to help the government achieve universal healthcare.

SERVING CONSUMERS **LIPPO**MALL

Lippo Malls is the largest mall owner and operator in Indonesia, with over 60 shopping malls in 29 major cities across the archipelago. The malls occupy more than 2.3 million square meters of retail space and accommodate more than 10,000 retailers.

The Lippo Group's MAXX COFFEE arm collaborates with coffee farmers from Aceh to Papua to deliver high-quality coffee to discerning coffee drinkers in Indonesia.

A key arm of the Lippo Group is Matahari Department Store, Indonesia's oldest and largest retailer and leading consumer brand.

SERVING CONSUMERS ⚡MATAHARI

Hypermart is the nation's leading hypermarket retailer, a one-stop shopping and dining experience for Indonesia's rising middle class.

SERVING CONSUMERS

Cinemaxx brings a new level of cinematic entertainment to Indonesia with state-of-the-art technology. It is the first cinema chain in Indonesia to have theatres designed specifically for children, combining films and play areas.

PROVIDING LIFESTYLE ENTERTAINMENT

MatahariMall.com is Indonesia's largest e-commerce marketplace, bringing together buyers and sellers and offering online-to-offline services. It points to a future of technology-enabled business.

SHIFTING TO A TECHNOLOGY-ENABLED WORLD

BeritaSatu Media Group keeps Indonesia informed. More than 3.2 million viewers get their news from BeritaSatu's satellite and cable services. The group also has business and other publications and provides fiber optic internet services all over Indonesia.

CONNECTING INDONESIANS TO THE WORLD   **BERITA SATU** MEDIA HOLDINGS

BOLT, Indonesia's first 4G LTE high speed data service provider, has 2.2 million subscribers.

Data storage units, Google and Akamai Technologies are among the multinationals that rely on these storage units.

The group was the first company in Indonesia to commission a satellite launch. This important step has allowed the group to provide communications services to the most remote corners of Indonesia.

CONNECTING INDONESIANS TO THE WORLD

BERITA SATU
MEDIA HOLDINGS

LAND IS A RESOURCE
AND A RAW MATERIAL

"I decided to leave banking behind."

I t may seem extraordinary now in our digitally savvy age, but in 1999, the world was gripped by fears of the "millennium bug", which many people believed would render all computers inoperable on 1 January 2000. Neither physics nor philosophy could explain the cause of such an error, but Bank Indonesia nonetheless ordered every bank to set up a "disaster committee" and held several seminars to discuss emergency action.

A more pressing concern for me at that time, however, was the direction Lippo Group would take after the millennium. Where should we concentrate our efforts? In this, we had two potential directions: one was the financial industry and the other was the land resources industry.

Finance is a business that you can look at but not touch. It has a lot of swagger, but all power actually lies in the hands of the central bank. You need Bank Indonesia's approval to hire mid-level personnel, and even a major shareholder of the bank such as myself had to obtain the central bank's consent before taking up a new role. Loans are the mainstay of banks, but Bank Indonesia had to agree to every single loan before it could be issued. Every expense had to be approved too.

All in all, even today, if you are running a bank in Indonesia, when it comes to the bank's real assets, you can look but not touch; it's a case of "drawing a picture of a cake and calling it a dinner". Bank Indonesia is so strict primarily because the country's banks are so susceptible to rumours. In 1995, Lippo Bank had suffered a major bank run; in 1998, we went through another serious bank run, this time caused by the financial crisis.

By 1998, I had been running banks for 38 years. During that time, I had experienced five bank runs, which is an average of one every seven years. Particularly alarming were the two big bank runs in 1995 and 1998. I couldn't help but reflect on whether passing on a business that would bring such regular stress to my children was the right thing to do. As a result of the economic troubles of 1991, the bank was unable to collect payments on many of its loans and it had land as underperforming assets. Practically all of the underperforming assets from 1995 and 1998 were land as well. We had become the owners of a sizeable amount of land. This new situation called for a clear and decisive strategy.

Before doing anything else, our standard practice was to determine the nature of a business, based on which we would establish a business strategy. After a lot of thought, we decided that land is a resource—a raw material—that could be processed into another form of product. After being commercialised, it could be sold or leased.

The direction and end-product of this land-processing would be flexibly adjusted based on geography, environment and population. The banking industry simply did not compare to the potential for adding value and bringing profit to a company through the processing of land.

Singapore has one of the world's most transparent housing policies. It introduced a "Home Ownership for the People" scheme in 1964. As early as the 1970s, it already had a consummate housing system that provided almost every resident with his or her own home.

For the last several decades, Singapore has continued to build new housing, and though prices are subject to cyclical fluctuations, over the longer term, house prices always go up. It is the same in Hong Kong; some say this is a feature of island nations. In fact, even real estate in the US is like this. In the US and other developed countries, real estate is an important driver of economic growth.

As noted earlier, Lippo Group had inadvertently amassed a huge amount of land resources. As a raw material, these resources could be processed in a number of ways and, following long-term development, their appreciation would be substantial. For Lippo Group, it was a revelation, and we were determined to make the most of it.

This was the gift that was given to me at the turn of the millennium, and I thank God for it.

I decided to leave banking behind, and only hold on to our insurance and investment divisions.

From then on, our core business would be the development of two natural resources: land and information networks.

THE ALCHEMY OF
REAL ESTATE

"Land = resource = raw material"

"Land = resource = raw material" was a new business concept. Because land was a raw material, it could be processed for agricultural, industrial or residential use. It could be processed into shopping plazas, supermarkets, department stores, cinemas, children's play areas, hotels, hospitals and schools. Development could also be taken a step further by combining all of these functions into one integrated building complex.

These different segments could also be spun off as their own separate operations, making them both an individual entity and an integrated part of a powerful industry chain with the potential for huge profits.

This huge industry chain would have the power to turn barren land into highly valuable land, and transform unappealing apartment blocks into mid- and high-grade communities. It was something akin to alchemy.

The reorientation in Lippo Group's strategy would produce eight different chains. Though each would be independent, all would be part of an interconnected, collaborative commercial organisation—one that was completely unique, with its own special business model.

At its foundation, however, would be the concept of making the whole chain standardised and quantified, starting with a meticulous division of labour from the lowest, most minor positions and then working upwards. Based on this principle, the whole process was to be written up as workflows entered into a computer system. This computer system would be at the core of the chain's management.

It took me several years to complete the IT system for managing the department stores, supermarkets and hospitals, but it was a prerequisite for the development of the chain concept. Only with this consummate computer system has it been possible to open 25 department stores, 25 supermarkets, 6 hospitals and other chain establishments.

Today, Lippo Group is Indonesia's largest chain. We have the biggest shopping plazas, the biggest department stores, the biggest supermarkets and the biggest hospitals, in addition to Indonesia's largest industrial park and largest residential community. Each year, we sell five hundred thousand square metres of building area. I feel very gratified to have achieved such success.

HOSPITALS ARE FOR THE PUBLIC GOOD BUT THEY ARE ALSO BUSINESSES

" Hospitals can both save people's lives and make a profit. "

I previously talked about turning Karawaci into a luxury residential complex equipped with a top-quality hospital, first-rate international primary and middle school, and Indonesia's most stylish shopping plaza.

Building the shopping plaza and setting up the school did not present any problems for us, but we had no experience to speak of when it came to the hospital. Where would we start? How would we apply for a licence to build it? How would we design it? How would we run it? How would we hire eminent doctors? We were at a complete loss.

In the end, I thought of the Gleneagles Hospital in Singapore as it was highly regarded by Indonesians and would add prestige to Karawaci. By pulling all the strings I could, I convinced Gleneagles to become partners in constructing the Karawaci Gleneagles Hospital.

After more than three years of construction, Karawaci Gleneagles Hospital was officially opened. Because the number of residents in the area was still small, it had few patients and suffered losses during its first four years. Unwilling to bear these losses, Gleneagles decided to sell their share and pull out. Left with no other options, we decided to run it ourselves.

Pertamina (a state-owned company originally specialising in oil and gas) owned several hospitals that were headed by a Chinese-Indonesian professor, Dr. Satyanegara, a gifted and distinguished neurosurgeon. I decided that he was the one for us. Having learned that he had recently retired, I sent numerous friends to try to convince him to become the director of Karawaci Gleneagles Hospital. He finally agreed. We also changed the hospital's name from Gleneagles Hospital to Siloam Hospital.

Dr. Satyanegara hired three eminent doctors to act as consultants. Things started to pick up at Siloam Hospital and business improved day by day, but it was still losing money. My colleagues had suggested shutting it down, but I did not agree, the reason being that Siloam Hospital was one of the promises we had made to the residents of Karawaci. It was also part of Lippo Group's social mission. Although it was losing money year after year, we could not give up on it.

Then came further disappointments: Dr. Satyanegara wanted to step down after serving as the hospital's director for three years. This was a great blow to me and I did everything I could to keep him, but in the end we had no choice but to reluctantly bid him farewell. Thanks to Dr. Satyanegara's hard work, Siloam Hospital had become widely recognised as a centre for neurosurgery. Eventually, Dr. Eka Julianta Wahjoepramono, a young neurosurgeon, took up the director's position.

Dr. Eka is a very ambitious and talented doctor whom I had encouraged to go to Japan to further his studies. He followed this up by gaining a doctorate in neurosurgery from the University of Western Australia School of Medicine and Pharmacology and becoming a member of the Asian Congress of Neurological Surgeons. I encouraged him to invite the association to hold their annual conference in Karawaci, where he could speak about his own experiences in medicine. This proved successful and three years later Karawaci also hosted the International Conference on Cerebrovascular Surgery.

Dr. Eka was subsequently elected president of the Asian-Oceanian International Congress on Skull Base Surgery from 2008–2012. It was a victory for him and an honour for us all. Siloam Hospital's reputation has grown in tandem with that of Dr. Eka. Today, Dr. Eka is Indonesia's foremost neurosurgeon, and Siloam is considered to be the best hospital for brain surgery in the country. Patients come from around Indonesia, and even from Singapore. I feel very proud of these accomplishments. It was my belief that an approach that combined medicine, education and research would be beneficial to the long-term growth of our medical division. As a result, in 1996, we began preparations to establish a medical school called Universitas Pelita Harapan (light and hope). The Indonesian government, however, had always taken a very cautious and conservative attitude towards medical education, which meant we only obtained approval to begin teaching following a huge amount of red tape and 10 years of hard work. In 2006, the Faculty of Medicine finally opened.

During its early years, Universitas Pelita Harapan followed the same model as other ordinary medical schools. But, like National University of Singapore's Yong Loo Lin School of Medicine, we wanted to innovate. To this end, I divided our entire teaching system into five parts:

- Curriculum formulation
- Teaching logic
- Teaching equipment
- Entry requirements for new students
- Entry requirements for new tutors.

In each of these five areas, the reforms would occur incrementally. New reforms would be introduced every year over the course of five academic years. This arrangement meant that old and new classes could carry on simultaneously, without being affected. The hardest part was teacher qualifications. The only solution was to hire retired professors from well-known institutes abroad. After everyone agreed, the reforms went ahead.

I appointed Dr. Eka as the school's first director. He was the backbone of our medical division and I felt he was worthy of being given another opportunity to nurture his skills. He worked hard in the position for five years, after which, the Indonesian Ministry of Education and Culture awarded him a professorship at the Universitas Pelita Harapan.

Dr. Eka leads a 17-strong team of brain surgeons at the Siloam Neurosurgery Centre, which is now known the world over. They perform over 1,000 operations a year. After 20 years of hard work, I had achieved my aim of turning Siloam Hospital into Indonesia's most renowned hospital.

But while Siloam Hospital was strengthening its reputation, it was still losing money. In my view, hospitals are intended to benefit society. It is normal and not surprising that they make a loss. I had previously carried out a cost analysis of a variety of the hospital's medical initiatives and the results showed that they were all profitable; in theory, then, the hospital should not have been losing money. But in 2009, I decided to again review the systems and processes at the hospital to reduce the continuing losses.

I arranged for a 13-person team to go to Siloam Hospital and learn about its workflows. There, they examined and discussed every single stage of treatment: hospital entry and registration, records of doctors' diagnoses, diagnostic imaging, blood tests, drug prescriptions, bed allocation, medical records, ward hygiene, surgical procedures, intensive care, waste treatment, drug sales at the pharmaceutical counter, drug storage, patient meals, accounting and so on.

Next, they wrote up the workflows and work practices, mapping out and talking over each one as they did so. In total, it took a year and a half to complete, after which the team spent another two years converting all this information into an IT system for the hospital. We thus achieved the digitalisation of the hospital's entire operations, covering everything from actual treatment to accounting, storage of diagnostic imagery and remote control applications.

Once the rationalisation and digitalisation of the hospital's workflows had been completed, I discovered many areas where there was either serious waste, or an overlap, or bottleneck in operations. These failings were the real reason why the hospital was making a loss.

If we made vigorous efforts to overhaul these shortcomings, the hospital would become a profitable enterprise much like any other business. It could save people's lives *and* make a profit, and would then be on its way to becoming another main industry of Lippo Group.

Medical treatment is a troubling issue for countries all over the world. The Americans are hailed as management experts, yet the country still suffers from problems with the management of its hospitals, problems with medical coverage and problems with medical liability insurance—none of which President Barack Obama has been able to solve despite his significant achievements in expanding healthcare. Many countries' healthcare budgets are increasing annually and have become their greatest burden.

Hospitals complain they are making a loss, while insurers complain that medical costs are too high. So where exactly is the problem?

Medical treatment should be divided into two separate industries: hospitals and health insurance. The latter should be handed over to companies and subject to commercial forces. Competition will rationalise prices and make service more customer-oriented. I believe the government, meanwhile, should stop subsidising hospitals and only provide medical insurance to civil servants and the poor. If medical fees can be rationalised through negotiation between health insurers and hospitals, I firmly believe that medical treatment issues can be resolved properly.

With this in mind, I decided that we should enter the medical industry. Our first move would be to create a hospital network in the Jakarta metropolitan area. We would set up three hospitals in each of the city's five districts, making a total of 15 flagship hospitals. Following this, we would open two smaller clinics in the vicinity of each of these hospitals for a total of 30. The pattern would be repeated by setting up five hospitals in each of Indonesia's seven largest cities—a total of 35. We would then build 25 hospitals in Indonesia's remaining 25 provincial capitals. Towns with relatively large populations would be chosen for the construction of a further 30 hospitals.

I hope that in 10 years we will have the beginnings of a network of 135 hospitals. Once the network is in place, we will complement it with the release of high-quality health insurance. I am confident that Lippo Medical Group will be a world-class medical organisation, and I hope that its model can help promote change in the Indonesian medical industry and bring happiness and peace of mind to people across the country.

CHAPTER NINE

MY FAITH

" My faith in Christ has given my whole family an unshakeable oneness, a bond that cannot be replaced by any other. "

I have been a Confucian, a Marxist, a socialist and a nationalist. Yet my most profound philosophical questions went unanswered until I found my Lord and Saviour, Jesus Christ. I had embraced multiple philosophies, even at the expense of my own safety at times, yet none of these gave me the answers I was seeking. For example, Confucius's vision of proper behaviour—with its goal of attaining social harmony—left too many questions unanswered. Was there a higher purpose to social harmony? What was the source of its compassion? Confucius took me only part of the way to where I am today, even though it was deeply ingrained in me thanks to the careful instruction of my father and my teachers in my early years.

I was in the dark, blind to the truth of Christ, yet I was a proud man and felt that I was a good person. I felt that I was self-sufficient and had no need of God. Yet a sequence of events later in my life would force me to reckon with my Maker—God would touch me and I would not be able to deny His existence.

One of the contributing factors in my conversion was that all of my children had become Christians. Each of them found Christ and I saw how it changed them for the better. My four eldest children—Andrew, James,

Rosy and Lilian—had all been sent to Macau in 1966 and that put them on the path towards Jesus Christ. That was a time when Indonesia was engulfed in political and economic turmoil. Schools were closed and some politicians fanned the flames of ethnic tensions. My wife and I thought it was better to send the children abroad where they could safely continue their studies. The boys were enrolled at the Perpetual Help School and later at Yuet Wah College, both of them Roman Catholic institutions. The girls studied at a convent in the Portuguese-run enclave, Santa Rosa de Lima. Four years later, Stephen and Minny were sent off to Singapore for schooling, and they stayed with the family of a close friend and business associate, Andrew Tan. Faith had not been the reason why I entrusted my children to the Tan family, but this turned out to be a happy coincidence. The care and guidance from these devout Christians made a deep and lasting impression on Stephen and Minny.

The change I saw in my children was especially true for Rosy and James. Rosy was always diligent in sharing her faith and bringing me to Christian fellowships. While I did not pay too much attention to it, I certainly didn't object. I did not want my scepticism toward their faith to get in the way of our relationship. In fact, I felt that I needed to continue to connect with them and understand their faith. It was for this reason that I chose to accompany them on religious outings.

Then came a pivotal weekend in September 1989 when my son James was particularly insistent that my wife and I join a church retreat. Again, wanting to avoid any intergenerational gap between me and my children, and knowing that Pastor Dr Stephen Tong, someone I respected, would lead the retreat, I went.

I attended with an attitude of indifference—not expecting much and not willing to make any commitments. I sat in session after session. Pastor Tong was a powerful preacher, yet I did not find his sermons compelling. Little did I know that the next sermon I heard would change me forever.

At the next sermon, Pastor Tong preached about the utterly sinful nature of man. He preached that this was true of every man throughout history and I knew that he meant to include me. I remember thinking to myself that Pastor Tong did not know me. I felt that if he really did know me, he would realise that I was a good man and that I contributed generously to many different religious causes whether Buddhist, Christian or Muslim. How could I be considered a sinner? As I resisted his assertions, Pastor Tong started to challenge the audience with a series of cutting questions.

He began by pointedly asking his listeners to "raise your hands if you have never cheated on your taxes." The gathering included many successful businessmen. Yet no hands went up. Reverend Tong then asked the men in the group: "Who among you has never lied to your wife at some point? If so, please raise your hand." Again, no hands went up. Those questions pierced through my heart and for the first time in my life I felt a sense of unworthiness, sinfulness and inadequacy. I broke down in tears although I tried to hide them. The failings he had raised, I could not deny. That afternoon I knew something had changed in my heart.

Unfortunately, I resisted Pastor Tong's call to accept Jesus as my personal Lord and Saviour. I was stubborn and proud. Furthermore, in my mind I was still responsible for the ancestral worship at home. Who would bring offerings of food to my parents and ancestors? I could not just run away from those responsibilities.

It was not until five months later, in February of 1990, that my mind and heart were forced to accept the truth of Christ. I was due to undergo heart bypass surgery and felt that I needed to make key decisions about certain matters in the event that the surgery was not successful. It was during this time of contemplation that my mind and heart were opened to the irrational nature of ancestor worship. In thinking about who could take over my duties to my ancestors, I realised that the practice itself did not make sense. If it were true that our ancestors depended on our providing food and worship then wouldn't it follow that the earlier generations would have been left neglected and uncared for? Just as I was not able to continue in this tradition once I passed, ancestors before me too would no longer have provided that service to their ancestors. The practice was not exactly Confucian either, since in Confucian philosophy merely feeding your parents did not constitute filial piety. Filial piety was much more than that; it required obedience and respect—behaviour that can only be exhibited while one's parents are alive. Therefore, ancestor worship was hardly a satisfactory response to the Confucian insistence on filial piety. Rather than worshipping my past ancestors, now I honour them while having a deeper thankfulness for God—the one who in His limitless grace gave me my parents in the first place.

Another significant moment of understanding occurred as I was awaiting surgery. Li Mei was constantly by my side and I realised that I had often taken her loyalty for granted. As a wife, she had supported me in good times and bad, sacrificing her own interests and helping me overcome whatever difficulties I encountered. I realised that while I paid my respects to my ancestors, I often ignored the needs of the family around me. Again, I was acutely reminded of my personal failings and felt the undeniable and merciful presence of the Lord.

It was then that I felt reconciled with my Maker and I calmly awaited my operation. What had appeared at first to be a distressing procedure now gave me peace. I had faith in Jesus. My entire family had also come to support me during this time of need and that too was a source of strength and comfort.

The operation was a success. Following my conversion, I went to Bible study daily, from Monday to Saturday, 6–7am, for at least three years. On Sundays I would attend church service at my newfound home—Pastor Tong's Reformed Evangelical Church (GRII). I was led to that church by its strong reformed traditions and focus on a cultural mandate, and Pastor

Tong's great example and testimony of evangelism. My wife also became increasingly active in the church.

My daughter Rosy's mother-in-law, Weng Wenying, was another individual who had persistently encouraged me to deepen my understanding of the faith. As a devout Christian, she was steadfast in her belief that I needed to immerse myself in the teachings of Christ. When she found that I had a change of heart and was open to the faith, she would come early each morning to fetch me and make sure I attended Bible study. I was eventually baptised at the Local Church in Jakarta in 1989 – shortly before my operation.

The Local Church had its roots in the work of two eminent Chinese pastors—Watchman Nee and his follower, Witness Lee. Pastor Nee was active in spreading the Christian faith in China in the early 20th century and Brother Lee carried on his work. After the communists came to power on the mainland and tried to eradicate all religious influences, Brother Lee continued his preachings in Taiwan and elsewhere. He founded the influential Living Stream Ministry, and I later began making an annual pilgrimage to its offices in Anaheim, California. There I would spend two to three weeks in intensive training in the Christian faith.

For me, my faith in Christ has become a central part of my life, and I truly feel that I have been born again. I am more aware than ever before of all of my failings and weaknesses. Yet knowing that I have been redeemed through Christ and His sacrifice on the cross, I have been transformed and granted a peace I never felt before. I like to say that I now have three basic tenets that guide me in my personal life and business dealings. First is the requirement that my actions glorify God. Whatever I do must meet this fundamental test. If some behaviour appears to contradict this, then it should be avoided. Second, I believe in refraining from activities that "bind" or ensnare you in addictive, evil or harmful behaviour. I have only one God in my life, but some forms of irrational or obsessive behaviour could lead me to value material things over my love for Christ. The single-minded pursuit of wealth is one kind of obsessive behaviour. It leads one to value material wealth more than pleasing God. Gambling and drinking are also examples of activities that can bind you. One who is addicted to gambling values winning above all else. The gambler may be willing to forfeit everything he owns—even if it denies him the ability to provide for the ones he loves—just to feed the desire to gamble. The list of such types of behaviour is long. Binding oneself in this way is contrary to the Christian faith, and this type of behaviour must be avoided. Finally, I strive to avoid behaviour that would cause others to stumble. What do I mean by that? Others judge you by your behaviour, so when a Christian behaves in an unchristian-like manner it causes others to question the basis of your faith. This is equivalent to placing a stumbling block in the way of someone else's journey to faith, which is clearly the opposite of what we are called to do as believers and warriors for Christ. Therefore, we should always conduct ourselves in such a manner that others will not have reason to question the validity and reality of what Christ has done for us.

The Christian faith has also been a guiding light for me in other respects as well. Education and medical care are two basic needs of any society, and our family has made a commitment to helping meet these needs. I will discuss our activities in these two key areas in greater detail in a later chapter of this book but let me just say that it was James who pushed us in the direction of education in Indonesia. The Pelita Harapan Educational Foundation, translated as "light and hope", started setting up schools with a vision of integrating faith and spiritual formation in the pursuit of academic excellence. The Foundation partnered closely with leading Christ-centered universities in the US to recruit well-qualified Christian teachers for the schools. Today, the Foundation schools offer quality Christian education from kindergarten to university, and some 27,000 students are enrolled in them at this point.

The Lippo Group's hospital arm—Siloam—takes its name from the ancient Biblical healing pool. Our hospitals and clinics take healing seriously, and it is healing in the broadest sense—physical, mental, emotional and spiritual. More than three million people are treated each year and this figure is projected to grow by more than 20 per cent annually. New hospitals are opening every year and by the end of this year, Siloam aims to extend its health services via a network of 32 hospitals across Indonesia.

These healthcare services, like our schools, are open to all. While the schools offer a Christian perspective, our hospitals eschew outward symbols of our faith out of respect for the local community. This, I might add, is a tenet of our reform church's beliefs, which strives to engage the community at large. We help our neighbours whether they are Christian, Muslim, Hindu, or of any other faith. Through these important activities, my family looks to glorify God by spreading the love and grace that He has given and taught to us.

One of the things that brings me greatest satisfaction is the fact that four generations of our family—now numbering close to 100 members—are all Christians. Most of us attend services at GRII. Even if we don't all worship at the same church all of the time, we are steeped in the teachings of the same faith. My coming to faith in Christ has brought my whole family into an unshakeable oneness, a bond that cannot be replaced by any other. Our love for Christ unites us.

CHAPTER TEN

THE IMPORTANCE OF INVESTING IN EDUCATION

"A nation's prosperity depends on access to education."

When I was young, my father would often say to me: "A family's wealth depends on the upbringing of its children, a company's success depends on talent, and a nation's prosperity depends on access to education." These three precepts had a great influence on me; they were what motivated me to learn, and they became the foundation for how I made my way through life.

My father taught me how to read Chinese characters, write letters and compose essays. He made sure I was a good neighbour, showed respect for my elders and understood the importance of faithfulness and loyalty to one's friends. He also instilled in me the need for thrifty living, assiduousness, and the ability to bear hardship. In all this, he set an example through his own actions.

He lost his wife at a young age but never remarried, treasuring her memory until the end of his life. This, too, had a profound effect on me. In my ancestral home in China, my grandfather opened a school and hired teachers to educate our neighbours' children in his home. These were the only educational facilities in the village, and my grandfather would often go around the village exhorting children to study. I think this had an effect on my father's character. I feel pride when I think of my father and grandfather; they both cared deeply about the next generation's upbringing.

In 1980, whilst I was in Hong Kong, a teacher from Putian named Lin Wenhao called on me to help with a project that was important to him. He was accompanied by a Taiwanese man, also surnamed Lin and whose family was from Putian. The two of them wished to discuss ways to help develop this small part of China that had been home to their forefathers.

I suggested that the first thing to do was build a university, and they both agreed. I invited them to Jakarta and Singapore to solicit contributions for the construction of a campus comprising 20 multi-storey buildings, and proposed that the main building—to be named the Mochtar Riady Teaching Building—be constructed first. This was met with an enthusiastic response, and with that Putian College was founded. It would play a major role in promoting education in Putian.

Around the year 2000, I took it upon myself to visit Minister of Education Chen Zhili and Deputy Minister of Aviation Min Guirong, another Putian native, in Beijing to gain their backing for a plan to upgrade Putian College to a university. Minister Chen was very supportive, and three years later Putian College was awarded university status. With competing universities in Fuzhou to the north and Xiamen to the south, Putian's location made it difficult to turn the university into a first-rate institute of higher education.

In order to overcome this difficulty, we had to innovate. We decided to set up accounting and computer courses in which English-language textbooks were used. This would cater to the need for English-speaking talent as cities across China opened up to foreign investment. Of the money I donated, some was used to send tutors to the UK and the US to learn more about accounting and computers, and some was used to hire

American tutors. The courses would be beneficial to the students because they would be able to find work in foreign firms in large cities once they graduated. This was my own small contribution to Putian's development.

Many Southeast Asian Chinese are alumni of Xiamen University, and they celebrate its founding by Tan Kah Kee, a Filipino-Chinese whose family originated from Fujian. They care about the university's progress and contribute whatever they can to show their respect for Tan. I am no exception.

On one occasion, I visited Xiamen and was received by then secretary of the municipal Communist Party committee, Hong Yongshi. During our meeting, I put it to him that Xiamen, as a small island with limited space, was not ideal for developing labour-intensive manufacturing, but it could become a base for high-tech industries.

High-tech industries required foreign technical talent, and they would be very glad to have a good hospital in Xiamen. I thus suggested setting up a medical school at the university to add to the range of courses offered and to enhance the level of service provided by local hospitals. The latter would ultimately make Xiamen into a medical centre for Fujian Province, particularly in the field of cardiology.

Secretary Hong, who was also Xiamen's mayor, enthusiastically supported the idea, and said he would help in any way he could. At the time, however, the local government did not have much money, so I decided to donate a teaching building to the medical school, to be called the Mochtar Riady Medical School Teaching Building.

Next, Professor Lim Yean Leng from Australia was hired as the first dean of the medical school, which would specialise in cardiology. The Xiamen University School of Medicine grew quickly and soon became one of China's most renowned medical schools.

Xiamen University also became a sister university to Putian University, and this helped improve the teaching standards at Putian. I am grateful to the president of Xiamen University, Professor Zhu Chongshi, and Vice President Pan Shimo for their strong support in this effort to assist Putian. I feel honoured to have been able to contribute to education in Fujian Province.

In 2003, Tsinghua (Qinghua) University Communist Party Secretary Chen Xi made a trip to Indonesia, during which he visited Universitas Indonesia. At the time, I was chairman of the university's board of trustees and oversaw all of its personnel and financial matters. Since the post was similar to that of a party secretary, I was asked to receive Secretary Chen.

As we began talking, we were surprised to discover that we were both natives of Putian. We quickly switched from more formal Mandarin to the comfort of our local dialect. I arranged a dinner reception for him at my home, and soon discovered we had much in common. Since then, I have often visited him at Tsinghua University, asking for his advice on educational matters. I have gained a lot from my friendship with Chen, and have also learned valuable lessons in running a university as a result of my association with Tsinghua University.

In 2008, Chen was promoted to the position of Liaoning Province's deputy secretary, and I made a special trip to Tsinghua University to congratulate him. Over dinner, he spoke of his wish to leave something behind for Tsinghua University, and politely inquired if I would be willing to help build a library that would be named after me. I was extremely pleased to hear this, and the next day we signed a letter of intent to build a library. It was an honour to make a contribution to China's most prestigious institute of higher learning.

UNIVERSITAS INDONESIA

" The workflow reforms . . . were a breath of fresh air. "

I ndonesia's most prestigious educational institute is Universitas Indonesia. It is the alma mater of many of Indonesia's academic, cultural, economic, and political elite. It was a great honour to be selected as the chairman of the university's board of trustees, a post I held for five years.

Elected by the faculty, students and the Minister of Education and Culture, the board is the university's highest executive body and is responsible for appointing the university rector, vice rectors, and other senior personnel. It also has overall responsibility for the university's curricular and financial matters. The board has a total of 21 members. The entire council meets once a week.

Following my appointment as chairman, the university rector presented me with the university's educational programme for the next 25 years. It filled four volumes and had been written by an expert hired from the World Bank. After poring over it for almost three weeks, I was still unable to identify any valid, practical measures. Perhaps my English wasn't good enough or maybe it was too complicated for me to understand. At one of our council meetings, I asked the rector if he could explain it to me—but he confessed he couldn't understand it either.

I smiled and said to my colleagues on the board: "I'm old. When I read a book, by the time I've reached the middle I've forgotten the beginning. When I get to the end I've forgotten the middle. Once I put the book aside, I've forgotten the lot."

I suggested that since we were appointed for five years, the work plan should also be for five years. These five years would be split into two phases of two-and-a-half years each. This way, everyone would be clear about what he or she had to do and what tasks were supposed to be completed. Instead of setting unrealistic goals, these tasks would be real and concrete. Everyone agreed.

I submitted a two-page work plan. One page advocated the digitalisation of the university's accounting and the other pushed for more research and education in the fields of IT, life sciences and nanotechnologies. After some deliberation, the board agreed to follow this clear and concise five-year work outline. We instructed the rector to launch three, new state-of-the-art courses, while I volunteered to take responsibility for digitalising the university's accounting.

Universitas Indonesia had over 10 faculties, the largest of which was the Faculty of Political and Social Sciences, with over 10,000 students. I selected this faculty as the first beneficiary of the accounting reforms. If I was successful here, then I would already have completed a quarter of the digitalisation work for the entire university. Focusing my efforts on reforming this faculty would also encourage other faculties to get involved.

The dean of the Faculty of Political and Social Sciences was Professor Gumilar Rusliwa Somantri. He had only been in the position for two months and wanted to make an impact. He immediately agreed to my proposal and said he was willing to cooperate in pushing the reforms through. I suggested putting together a six-person team. The faculty sent its deputy, who was responsible for managing the faculty's finances, as well as his two assistants, and I called on the help of three accountants from Lippo Bank.

The work got off to a very unassuming start. The team began by selecting major departments in the faculty and writing out their workflows.

Once this was complete, the process was repeated for the whole faculty. Writing out all the workflows took four months, after which they were digitalised along with the faculty's accounting procedures. After a total of six months, the Faculty of Political and Social Sciences' administration had been standardised, and its accounting had been digitalised.

I arranged for Bank Negara Indonesia to collect student fees and deposit them directly into the Faculty of Political and Social Sciences' account. In short, the bank now handled all payments to and from the faculty, meaning that everything was recorded. At the end of each day, each department in the faculty had to check financial income and expenditures, and each department head and the faculty dean could only leave after these checks were completed. Taking stock of the faculty's accounts on a daily basis gave the dean a clear idea of whether the department's operations were meeting their targets and staying on budget.

After the reform, each department's income and expenditure could be understood at a glance, and any suspicious payments could be immediately discovered and addressed by the dean. This was a real step towards achieving "zero waste and zero fraud". For a department whose income did not meet targets, a review would be carried out and efforts would be devoted to making improvements. All of this produced a large increase in the Faculty of Political and Social Sciences' income and was accompanied by a pay raise for the entire staff, much to everyone's delight.

The workflow reforms of the Faculty of Political and Social Sciences were a breath of fresh air. It now had a reliable accounting system and financial reports that painted a clear picture of each department's finances. Other faculties emulated the model, and the digital accounting reforms were quickly rolled out across the entire university. Overall, Universitas Indonesia's income increased dramatically between 2002 and 2007.

Universitas Indonesia had two campuses. The new campus was in the suburbs, while the old campus was in the centre of Jakarta. The latter covered an area of nine hectares and had a very high commercial value thanks to its prime location. However, there was no logic in the way the buildings had been laid out. Most had only been intended to be temporary, and they were old and inefficient.

I submitted a plan to the board to transform the campus. We would pull the whole thing down and build four new levels: three below ground and one above ground. Each level would cover an area of 80,000 square metres, making a total of 320,000 square metres. On the ground level, 30 one-storey buildings would be constructed. The lowest floor below ground would serve as a car park, which, combined with the two levels above it, would cover an area of 240,000 square metres. These three levels could be used for shops with a 30-year lease.

The income from the long-term leases would be Rp50 million per square metre, or a total one-off income of Rp12 trillion. Building costs would be Rp6 million per square metre, meaning that the total cost of these 320,000 square metres would be close to Rp2 trillion—leaving a net profit of Rp10 trillion. The 30 one-storey buildings could be used as classrooms, student and tutor dormitories, a hotel, and research facilities. I was confident that I could find 30 companies that would contribute to the construction of each building in return for having it named after them.

At minimal cost, the scheme above would rebuild the old campus and provide profits of Rp10 trillion. This money could be used as an investment fund that would cover teaching and research fees, training costs, scholarships, a technology incubator fund and maintenance expenses for all the buildings.

Most of the council agreed to the scheme, but one member objected. He believed that education should not be profit-oriented, and that there should be more focus on history and culture. As such, he was opposed to pulling down the century-old buildings and one small, dilapidated church.

He called on the support of various figures in the university to oppose the plan. I was unwilling to stir up any trouble, and to my great disappointment abandoned the scheme. In my opinion, those who opposed the project did not have the university's long-term development in mind when making the decision. They preferred that the campus remain in its current run-down state, and because they were in control of the university, there was nothing I could do.

NANOTECHNOLOGIES AND BUSINESS MANAGEMENT

" Management principles should extend from small to large. *"*

W hile I was serving as chairman of the board of trustees at the University of Southern California and later at Arkansas State University, I would often hear the other trustees speak of nanotechnologies during our board meetings. Later on, when I asked professors at Tsinghua University about the future direction of the university, they also brought up nanotechnologies. As such, I was gaining an appreciation of their importance even though I did not understand what they were. When I proposed more research and education on nanotechnologies to Universitas Indonesia's board of trustees, the other members were no more informed than me. I had no choice but to read whatever materials I could before going back and explaining why I thought we should pay attention to them.

I read a total of 16 books on the subject, most of which talked about the commercial value of nanotechnologies. Only a few discussed their academic value. It is both a wondrous and very simple discipline, and its essence is this: all matter on earth is made up of different atomic and molecular structures, and if there were a means of splitting up these atomic and molecular structures and rearranging them into a structure of a different form, then a different substance could be produced.

To give an example, once common coal has been broken down, the carbon atoms could be rearranged to form graphite or even diamonds. This is what nanotechnologies are all about, and they are thus named because of the minuscule size of atoms, which fall within the nanoscopic scale (one million nanometres are equivalent to one millimetre).

In the early 2000s, I travelled to Nanjing to visit my alma mater, Southeast University (formerly National Central or Chung Yang University), where I was received by the university president, Gu Guanqun. I had previously donated funds for the construction of the Mochtar Riady Science Building, which is situated at the site of the four arches that are the remains of the original university.

Gu shared his plan to build a new campus, and I told him I thought it was an excellent idea. I decided to donate another building—to be called the Mochtar Riady Library—and this would be the centrepiece of the new campus. I felt this was my social responsibility, since so much of my success was made possible by the education I received at my alma mater.

Gu invited me to give a speech about my experience in business management at a conference. My view was that, in effect, running a business is a kind of "nanotechnology" management.

I likened this to the teachings of the Chinese philosopher Lao Tzu, who wrote that, "A journey of a thousand miles starts from a single step," "A tree as wide as a man's embrace springs from a small shoot," and "Being is born out of non-being." The single step, small shoot and non-being all have the same significance as the prefix "nano".

By the same token, when studying a company's operations, you should start from the lowest level and most minor position, and management principles should go from small to large, from bottom to top, from internal to external, from a single point to the whole.

Changes in things start small, and build up from there; similarly, the larger picture reveals itself in the smallest details. In effect, Lao Tzu was the first person to advocate a "nanotechnological" mindset. This is the core idea behind the application of nanotechnologies in business management.

In the last century, scientists working in the field of life sciences discovered that all living matter is based on DNA. DNA consists of a double-helix structure formed by two interconnected bases, and these bases, which are like the steps on a spiral staircase, can be divided into four fundamental types: adenine, thymine, cytosine and guanine. The different configurations of these four types determine differences in DNA, and differences in DNA determine different species.

A company's operations are based on numerous internal workflows, in much the same way that the cells in a person's body function according to the configuration of the four bases mentioned above. Workflows are made up of four elements:

- Work posts: these depict the steps, positions and supervising personnel for the entire workflow.
- Work tasks: these describe the specific tasks of relevant personnel.
- Work rules: these describe how tasks are to be carried out.
- Main body of work: this describes which documents or materials are to be worked on.

Only when these four elements work in harmony can a company produce high-quality products at low cost, which is what is meant by productivity. Production line workflows determine the dynamism of a company—and this is "nanotechnologies" business management.

If we apply this to hospitals, for example, we can see they contain two systems: hospital property (such as buildings and equipment) and medical treatment. These are two different operational units, which include many small work units. The whole hospital is a combined system integrating a number of units (equivalent to molecules), each of which is both independent and interconnected. Based on the principles of nanotechnologies, we can separate these two operational units (equivalent to cells or molecules), divide them into property companies and management companies and create a relationship in which the management company leases real estate from the property company.

Such an arrangement can lessen the investment burden on the hospital and allow it to open more branches. The property company can also sell its leasing business to real estate investment trusts (widely known as REITs), providing it with funds that it can use in the construction of more property, in much the same way a public stock offer would. At the same time, the hospital management company can go public, thereby giving it more funds to open branches. In this way, both sides complement each other and are able to expand continually.

Such a business expansion model corresponds to Lao Tzu's principle of "One gave birth to two. Two gave birth to three. Three gave birth to all things," and also reflects the essence of nanotechnologies. If we were to take this a step further, a hospital's large-scale medical equipment could be spun off to form an independently run leasing company, which would be yet another form of "nanotechnologies" in a company's operations. In short, there is a close correlation between nanotechnologies and ancient Chinese philosophy, and the principles of both can be put to good use in the management and operation of a corporation.

UNIVERSITAS PELITA HARAPAN

" *There is a pressing need to nurture morally conscientious talent.* *"*

I n 1996, my son James proposed setting up a university in Indonesia. This was a perfect fit with my educational aspirations, and I actively encouraged him to make this goal a reality.

In Indonesia, private universities are generally established as a collaborative enterprise and they raise funds through public contributions. This often results in a barrage of opinions, endless discussions that do not come to any decisions, and decisions (when they have finally been reached) that are often not carried out. In most cases, there are also power struggles and factional disputes that lead to poor management and ineffective teaching. In light of this, James suggested that the Riady family supply all of the funds for the university.

After several years of hard work, and with the assistance of the then-Minister of Education and Culture Professor Wardiman Djojonegoro, we were finally successful in opening the university. Johannes Oentoro was appointed as the first rector. The university started with only four departments but more have gradually been added since then.

From the very beginning, James referred to the university as the "Universitas Pelita Harapan" (light and hope), a name that comes from the Bible and is a clear indication that this is a Christian university. Bible study is one of the required courses.

Universitas Pelita Harapan gives first place to moral education. Smoking is strictly forbidden on campus, and the university is very rigorous in carrying out drug tests. This is in stark contrast to other universities, which take a very lax approach to moral education. Thanks to James's diligence, the university has made rapid progress and built a reputation for scholastic excellence in just 10 years. Today, it is one of Indonesia's best-known institutes of higher education.

From 1998 to 2002, there were several protests against Universitas Pelita Harapan, during which many newspapers and radio stations attacked the religious component of its education. Several politicians and religious figures who were close to us advised us to abandon our aim of running a Christian university, in order to avoid further criticism from other religious groups.

I was beginning to waver, but to my surprise James stood firm. Such was his resolve. He firmly believed that the Lord's will was correct, that the Lord was with him and that righteousness would win out over intolerance. I was moved by James's unshakeable belief in the Lord, and continued to support him in his stance towards the university. James spent almost all of his time involved in university matters, and it warmed my heart to see that his educational aspirations were even stronger than my own.

Prior to the 1970s, many of Indonesia's eminent doctors and lawyers were of Chinese descent. After President Suharto came to power, however, he introduced an array of policies that outlawed Chinese-language schools and Chinese-language media and discouraged the use of Chinese surnames. These measures had much in common with legislation introduced by autocratic regimes elsewhere.

Although the government did not expressly stipulate it, Universitas Indonesia's School of Medicine and School of Law had stopped admitting ethnic Chinese students. This created a big gap in the country's medical and legal professions, and by the year 2000, only a tiny number of ethnic Chinese doctors and lawyers remained. This is the reason why many wealthy

Indonesians choose to go to Singapore for medical treatment. It was and remains a great loss for Indonesia.

On the other hand, the political situation in Indonesia has continued to progress towards democracy and the rule of law. As a result, law is becoming ever more important. In the fields of medicine and law, there is a pressing need to nurture morally conscientious talent.

In view of this, I personally oversaw the setting up of the Universitas Pelita Harapan School of Law and School of Medicine. After a huge effort, these two schools became a reality, helping to fill this urgent need. Today, a doctorate from the Universitas Pelita Harapan School of Law is a highly regarded qualification. Graduates from our School of Medicine are among the top performers in the National Doctors Association Exam. Alumni from the Universitas Pelita Harapan School of Law and School of Medicine are achieving ever-greater status in mainstream society. One important reason for this is that Universitas Pelita Harapan alumni all have very high moral standards.

When James's eldest son John finished his MBA at the Wharton business school in the US, he was accepted into the Columbia University School of Law where he received his Juris Doctor degree. After returning to Indonesia in 2011, to my delight, he chose to take up a professorship at the Universitas Pelita Harapan School of Law as his primary focus instead of joining the commercial sector. I was overjoyed: he will continue to make my educational aspirations a reality.

SEKOLAH PELITA HARAPAN

"Cultivating perseverance and a good moral character among students."

As previously mentioned, developing Karawaci into a luxury residential complex required building a top-quality hospital and first-rate international primary and middle school.

James named the school Sekolah Pelita Harapan (light and hope). The school was also founded as a Christian institution at which Bible studies were compulsory. Just as at the university, we placed a strong emphasis on morals, forbidding smoking and drugs, and we encouraged the students' all-round development by including sports and music in the curriculum.

The school is bilingual, with lessons conducted in English and Indonesian. To this end, we hired over one hundred American teachers, which provided a teacher-to-student ratio of 1 to 10. The teachers had to be Christians and graduates of American teaching colleges; they all had abundant teaching experience and a strong sense of responsibility. We hired a veteran American educator to be the school's principal, while James's wife, Aileen, filled the position of vice principal and handled public relations and administrative matters.

The school boasts highly competent administrative and financial management, which is one of the reasons why it has grown so quickly. Most of Sekolah Pelita Harapan's students come from well-off families and almost all of them go abroad for university. Thanks to the school's reputation for rigorous educational standards, they are able to get into America's top 50 universities.

Karawaci also has mid-level housing. For these residents, there is Sekolah Dian Harapan (ray of hope) primary and middle school. The curriculum is designed to the same standards as international schools, but lessons are taught exclusively in Indonesian and there are no American teachers. The school's buildings and equipment are far superior to most national schools, and it also has a swimming pool, sports field and library—none of which is available in the country's state schools. Fees are only slightly higher than those of the national schools.

Graduate exam results are also excellent. As we had predicted, the quality education provided by Sekolah Dian Harapan encouraged many families to move to Karawaci. Today, this housing complex has also become a premium residential area and its price per square metre has risen from US$300 to US$3,000. No one has worked harder for these two schools than James, who has assembled the talent needed to run these exceptional schools.

The successful development of Lippo Karawaci became a model that we used in other commercial and residential projects. These include Lippo Group's Cikarang Industrial Park, Tanjung Bunga Village in Makassar, Sentul holiday resort, St. Moritz in the centre of Jakarta (luxury commercial and residential complexes covering a total area of 1.4 million square metres), Kemang Village (another high-end commercial and residential complex in the south of Jakarta covering 1.1 million square metres), Holland Village (located in the centre of the capital and covering 600,000 square metres), and other developments such as the North Sumatra provincial government compound and the Orange County complex, currently being constructed at Cikarang. They all have a Sekolah Pelita Harapan and a Sekolah Dian Harapan, as well as a Siloam Hospital, and, of course, a luxury shopping mall.

Our experience in building and running so many commercially operated primary and middle schools has reaped rich results. Over the course of 20 years, we have helped nurture a number of great talents. Pelita graduates hold important positions and have made vital contributions to Indonesian society. All of my 22 grandchildren are graduates of Sekolah Pelita Harapan and all were accepted into renowned universities in the US. After finishing their studies, they returned to Indonesia and have contributed to this nation's development.

Looking back at the early years of Sekolah Pelita Harapan, I was struck by the school's luxurious facilities: over 20 soundproofed music rooms, an Olympic-size swimming pool, an equestrian centre, beautiful classrooms, and a very pleasant library. All the teaching staff came from the US and the campus had a quiet elegance to it. Someone once told me it was a school that could be described as the Eton College of the East.

My own youth involved great hardship, but it also nurtured in me a work ethic and determination that contributed to my success in later life. I often worried that perhaps the school's' facilities were too good and the surroundings too comfortable. Would this spoil the children, make them too soft to deal with life's challenges?

I frequently reminded James and his wife that they must place a strong emphasis on cultivating perseverance and a good moral character among students, so these students would be able to make their own way in the world. It was only when my grandchildren returned from their studies abroad that I saw how capable and hard-working they were. It was then that I stopped worrying. Sekolah Pelita Harapan is worthy of parents' trust.

After James's success in managing Sekolah Pelita Harapan and Sekolah Dian Harapan, he told me that he wished to open a free school in a remote and underdeveloped part of Indonesia. The school would provide compulsory education to impoverished children and be called Sekolah Lentera Harapan (lantern of hope). I thought it was a wonderful idea.

Opening a school in such an area presented many difficulties, the first of which was finding good teachers. Unable to put up with the conditions there, many people were unwilling to work in these out-of-the-way areas. In the end, our only option was to open a teacher's college in Universitas Pelita Harapan in partnership with an Australian university. The Australian side provided the teaching materials and tutors, and graduates received a diploma from both universities. Students are recruited from under-developed areas, and required to return there to teach for four years after graduation.

Each year, 600 scholarships are provided that cover all fees as well as meals and accommodation. This approach has so far proved very success-ful, and I am confident that it will be able to provide a free, high-quality education for Indonesia's poor.

I have told James that, God willing, we should provide 1,000 Sekolah Lentera Harapan schools in poor regions across Indonesia. This will be the Riady family's social mission, and will help make Indonesia a more prosperous and powerful nation.

CENTRAL MALANG UNIVERSITY AND MALANG MIDDLE SCHOOL ALUMNI ASSOCIATION

" I felt I had repaid my alma mater for everything it had given me. "

Huang Yiping (Oei Yi Pan), who was a prominent member of Malang's Chinese population, set up Ma Chung Middle School (Malang Middle School) following the Japanese invasion in World War II. Its first principal was Wang Shiming, who was later awarded a professorship at a university in the United States. Thanks to the combined efforts of Huang and Wang, Java Middle School had become the best middle school not just in East Java, but the whole of eastern Indonesia within a year.

In 2001, the Ma Chung Middle School Alumni Association met at Xiamen University in China. Approximately 900 alumni arrived in Xiamen from all over the world to attend this reunion. It was a chance to renew friendships that in some cases were from decades ago. There were touching scenes as everybody excitedly chatted about their school days and recalled their beloved alma mater. All of them had one wish: to see Malang Middle School reopen again.

I had been asked by my classmates to address the gathering, and I spoke about Xiamen University founder Tan Kah Kee. Venerated by

Chinese communities all over the world, it was Tan who inspired Huang Yiping to set up Ma Chung Middle School. I said that today, we should ensure that we pass on Huang's educational spirit to future generations. We should not just reopen the school, but should also set up a university in Malang to commemorate Huang's achievements.

The audience met my proposal with cheers of approval. There and then, we elected several alumni to a committee tasked with setting up the university. I was named head of the committee that would take charge of this important task on behalf of the Ma Chung Middle School Alumni Association.

Major cities all over Indonesia have their own Chinese schools, and there are also many alumni associations. Most of them are beset by conflicts of interest, some of which are so bitter they end up in court. I observed that in many cases the biggest problems came from those who had contributed the least. They often had unreasonable expectations of how schools should be run.

Many years ago, the Ma Chung Middle School Alumni Association had raised money from its members, and the funds had since increased to approximately US$500,000 through the purchase and sale of land. There had been no end of disagreements about how to use this money, and things only got worse once it became clear we were about to open a university. Decisions had to be made about who would be responsible for managing the project, and it was a very frustrating situation. Before long, four alumni from Surabaya, including businessman Huang Qizhu, came to see me to ask for my views about Universitas Ma Chung (Central Malang University).

First, I reminded the alumni of a fundamental question faced by Chinese Indonesians: would we ultimately return to China, like a leaf that falls to the base of a tree, or did we plan to set down roots in Indonesia? My opinion was that since we were Indonesian nationals we should set down roots here. As a result, Universitas Ma Chung should be an institution that nurtured Indonesian culture, and it should become a melting pot that was part of the great family of the Indonesian people.

With regard to teaching Chinese language and culture, this was no different from the principle behind learning English: we were living in the age of China, and it was vital that people learn about it. It was not being taught because we ultimately wanted to return to China. Universitas Ma Chung should devote itself to becoming a cultural melting pot as this was one of the great premises and principles of education. I hoped everyone would agree with my views.

Second, I suggested abandoning the usual approach of setting up a university directly through the alumni association. Instead, the alumni should establish a joint venture company that would be responsible for setting up the university. Everything would be carried out according to well-established company procedures; furthermore, we would agree that this company's sole task would be to set up the university, and it would not engage in any other commercial activities. This would get the university in operation quickly and avoid disputes.

Third, the budget for setting up the university should be approximately US$13 million. A sponsor would be responsible for providing half of these funds, and the remainder would be raised through donations. The funds had to be put in place first—otherwise the project would never get off the ground.

Fourth, the school's rector had to be someone with a doctorate degree. The individual also had to be tolerant, open-minded and willing to learn.

Fifth, someone dependable had to be entrusted with recruiting the rector.

Huang Qizhu was very much in agreement with my proposals, and committed to providing half of the costs needed to set up the school. He also suggested that I serve as chairman of the School Building Committee, and be responsible for recruiting the rector and other teaching staff. I agreed, and we got to work.

Setting up the university proved to be a lot more troublesome than establishing Universitas Pelita Harapan. I had to spend a lot of time sorting out trifling problems in which emotions often took precedence over the actual matters at hand. However, thanks to Huang's integrity and selflessness, as well as his complete trust in me, things still went fairly smoothly.

To give an example, Huang had already selected two plots of land for the university: one in the southeast of Malang and another in the southwest. He very politely insisted that I decide which one we use. I chose the southwestern plot, the reason being that it was near the city's wealthy district and boasted beautiful scenery. It had great prospects.

I hired Dr. Leenawaty Limantara, then vice director of the Mochtar Riady Institute for Nanotechnology, to be the university's first rector, and personally discussed the curriculum, administrative management and selection of teachers with her. Before she took up the position, we arranged for her to spend a month working at Universitas Pelita Harapan, where her work was widely praised by the faculty staff. Later on, with support from Huang and myself, she set up a botanical institute at Universitas Ma Chung, and it has since won praise for its research.

After approximately three years, construction of the university was completed and classes began. My responsibilities had come to an end, and I felt I had repaid my alma mater for everything it had given me. Universitas Ma Chung was very quickly recognised and accepted by the public, much to the satisfaction, I am sure, of the Malang Middle School Alumni.

CHAPTER ELEVEN

FAMILY
IS OUR FUTURE

" Love is at the heart of our family and the foundation of our business. "

A t this point, we reach the end of the fourth period of my story. The greater part of Lippo Group's business had been conducted in Indonesia, which is where I have lived and focused my attention for so many years. Apart from two years in Hong Kong, from 1984–1986, helping Stephen set up a company, the rest of my time had been spent living together with my wife and son James in my homeland. From 1991 onwards, I left almost all of Lippo Group's Indonesia operations in James's hands; as such, the accomplishments of Lippo Group described in this book are as much his story as my own.

In 1991, I parted ways with Sudono in order to concentrate on building up my own business. This was the year of Lippo Group's shift from finance to the development of land resources and its subsequent involvement in medicine, education, retailing, and telecommunications.

In all these businesses we started from nothing, and we launched them all at the same time. It was very challenging, but I had faith in the philosophy of Lao Tzu: "A tree as wide as a man's embrace springs from a small shoot. Meet the difficult while it is easy. Meet the big while it is small." After many years of hard work, Lippo Group is among the largest corporations in Indonesia. Being has truly been born out of non-being; small has grown to become large.

On one occasion, I was invited to give a speech at the National University of Singapore, and a member of the audience posed the following question: "Universities teach that a company can only be successful if it is very concentrated on its efforts; Lippo Group's operations are extremely diversified, and cover a number of different sectors, yet every one of its divisions has been successful. What is the secret of its success?"

I replied that the secret of our success is: "I know I do not know". When you are aware that you do not know something you must humbly seek out someone who does. You must be willing to turn over the operations to someone who thoroughly understands the business.

To give an example, I knew that I did not understand supermarket chains—nor could I even pretend to—yet I found myself operating just such a business. The correct approach was to invite an expert in running supermarkets to be in charge, so I hired a competitor's CEO. Thanks to his professionalism and dedication, Lippo Group's supermarket chain grew very quickly. In essence, there is no contradiction between being diversified yet concentrated in your efforts.

When it comes to recruiting talent, James and Stephen are masters at networking and putting together teams of skilled people. They are also experts at analysing business and financial issues. The depth and accuracy of their analysis make it easy for us to spot problem areas and address them. The combination of the right remedial measures and strong execution is what has given Lippo Group such dynamism.

While presiding over the company's expansion, James has also made good use of data, and this has allowed him to quickly see to the core of complex issues. After the importance of data became clear to me, I began to place a stronger emphasis on gaining accurate and comprehensive information on our businesses. I advocated the use of standardised workflows to direct every member of staff in their work, and the use of computers to record every transaction accurately. This has made it easier to provide reliable and highly detailed data for use in decision-making.

James is also good at quickly identifying weak points in our operations and rectifying them. He can also be very stern in reproving colleagues who don't pull their weight. This has made Lippo Group into the success it is today.

Meanwhile, Stephen has worked alongside James in directing the educational initiatives that I care so much about. He has provided the funds for creating the National University of Singapore Business School's Mochtar Riady Building, donated the Mochtar Riady Auditorium at the Singapore Management University Administration Building, and sponsored the construction of the Mochtar Riady Building at Hong Kong Baptist University. Stephen strongly believes in giving back to society and insists that we give priority to fulfilling our corporate social responsibilities. These are qualities that fill me with admiration.

James and Stephen understand my overall philosophy, and have a profound grasp of my "nanotechnological" approach to business management. They are both adept at bringing out the best in those who work for them—and the teams they have assembled are very good indeed.

My sons are also both very devout: they obey the Word of God and are faithful in their service to the Lord. The Bible tells us that reverence of God is the source of all wisdom, and the two of them have gained much enlightenment from their diligent study of the Bible. All of us love our family, and as the saying goes: "If a family lives in harmony, all affairs will prosper." Love is at the heart of our family and the foundation of our business.

The ancients said: "A contented person is happy with what he has." The next generation of my family is both capable and hard-working, and I am very content.

MY CHILDREN ARE
STRONGER THAN ME

" Making mistakes is far better than never having the courage to try. "

L ike all parents, I hope that my children will be even more successful than me, and so by the age of 60, I had already begun planning how to hand the company over to them. My oldest son, Andrew, wanted to go his own way. I respected his decision to set up his own business independent of the family firm. James and Stephen would head Lippo Group instead.

Many years ago, I watched on television how eagles teach their young to fly. They pick them up, hoist them into the air, and then let go. The young have no choice but to attempt to fly, and just as they are about to hit the ground, the adult eagle will swoop down and grab them again. Over and over, the young will fail, but the eagle will keep repeating the process until the young have finally learned to fly on their own. This was a real inspiration to me.

In teaching your children to make their own way in business, you have to be brave enough to let them learn from their failures. Instead of trying to tell them what to do, you should let them gain their own experience. Making mistakes is far better than never having the courage to try. Failure is indeed the mother of success.

Several sections of this book—"Indonesia and the 1997-1998 Asian Financial Crisis", "Land is a Resource and a Raw Material", "Business Clusters Derived from Land Resources", "Hospitals are for the Public Good But They are also Businesses" and "Universitas Pelita Harapan"—are also James's story.

Particularly when it came to dealing with the myriad problems caused by the Asian financial crisis, I deliberately stood to one side and let James address these daunting challenges on his own. I believed that it would be a once-in-a-lifetime learning opportunity for him. Only under such conditions would he learn real skills in the face of adversity. At the time, if I had stepped in and taken over, he would have been denied these valuable lessons.

From the challenges he faced dealing with various business partners, Stephen also learned the treacherous side of business. He learned to be tenacious and persistent. From setting up a new company, he also learned about recruiting talent, putting together teams of people who could work together to a common purpose and weeding out people who were not right for those tasks.

These challenges have made James and Stephen more mature, and I am delighted at how they have excelled themselves.

So what gives me the greatest pride and satisfaction? There is no right answer to that, but one very straightforward reply springs to mind: if each of my children can run a business or a household, and if they can teach their children to do the same, and if they are all children who love and respect God, then nothing would give me greater pride and satisfaction. It is that simple, and I am very fortunate that my three sons and three daughters have achieved this.

Andrew's oldest son is Michael. After he graduated, I placed him under James's tutelage. James is very good with young people and has been happy to take them under his wing. After 10 years of learning from James, today Michael knows the business of running shopping malls inside and out. It is a surprisingly diverse business that requires instinct and experience in selecting locations, a knack for determining building design, colour schemes and market positioning, and skill in attracting tenants. It also requires a knowledge of rental procedures, staff training, advertising, financial management and budget formulation. Having mastered all of these aspects of the business, he is now able to get new shopping malls up and running in just one year—a very brief period for this kind of complex project. Moreover, he has become adept at negotiating the financing of these projects with investment funds.

Andrew's second son is Howard. After graduating from college, he went straight to the University of Chicago for a doctorate degree in economics. He is in love with academia and his ambition is to be a research professor. I feel fortunate to have a grandson like Howard who is so dedicated to the pursuit of knowledge.

James's eldest son is John. He has done very well in his studies. After graduating as a Palmer Scholar from Wharton School of Business, he was accepted into the Columbia University Law School, where he gained top marks and was awarded a Juris Doctor degree. After returning to Indonesia, his choice for his first appointment was as a professor of law at Universitas Pelita Harapan. I am delighted that he is so passionate about education and the people of Indonesia. He is also very talented at business and politics and is destined for great things.

James's second son Henry is the most eccentric of all of them. He gained a master's degree in communication management in the minimum time necessary at the University of Southern California. Henry is a great people person, and got on extremely well with tutors and fellow students. After completing his studies, he chose to work in the media industry and there he is thriving.

Stephen's son Brian returned to Indonesia after taking a year-and-a-half apprenticeship at an investment bank in New York following graduation. I also arranged for him to be taken under James's wing, so that he could develop our cinema business from scratch. Indonesia's cinema chains have a long history in the business and enjoy a practical monopoly over showing films. Breaking into this market was no easy task, yet Brian found a solution and has quickly expanded our cinema division. He has a special knack for film selection as well as cinema design, evaluating equipment and putting a network of talented people in place. The business is already benefiting from his significant contributions.

STEPHEN CHOOSES SINGAPORE AS A BASE FOR DEVELOPMENT

" I am confident he has made the right choice. "

T he 1997–1998 Asian financial crisis wreaked havoc on the economies of Indonesia and South Korea. The two countries' currencies depreciated by almost 80 per cent, interest rates shot up, and credit was in short supply. There was a fire sale on stock and the price of goods plummeted. Unable to bear the high interest rates on loans, companies went bankrupt one after the other—quickly followed by their banks.

During this time, only Hong Kong and Singapore stood firm, which was a testament to their strengths. The real estate industries of these two markets, however, were badly shaken and property prices dropped by almost half. Hong Kong's real estate proved more resilient than Singapore's due to the fact that the 10 largest firms held a tight grip on the industry. They were financially strong and had little debt. As a result, by the year 2000, Hong Kong real estate had already recovered.

This financial crisis had exposed the near-monopoly characteristics of the real estate and financial industries in Hong Kong. Stephen concluded that breaking into the market would be difficult, and there was little room for growth. He saw that Singapore's real estate industry was more diffuse, which would allow new companies entering the market more room to grow. In addition, Stephen cared a lot about his children's education, and he felt that Singapore provided a stronger educational environment. For the sake of his children's future, he moved his family to Singapore in 2000.

James also cared a lot about his children's education, and he devoted much of his time to setting up Sekolah Pelita Harapan so that he could look after their schooling. I am delighted that my children value education so highly, as this is the basis of a family's long-lasting prosperity.

After Stephen graduated from the University of Southern California in 1984, I arranged a three-month apprenticeship for him at Citibank in New York. Following this, he spent a further three months at Standard Chartered in Hong Kong. The year 1984 also happened to be when I bought Hongkong Chinese Bank (HKCB), which was a rare opportunity for Stephen. He was involved in the acquisition of a bank in the financial heart of Asia and learned from the dealings with the Overseas Trust Bank (the former owner of the bank). He also played a role in reorganising HKCB's workflows and mapping out a new business development strategy. In addition, he learned how to formulate budgets, select locations for new branches and choose the right customers. He helped increase the bank's deposits— from HK$300 million to HK$4 billion—in just two years and can be proud of his achievements in turning a money-losing bank into a profitable one.

More importantly, he experienced first-hand how local regulatory authorities discriminated against banks with ties to Indonesia. For example, the capital adequacy ratio (CAR) for most banks in Hong Kong was 8 per cent, but for HKCB this figure was 12 per cent. That was in addition to even stricter rules on lending. As I mention elsewhere in this book, we sold a 50 per cent share of the bank to China Resources Group, the largest mainland Chinese enterprise in Hong Kong. This move was aimed at overcoming discrimination as well as improving HKCB's reputation among Hong Kong residents.

Stephen was involved throughout the entire process of this stake sale. In so doing, he worked with his counterparts at China Resources Group, built a consensus and coordinated efforts to ensure the growth of HKCB. He gained the trust of the chairperson of China Resources Group, Zhu Youlan, and also played a role in our dealings with the famed chairman of the Cheung Kong Group, Li Ka-shing.

More importantly, in Hong Kong he had experienced the rule of law and the way market economies worked. I was reassured to see how he showed increasing maturity through his ability to analyse Hong Kong's economic structure. In the year 2000, when Stephen decided to move his family to Singapore as a result of what he had learned over 15 years in Hong Kong, I was confident that he had made the right choice.

OUR STORY IN SINGAPORE

"Learning from setbacks"

After Stephen and his family moved to Singapore, I gave him time to settle in and then tasked him with managing a listed company. He spent three years familiarising himself with Singapore, and in 2004 he told me: "Movement is life and staying still is death; making the wrong move, furthermore, is better than doing nothing."

In 2004, Stephen took part in a public tender for some land that was being sold into the market. He lost and he lost badly. His bid was almost 70 per cent lower than the winner's. This was his first taste of defeat. Where had we gone wrong in our analysis? We learned some lessons about the pricing and use of land in our profit estimations. When another piece of land was auctioned soon after, Stephen was already more adroit in his calculations. He was unsuccessful once again but this time his bid was just a few percentage points off the winning price. Several months later, there was another land auction, and this time Stephen's tender was successful. After consulting several architectural firms about building proposals, room layout, quality positioning, price positioning, and other key issues, Stephen decided we would position ourselves as a premium land developer. He set out to establish the Lippo brand in Singapore, working hard in this pursuit. Success followed in short order. He went on to construct seven more building complexes that made Lippo Group a well-known real estate developer in Singapore.

Property owners and estate agents came from far and wide offering to sell Stephen their real estate. Stephen believed that Singapore's real estate industry was still in hibernation, and that land prices had yet to return to pre-1998 levels; as such, we had to make the most of the opportunity. At the time, an office building at 78 Shenton Way had caught my eye, and after negotiations, we purchased it at the price of S$500 per square foot.

In 2005, Stephen took an interest in another office building in the city's financial district at 79 Anson Road, which we bought for S$90 million. In 2006, as we concentrated our resources on acquiring Overseas Union Enterprise Limited, we sold 79 Anson Road for S$230 million and 78 Shenton Way for S$1,300 per square foot.

Incidentally, we made another very interesting real estate deal in 2000, the year we decided to relocate Lippo Group's overseas headquarters to Singapore. As luck would have it, there was a building at 1 Phillip Street that was being rebuilt and was just the modest size we needed. We bought it for S$30 million. Having acquired 78 Shenton Way, we sold the Phillip Street building for S$90 million. Soon after, the buyer sold it back to us for S$33 million, and two years later, we sold it again for S$99 million!

Stephen had established a firm base for further growth in Singapore.

OUR MOST IMPORTANT MILESTONE: BUYING OVERSEAS UNION ENTERPRISE LIMITED

"This was the biggest acquisition of my life."

In 2004, financial regulators in Singapore decreed that banks in Singapore had to separate their financial and non-financial operations as part of Singapore's ongoing reforms to strengthen the domestic banking sector. As a result, United Overseas Bank (UOB) was required to divest its shareholdings in the real estate entity, Overseas Union Enterprise Limited (OUE). UOB and OUE were both listed companies in Singapore, which meant they were subject to different regulatory mechanisms. The sale had to be conducted via a designated bank through an auction.

At that time, OUE owned two Mandarin Hotels in Singapore, a landmark 60-storey office building—the tallest in the city—as well as a plot of land by the waterfront that had been earmarked for commercial use. In China, it owned two Mandarin Hotels, one in Shantou and one in Hainan Island's capital Haikou, and was also a shareholder in Shanghai's JC Mandarin Hotel, which it managed.

It was an arduous process, but in the end, we were successful in our bid for OUE, paying US$1.6 billion. This was the biggest acquisition of my life. It was an example of "a snake swallowing an elephant", and was instrumental in our successful growth in Singapore. Despite encountering many obstacles along the way, Stephen proved to be patient, modest and resilient. He was able to adapt to changing circumstances and emerged stronger and considerably more experienced.

MEASURES TO INCREASE OUE'S MARKET VALUE

"The biggest weak point of any company is waste."

The biggest weak point of any company is waste. Waste refers to many things, but the greatest waste of all is using a valuable location for a purpose that has no value. The focus of business reform plans and development plans is either how to enhance the way land is used in order to increase income and value, or how to transform a low-output business into a high-value one.

After taking over OUE, we noted that Singapore's Mandarin Hotel was open on three sides, one of which faced onto Orchard Road. Orchard Road is one of Singapore's busiest streets, and home to most of the city's luxury shopping malls. If we relocated the entrance of the Mandarin Hotel to its right-hand side and moved its lobby and hotel to the fifth floor, we could transform the first four floors into a luxury shopping mall that would significantly boost income. The first four floors could be spun off as an independent company with an extremely high property value. Annual rent for the shopping mall could be up to S$40 million, and as an asset, the shopping mall would be worth as much as S$1 billion. This would be the first step in reforming OUE.

The second initiative we carried out was to add three storeys to One Raffles Place (formerly OUB Centre), which was then Singapore's tallest building. The uppermost floor would be transformed into a rooftop restaurant, where guests could look out over the entire city as they dined. It would be a popular tourist destination.

The third initiative was to transform the former Overseas Union House, which housed a car park, into a high-end office tower that was renamed the OUE Bayfront.

Thanks to these initiatives, OUE's earnings increased from around S$30 million in 2009 to almost S$1 billion in 2014. From an original market price of approximately S$1 billion in 2006, today OUE is worth over S$4 billion. We have completely changed the face of OUE.

A SKYSCRAPER IN LOS ANGELES

"
Lippo Group was now a fully international company. "

In 2008, the subprime mortgage crisis in the US created financial turmoil across the globe. In addition to causing great damage to America's financial industry, the crisis also had a huge impact on the US real estate market. Property prices slumped and transactions came to a halt. Even six years later in 2014, the market had yet to fully recover. We saw this as an opportunity, and began preparing to break into the US real estate market.

Our chance came in early summer 2014, when the landmark 72-storey US Bank Tower in the centre of Los Angeles was put up for sale at the price of US$300 per square foot. After hard negotiations, we purchased it for US$257 per square foot. Beside it was a four-storey building that we had also planned to buy, but we had taken a step-by-step approach. To our surprise, by the time we were ready to move it had already been purchased by someone else. We were disappointed but this suggested to us the real estate market in the US had already started to recover. We were fortunate to have been able to break into the US market and acquire a landmark building when we did.

At that point, we had landmark buildings in Singapore, Hong Kong, Shanghai and Los Angeles. This showed that Lippo Group was a fully international company. I also hoped to ultimately own a landmark building in Jakarta, which would show that we were entering a new century centred on the Pacific Basin.

Incidentally, Lippo Group's success can be attributed to both skill and luck. It has to be said that our purchase of the two buildings in Singapore's financial district that had previously belonged to DBS Bank were due to Stephen's good fortune and keen business sense. He had been able to purchase these buildings for less than S$1,000 per square foot at a time when the market price was generally S$1,300.

Today, we have begun renovating the first three floors of these two buildings into shopping malls. I firmly believe that once these renovations are complete, they will become a new model for shopping malls and office buildings that will prove very popular with the public.

LIMEI: A GOOD WIFE AND A LOVING MOTHER

" I am fortunate to have such a great companion. "

Limei is the heart of our family, and a very virtuous one at that.

While I was still working in banking, a customer once gave me a very precious gift: four gold bars. I had never seen a gold bar with my own eyes, and returned home with them in a state of great excitement. After laying eyes on the gold bars, Limei cross-examined me about where they had come from. Having found out they were a gift from a customer, she very sternly warned me that I had to take them back—the reason being that if I accepted such an expensive gift, it would leave me in my customer's debt; it was like selling my freedom for riches. Limei's warning reminded me of my father who, when I was a child, had told me not to accept gifts from others because that would become a debt that would have to be repaid. I accepted Limei's advice and immediately returned the gold bars.

Limei has always kept an eye on my morality and integrity, and frequently reminds me that she wishes me to be honest and upstanding.

Limei has inspired all of us to keep improving ourselves. At the age of 50, she went to the US on her own to complete a degree in sociology at the University of Southern California. After that, she was tenacious in making sure our sons-in-law, Dr. Tahir and Jeffrey Wonsono, and our sons Andrew and Stephen, finished their master's degrees.

In May 1999, she singlehandedly took a group of 13 children – which included a few of our grandchildren and the children of family friends, to summer school at Shanghai's East China Normal University. The following year she arranged a similar kind of summer program at Peking University. She and the children lived in university dormitories so that they could experience living in such close proximity to so many others. At home, she insisted that our grandchildren practise writing Chinese characters before going to bed. Before that they had other chores such as helping her sweep the road in front of our house.

She also kept a close eye on their personal appearance and behaviour: they were not allowed any outrageous hairstyles; their clothes had to be simple and unostentatious; they had to lead calm and tranquil lives. They were expected to be gracious and forgiving, humble and hard-working as well as diligent when it came to their education. They were expected to abstain from anything indecent or improper.

Limei is a woman of patience and perseverance. At the smallest hint that our grandchildren were going astray, she would insist they mend their ways. She wouldn't rest until she had worn them down and reached the desired result.

Limei has always said that tranquility is good for the soul and thrift is good for one's moral character. In this, she has set an example by leading a very peaceful and serene life. She believes that "a wife should treasure her husband and take glory in her sons," and has never wanted anything more than to be a good wife and loving mother. I am fortunate to have such a great companion.

My eldest daughter is Rosy. After giving birth to three daughters, she had given up hope of having any more children. But Limei was a firm believer in the old Chinese saying that "there are three types of unfilial conduct, and the worst of them is having no (male) descendants." She felt that Rosy should not give up on this important task. She kept urging her to persist, and took her and her husband to doctors in Singapore and Tokyo. In the end, the Heavenly Father blessed Rosy with a son. I suggested the name of Dachuan. He is bright, studious and capable, and will be a worthy successor to his father's business. I am very happy for Rosy's family, and very proud of the achievements of her husband Dr. Tahir. I am even prouder of the efforts that Limei has made towards our offspring.

My second daughter, Lanny, married Cai Huangde and has two sons by him. Huangde runs a shopping mall real estate business, while their eldest son, Youhui, operates a zirconium mine. Youhui is very competent and hard-working. Their second son, Youbang, runs an investment fund that he has built up from humble beginnings. Their two daughters are also very capable, and they all have chosen careers they enjoy.

My youngest daughter, Li Ming, is married to Huang Chaolong and they have two sons. Chaolong is a very determined man who runs a coconut processing business. Every part of the coconut is valuable, he likes to say. Nothing is wasted. He has worked very hard at his business and great success lies ahead.

THE FIFTH PERIOD
2011–PRESENT

CHAPTER TWELVE

BECOMING A ROLE MODEL FOR MY CHILDREN AND GRANDCHILDREN

"
China is already becoming the Asia-Pacific region's leading power, and the 21st century will be its century. "

The fourth period, 1991–2010, covers the era of a shift in economic power from the Atlantic to the Pacific Basin. I talked about the "Chinese century", and summarised by saying that given China's vast population, the people's keen desire for reform, and the strong Chinese work ethic, the next 10 years would see the rise of China. I predict that it will be a rise that produces positive effects. China is already becoming the Asia-Pacific region's leading power, and the 21st century will be its century.

In 2008, CNN host and Newsweek editor Fareed Zakaria published a book called *The Post-American World* in which he said that the rise of China would create a "post-American" world. Later, in 2013, the director of the National University of Singapore's School of Public Policy, Professor

Kishore Mahbubani, published *The Great Convergence*, in which he described the fundamental changes brought about in economic globalisation as a result of China's entry into the World Trade Organisation. China's performance during the 2008 economic crisis presaged a shift in the world's economic might. The paradox of the trends of globalisation and the regional interests of each country will be the primary problem of the 21st century. Professor Mahbubani believes that the world is already one integrated whole, and that countries all over the world—whether they are in the East or West—can only survive on this planet if they achieve agreement and integration based upon a broader ideological foundation.

Today, everyone can see how, in just 30 years, China has developed. It has constructed high-speed railways, highways, modern airports, power plants and other facilities that are among the best in the world. China's aerospace technology, laser technology, nanotechnology, military technology and deep-sea marine technology are all closing in on those of the US, and the country is already a world leader in certain spheres of technology. This is the reality of the "China factor".

The China factor has already brought about fundamental changes in the geopolitics of the Pacific region. When President Xi Jinping bluntly told President Barack Obama that the Pacific is big enough for both China and the United States, it was evidence of the contest between China and the US, and of the strategic importance of this region.

Now, as I relate the fifth period of my life, I will write about my hopes rather than my experiences, for I do not know how much time I have left on earth. In fact, all I have is hope: I hope to see my grandchildren contribute to the rise of Indonesia; I hope that when China and the US discuss matters in the Pacific, they will invite the President of Indonesia to take part; and I hope to soon see the rise of Indonesia.

THE RISE OF INDONESIA

" If we are to make the most of these advantages, we must first understand our shortcomings. "

I ndonesia sits midway down the Pacific at the confluence of the Indian Ocean and the Pacific Ocean. Its geographic position has high military value, and the country is also a trading hub between the two oceans. Indonesians must position themselves as the defenders of peace and as a force that can help stop war. During the post-American age and the redistribution of the world's wealth, how can Indonesians establish a foothold and create our own opportunities? This era of change will see many crises, but there will also be limitless opportunities hidden within. I am confident that this period will also see the rise of the Indonesian people.

In addition to the strategic significance of its location, Indonesia enjoys almost inexhaustible marine resources. It is a global shipping hub and a centre for the repair and resupply of commercial vessels. If we take this a step further, we could become a global shipbuilding centre. Indonesians must have the boldness to establish a place for ourselves in the world.

Today, the world's developed economies are facing the burdens of an ageing population and the cost of caring for the growing ranks of their elderly citizens. Indonesia, however, enjoys abundant labour resources and a young population. A romanised writing system and a simple, straightforward language are great benefits in providing universal education.

Combined with universal middle school vocational education, this can be a great help in developing the economy.

Indonesia also has a great deal of arable land. I believe that together with the land's fertility, plentiful supply of water, as well as the country's favourable climate and ample labour resources, there is no better place to develop agriculture and forestry. We should position ourselves as the granary of Asia and a base for forestry and livestock. These are the prerequisites if we are to become a prosperous and powerful nation.

Indonesia is also home to much of Asia's mining industry, and every effort should be made to develop industries specialising in the mid- and downstream products of this sector in order to add greater value to the ore that is extracted. This will be another key factor in Indonesia's future.

Indonesia possesses strategic geographic advantages that can be used to support the development of infrastructure; a marine economy; an agricultural, forestry and livestock economy; a mining economy; a travel economy and a medical tourism economy.

At the beginning of China's reforms, Deng Xiaoping uttered his famous saying that it was "glorious" to become rich. One of his lesser-known observations was that in order to become rich, a nation needs to build roads. These "roads" were another way of saying basic infrastructure. Likewise, if Indonesia is to prosper, it must first build up its infrastructure. As it happens, the underdeveloped state of our infrastructure is a solution to the overcapacity in China's own basic industries—Indonesia can take advantage of China's excess building capacity to modernise at low cost. The two countries complement each other to a high degree, and this is something we should capitalise on.

I have just outlined Indonesia's advantages, but if we are to make the most of these advantages, we must first understand our shortcomings. These shortcomings are, without doubt, an obstacle to Indonesia's prosperity and must be overcome if we are to reach our full potential.

Today, Indonesia has three major weak points:

- A budget deficit, which has led to a deficit in the treasury
- A trade deficit, which has led to an imbalance in the values in our markets
- A high-cost economy, which has made us uncompetitive and has hindered economic growth.

There are various reasons for these shortcomings.

Three things have caused the budget deficit:

- Irrationally set budgets (reflecting waste and corruption)
- Overspending (due to corruption in purchasing)
- Energy subsidies of the past.

There are three causes of the trade deficit:

- The raw materials that Indonesia exports lack added value.
- The industrial materials that are imported have already been processed and thus have a high cost, meaning the value of imports is higher than that of exports.
- Oil subsidies of the past have encouraged waste and increased oil imports.

There are three reasons for the high-cost economy:

- Basic infrastructure is incomplete, meaning that logistics costs are high.
- Upstream raw materials are imported, which means the costs of downstream industries are high.

- The government's administrative efficiency is poor, which adds high hidden costs.

All this can be rectified if we take the following steps:

- First, when the supply of oil is stable, the price of goods is stable, the currency is stable and the political situation is stable. With oil prices at low levels, our subsidies have disappeared. If prices rise, subsidies should not be reinstated. Money saved should be used to construct basic infrastructure and thus reduce logistics costs.
- Second, the money saved from the end to oil subsidies should be combined with foreign investment to immediately build a ferronickel industry and other building material industries to support infrastructure construction.
- Third, politicians should be encouraged to pass laws enabling the procurement of land for use in the construction of basic infrastructure.
- Fourth, manufacturing plants should be set up to process primary raw materials.
- Fifth, efforts should be devoted to expanding Indonesia's marine resource industry.
- Sixth, a team should be put together to rewrite the state's administrative workflows, from top to bottom, from the most minor position to the most important.

Workflows should be introduced to every work post in order to standardise administrative work, improve efficiency and eradicate corruption. Workflows should also be used to establish a budget for each position, which will help prevent losses and make Indonesia more prosperous.

THE FORMATION OF THE INDONESIAN MIDDLE CLASS

" Department stores and supermarkets were flourishing. *"*

T he 1997–1998 Asian financial crisis inflicted catastrophic damage on many industries in Indonesia, but after six years of hard struggle, the economy began to recover. By 2010, land prices in Jakarta's financial district were 10 times higher than in 1998. We owned three building complexes in the centre of the city, each covering an area of approximately one million square metres, and each building was snapped up as soon as it went on sale.

Evidently, the Indonesian people's purchasing power was rocketing. Every major shopping mall was packed with people, and restaurants were full. Lippo's Sun Plaza department stores and Hypermart supermarkets were flourishing and we were opening 25 new stores per year. In 2012, automobile sales in Indonesia exceeded one million vehicles, and the country's highway network, despite its rapid expansion, has since been unable to keep up with the number of new cars on the road.

The agricultural, forestry and mining industries of each Indonesian island are doing very well. Though more inter-island air services are added every month, the flights between islands are fully booked. New buildings are also sprouting up all over the country. These thriving scenes speak of the rise of Indonesia's middle class, which has been accompanied by a boom in the service sector.

The Lippo Group has focused on businesses in this growth area. They include shopping-related real estate, office real estate, housing, leisure real estate, and medical real estate, as well as associated industries such as retail, education, hospitals, health insurance, life insurance, finance, telecommunications, TV (cable, terrestrial and satellite), and online shopping.

Broadly speaking, we have two main businesses: the development of land resources and the development of IT networks in addition to the business clusters derived from them. I am confident that Lippo Group will stand by these two main businesses and continue to expand them.

THE LONG-TERM PROSPERITY OF A FAMILY FIRM

"Identities. . .come with responsibilities"

I n China there is a saying that "a family's wealth stops at the third generation". There are, of course, some exceptions to this Chinese view of the impermanence of family wealth and power. The House of Medici, the standard-bearer of the Renaissance, lasted for several centuries and the Rothschild family has enjoyed wealth for many generations and continues to prosper. Many large Japanese trading houses are also family firms that are still a dominant force in the country's economy.

So why is it said in China that "a family's wealth stops at the third generation"? I believe the wisdom, abilities and personalities of the next generation of a family are given to them at birth, and cannot be fashioned according to one's own desires. After three generations, a family becomes an extremely complex entity, one in which there are disparate characters and everyone has their own preferences and intentions. It becomes very difficult to unify.

Much can, however, be learned from Japan's family trading houses. These family firms separate ownership rights and management rights, with companies taken public so that they become autonomous legal entities that are independent from the family. Only the most capable and intelligent family members are allowed to participate in managing these companies, and as this pattern is repeated down the generations, the trading houses achieve long-lasting success.

For a company to thrive from generation to generation, it must be exceptional. In this, the strengths and weaknesses of national enterprises are intimately connected to the rise and fall of a country. A government's coffers are filled by the taxes paid by the nation's companies; the more companies there are, and the more profitable they are, the greater a country's tax revenue. The more wealth in the national treasury, the more a country can provide for its people's welfare and put basic infrastructure in place.

To put it another way, the government is analogous to a special shareholder in all the companies in the country. It shares in the profits without making any investment, and if there are losses, it accepts no responsibility. As a result, it is the responsibility of business owners to ensure their companies are viable over the longer term.

How should one handle the relationship between a company and the family so that there is a separation of ownership and management but each is also present in the other? How should one give a company the right level of independence from the family? How should one nurture the next generation of management into one in which there is both a high level of ability and continuity? This is the responsibility of the first generation of business owners.

With regard to the separation of ownership and management rights of family firms, the Japanese and US models are entirely different. If the Japanese trading houses are publicly listed, their management will be promoted from within following a rigorous process of assessment and elimination. As such, there is a strong emphasis on long-term strategic objectives.

Publicly listed companies in the US, meanwhile, are directed by a large body of shareholders who stress returns on their investments. They are simultaneously concerned with the real and the imaginary, and are often short-sighted, seeking profits by any means. This places a tremendous amount of pressure on management, which has to be flexible and ready to make frequent tactical shifts. Such companies are highly competitive and innovative, but they often ignore their long-term interests.

Each of the management models described above has its pros and cons. In each, there are things to be emulated and others to be avoided. My observations tell me that we should adopt the organisational structure of a Japanese trading house, but also incorporate an American approach to talent in which we seek out the best at all times to help drive innovation. This should be the way Lippo Group is run: we should constantly nurture new talent.

Earlier, I mentioned my fascination with a television programme about eagles teaching their young to fly. It was a great inspiration for me. I tried the same approach with James and Stephen, forcing them to fly at an early age. They endured many failures, but from this, they gained experience, and their success today is the product of those failures. I hope that everyone at Lippo will give the next generation the chance to fail while learning to fly. This is the Lippo model.

I have mentioned the responsibilities of a company several times, but have said nothing of how they are connected to a person's identity. Every person has several identities, and the number of identities increases as you get older.

For example, when I was born, I had only one identity: I was my father's son. The following year, when my mother gave birth to a daughter, I gained another identity: I was both a son and brother. Before long I began school, where I gained another identity as the teacher's student. When I graduated I became an alumnus of the school, and when I started work I became the employee of a company, and a subordinate of my supervisor. After getting married another identity was added: I was someone's husband. Not long after, we had a child and I assumed a new identity as a father. When my son had a child, I became a grandfather, and now I am a grandfather many times over. I am also the chairman of many companies, the head of the board of trustees of many universities, and, more importantly, I am a citizen of the Republic of Indonesia.

However, many people overlook the importance of their identity. Even worse, they do not know what responsibilities are a part of their identities.

Identities come with a certain amount of authority, but they also come with responsibilities. As a child, you must do well by your parents; as a parent, you take responsibility for the education of your children and you must make sure they too have the necessary preparation to become good parents. If this is passed on from one generation to the next, a family will prosper. When the whole country is made up of good fathers, good sons, good mothers and good daughters, then the country and its people will thrive.

I turned 87 this year and my hope is that I can set a good example for my grandchildren and say that I contributed to the betterment of Indonesia.

MOCHTAR RIADY'S
LIFE JOURNEY

I t is a blessing to reach the age of 87; even more so when you can look back on so many achievements over that period and share the joys with a loving family that now numbers close to 100. Mochtar Riady's extraordinary life story begins in very humble circumstances. He endured numerous setbacks in a tumultuous period of history but eventually succeeded in building a series of nimble and innovative banks and, ultimately, a globally competitive conglomerate. Along the way, he played an enormous role in Indonesia's economic, financial and social development and made major contributions to the advances of his second home — China. The secret of his success has been a unique combination of business acumen, an uncanny ability to anticipate future trends and a knack for reacting quickly in times of changing circumstances. He has also displayed a mixture of tenacity and devotion to detail — as seen in what he calls a "nanotechnology" style of management. All of these qualities and more are on display in the pages of this book. The following is a brief outline of the key events that shaped his life and his career over these more than eight decades.

1929   Mochtar Riady was born in Batu in East Java on May 12, 1929. When he was five months old, his parents took him to his father's home village in China's Fujian province to be with Mochtar's ailing grandfather. Mochtar and his mother stay on for nearly six years. In later life, Mochtar's links to

Fujian—and particularly to the area of that province known as Putian—become an important bond with many Chinese businessmen in Indonesia—as well as officials in China.

1935   Mochtar returns to Indonesia, taking a boat from the port of Xiamen in Fujian to Surabaya on the Indonesian island of Java. The family settles in Malang, also on Java, where Mochtar goes to the Nan Qiang (southern strength) Chinese school.

1938   Mochtar's mother dies in childbirth.

1942   Japan occupies the Dutch East Indies, dismantling much of the colonial state in what is now Indonesia. Japanese troops land on Java less than three months after the surprise attack on Pearl Harbor—which draws the US into the war in the Pacific.

Mochtar's father is arrested for joining a Chinese association which Japanese authorities mistakenly confuse with another organisation opposed to Japan's occupation of China. (Japan's 1931 invasion of Manchuria leads to all-out war in 1937 and the occupation of much of China). In Indonesia, thousands of civilians are arrested on the mere suspicion of resistance to the Japanese.

1945   Indonesia declares independence on August 17, 1945—just two days after Japan accepts Allied terms to end World War II. Indonesia's struggle for independence continues as the Allies return to Indonesia and quickly reinstall the Dutch East Indies civilian government. Dutch attempts to extend colonial rule meet determined resistance. Key battle takes place in Surabaya on November 10, 1945.

1946   Even as a young man, Mochtar is sympathetic to the independence movement and joins a group led by Siauw Giok Tjhan, a Chinese Indonesian activist who later serves as a cabinet minister under Sukarno but is eventually imprisoned by Suharto. Mochtar leaves for China to avoid arrest for his anti-colonial activities in Malang. He later studies in Nanjing at the National Central University, now known as Southeast University.

In China, a power struggle resumes between the Nationalist (Kuomintang) government and the communists after a period of uneasy cooperation during the war of resistance against Japan. The US supports the Nationalist government headed by Chiang Kai-shek but corruption, chaos brought on by the years of fighting and economic mismanagement undermine public support.

1948–1949 China's civil war closes in on Nanjing, where Mochtar is studying. Mochtar makes his way to Hong Kong. The Nationalist government collapses on the mainland and retreats to Taiwan. The communists proclaim the People's Republic of China in Beijing on October 1, 1949.

The Dutch formally recognise Indonesia independence in December of 1949.

1950   Mochtar returns to Indonesia. Soaring inflation pushes the government to introduce the "Sjafruddin Scissors" policy—a crude form of monetary controls named after the finance minister at the time. Bank notes of the Dutch colonial government are literally cut in half—and retain only half their original value. The other half of the bank note is exchanged for a government bond—but the move fails to have lasting effect on stabilising the economic situation.

1951   Mochtar marries Li Limei — also known as Suryawati Lidya.

1954   Mochtar moves to Jakarta and starts a trading business. He later adds shipping operations, moving goods between Tembilahan and Rengat on Sumatra and Jakarta.

1959   Mochtar's father passes away. Two days later Indonesia announces another currency devaluation whereby Rp1,000 and Rp500 notes lose 90 per cent of their former value. Some bank deposits are frozen. The move has a severe impact on the economy—including Mochtar's business.

1959–1960 Mochtar starts his banking career, becoming president of Kemakmuran Bank.

1963   Mochtar takes the helm of Bank Buana, which has been acquired by investors from five key industries. His leadership helps the bank survive the 1965 political and economic crisis.

1965   Hyperinflation leads to another devaluation of the rupiah. This time the value of Rp1,000 notes is slashed to Rp1. But this fails to tame inflation which tops 600 per cent the following year.

Mochtar takes control of troubled Bank Kemakmuran, Bank Industri Dagang Indonesia (BIDI) in addition to Bank Buana.

1966–1967 Sukarno loses grip on power.

1971 Mochtar establishes Panin Bank formed through the merger of Bank Kemakmuran, Bank Industri Dagang Indonesia Surabaya and BIDI. This is coordinated with Bank Indonesia's plan to strengthen the banking sector through mergers, reducing the number of small and weak banks. This trims the number of banks from 129 at the end of 1971 to 77 by 1980.

1975 Mochtar leaves Panin Bank and joins Sudono Salim—also known by his Chinese name Liem Sioe Liong—at Bank Central Asia (BCA). Their banking partnership lasts for 16 years. Salim, founder of the Salim Group, is a close confidant of President Suharto.

1976 Mochtar agrees to acquire a stake in the National Bank of Georgia, but abandons the plan amid political controversy surrounding the bank's key shareholder, Bert Lance. Lance asks to back out of the deal when he is forced to step down from his position as budget director for US President Jimmy Carter—and no longer faces conflict of interest issues. There is a silver lining though—Mochtar forges a close friendship with Jack Stephens, the US investment banker who helped arrange the aborted deal.

1977 BCA Bank acquires Gemari Bank from a foundation under the military to obtain clearing and foreign exchange licenses

1979 BCA launches BCA Card—Indonesia's first credit card.

1980 Mochtar takes a stake in the Union Planters Bank, the largest bank holding company in the US state of Tennessee.

1981   Mochtar buys shares of Bank Perniagaan Indonesia (BPI), a bank founded by businessman Hashim Ning.

1983–1984 Mochtar invests in Worthen Bank of Arkansas. He becomes acquainted with Bill Clinton—then serving as governor of Arkansas and later to become president of the United States.

1985   BCA opens branch in New York

Mochtar receives honorary Doctorate of Laws from Golden Gate University of San Francisco

1988   Mochtar becomes member of committee drafting PAKTO 88, which opens up the banking sector in Indonesia. Thanks to the policies under PAKTO 88, BCA was able to open 150 branches in a span of 12 months.

1989   Bank Umum Asia merges with Bank Perniagaan Indonesia to form Lippo Bank. Lippo Bank and BCA launch the Tabungan Hari Depan (Tahapan) savings plan aimed at attracting deposits from customers from middle and lower income brackets. The plan, which offers a lottery to encourage deposits and pays competitive interest rates, proves highly successful.

Lippo Bank initiates public stock offer, lists shares on Jakarta Stock Exchange. Move is highly successful, gaining widespread support from public investors and the financial sector.

Mochtar attends gathering to hear sermon of Reverend Stephen Tong. This is his start on the path to Christ. He is baptised at the Local Church in Jakarta later that year.

1990   PT Tunggal Reksakencana is incorporated—the forerunner of PT Lippo Karawaci Tbk.

1991   Mochtar leaves BCA. Assets of the bank reach Rp7.5 trillion, or almost US$3 billion, some 3,000 times greater than the Rp998 million or US$1 million when Mochtar first started at the bank.

1993   Sekolah Pelita Harapan (SPH) is established, providing basic education from kindergarten to high school. It offers education that meets international standards but part of its mission is to provide a foundation in Christian values. The school is under the direction of the Yayasan Pendidikan Pelita Harapan (YPHH), or Pelita Harapan Education Foundation.

1994   Universitas Pelita Harapan (UPH) starts operations, offering university level education. It seeks to ensure that its graduates are able to compete internationally while they gain a firm foundation in Christian values. UPH later opens branches in Surabaya and plans for one in Makassar and Semarang

1995   Dian Harapan School (SDH) established in Lippo Village Tangerang to provide affordable education with a Biblical Christian foundation. SDH now has six campuses in different locations across Indonesia.

1996   Siloam Gleneagles Lippo Karawaci Hospital officially opened as Mochtar and the Lippo Group expand into the medical care sector. Initially formed in conjunction with the acclaimed Gleneagles Hospital in Singapore, Gleneagles later withdraws, citing financial losses. The hospital is renamed Siloam Karawaci Hospital, and Mochtar's son James vows hospital will offer international standard medical services to community.

1997   Lippo Cikarang lists shares on Jakarta Stock Exchange.

Mochtar, together with the Lippo Group, develops the Cikarang area on Java. Once a largely ignored stretch of land, this becomes a district for a highly desirable industrial park as well as upscale housing, shopping centres, educational facilities, sports and health facilities. Today, there are more than 45,000 housing units in Lippo Cikarang and a daily working population of 350,000 workers.

1998   Sekolah Lentera Harapan (SLH) established to provide educational facilities to those from middle to lower income backgrounds. SLH has a strong presence in a number of Indonesian cities.

2002   Mochtar is elected Chairman of the Board of Trustees at the University of Indonesia. Under his leadership, the university optimises the use of its property assets and strengthens financial management. Mochtar introduces corporate culture promoting efficiency and transparency.

2006   Mochtar Riady Institute for Nanotechnology (MRIN) established, coinciding with Mochtar's 77th birthday on May 12, 2006. The research facility worth $30 million is widely considered a manifestation of his social commitment to Indonesia.

Less than a year after its inauguration, MRIN obtains two patents from patent agencies in Hong Kong and Australia. The patents are for a genetic tool (single nucleotide polymorphism) and diagnostic device patterns for patients who suffer from cirrhosis of the liver.

2007   Mochtar Riady Comprehensive Cancer Center (MRCCC) groundbreaking ceremony takes place in May 2007 and construction completed in December 2008.

University of Ma Chung in Malang is inaugurated and Mochtar is one of the initiators of the project.

San Diego Hills Memorial Parks and Funeral Homes opens with the conversion of 500 hectares of underutilised land in Karawang. The cemetery project takes its inspiration from the Rose Garden and Forest Lawn Memorial Parks and Mortuaries in California in the US.

2008   UPH College is established. It offers an integrated high school curriculum system, with an emphasis on learning in English and an art and music appreciation programme.

2009   Mochtar receives honorary degree from Hong Kong Baptist University.

2011   Siloam Hospital acquires Asia Media Jambi and Balikpapan Husada Hospital. The inauguration of Siloam Hospital MRCCC in Semanggi, Jakarta and Siloam Hospital in Jambi takes place this year.

2012   Siloam opens four new hospitals—the Rumah Sakit Umum Siloam, Siloam Manado, Siloam Makassar and Siloam Sriwijaya Palembang. It also acquires heart clinic in Cinere, Depok.

2013   Siloam Bali and Siloam Simatupang in Jakarta inaugurated.

2014   Mochtar Riady acquires the US Bank Tower in Los Angeles, the tallest building in California, for US$367.5 billion.

President Joko Widodo inaugurates Siloam's 19th hospital in Kupang, East Nusa Tenggara.

2015   Construction starts on Millennium Lippo Village in Karawaci in Tangerang. Millennium Lippo Village is part of the 132-hectare central business district development and is estimated to cost Rp200 trillion.

Mochtar inaugurates the Mochtar Riady Plaza Quantum as a development centre for nanotechnology research at Universitas Indonesia.

INDEX